ENTERPRISE
CHINA

ABOUT THINKERS50

Thinkers50 is the world's most reliable resource for identifying, ranking, and sharing the leading management and business ideas of our age. Since 2001, we've been providing access to ideas with the power to make a positive difference in the world.

The Thinkers50 definitive ranking of management thinkers is published every two years. Its Distinguished Achievement Awards, which recognize the very best in management thinking and practice, have been described by the Financial Times as the "Oscars of management thinking."

ENTERPRISE CHINA

ADOPTING A COMPETITIVE STRATEGY FOR

BUSINESS SUCCESS

ALLEN J. MORRISON / J. STEWART BLACK

WILEY

Published by John Wiley & Sons, Inc., Hoboken, New Jersey.
Published simultaneously in Canada.

For general information on our other products and services or for technical support, please contact our
Customer Care Department within the United States at (800) 762-2974, outside the United States at (317)
572-3993 or fax (317) 572-4002.

Wiley publishes in a variety of print and electronic formats and by print-on-demand. Some material
included with standard print versions of this book may not be included in e-books or in print-on-demand.
If this book refers to media such as a CD or DVD that is not included in the version you purchased, you
may download this material at http://booksupport.wiley.com. For more information about Wiley products,
visit www.wiley.com.

Library of Congress Cataloging-in-Publication Data is Available:

ISBN 9781394153428 (Hardback)
ISBN 9781394153442 (ePDF)
ISBN 9781394153435 (ePub)

Cover Design: Wiley
Cover Image: © Gaid Kornsilapa/Shutterstock
Author Photos: Courtesy of the Authors

SKY10036528_101122

CONTENTS

PREFACE

As senior professors of leadership and strategy, our research and writing go back more than 30 years. Over that time, collectively, we have traveled to China (including Hong Kong) more than 120 times. We have written more than a dozen business case studies on Western companies in China and Chinese companies expanding abroad. We have served as visiting professors at leading Chinese business schools and have taught scores of executives and senior Chinese government officials. As well, we have run workshops for more than 3,000 Western executives about doing business in China or working with Chinese companies. In addition, we have interviewed dozens of Chinese executives and government officials, including mayors and members of Chinese state regulatory agencies and planning offices in China, as well as equal numbers of US and European officers in trade associations and business roundtables and Western executives with significant experience in China. We have served on governance and advisory boards of publicly listed Chinese companies and distinguished Chinese universities.

Our interest in China has only grown throughout the years. The country's growth and prosperity have surpassed everyone's expectations, including our own. We each traveled to China for the first time in the summer of 1989—one to Beijing and the other to Shenzhen. The impact of the protests in Tiananmen Square had a profound impact on the country and each of us. One of our first joint research trips to China took us to Shanghai in the early 1990s. The airport was not the shiny, sprawling edifice that people see today. In fact, part of the concourse was being repaired with only a dirt floor to walk on. We had to walk from the international terminal to the domestic terminal through the town streets. Flash-forward a few decades, and we recall a recent trip on one of the country's high-speed trains from Nanjing to Beijing. The journey of about 640 miles is not much different than the distance between Nashville, Tennessee, and Orlando, Florida, which by car would normally take between 10 and 12 hours. The trip took just over 3.5 hours. The train and the ride was as nice as any in Japan or Switzerland. Today the country's airports, seaports, subways, roads, and bridges are among the best in the world. We have been equally impressed by the level of digitization and advances in the cloud and online services, as well as by the staggering number of Swiss watch shops, glitzy high-rises, and German luxury cars on the roads. More recently, we were surprised to find panhandlers flashing QR codes instead of presenting tin cups at passersby.

These modern sights, sounds, and impressions have been experienced by virtually anyone and everyone who has traveled to China in the last decade. Those with long experience in China are astounded at the degree and pace of change. Those who have only visited China for the first time in the last few years are often shocked by what they see and experience. As one tourist we ran into before the COVID-19 pandemic stated, "I didn't expect rickshaws and people in Mao suits, but I also didn't expect this. The level of modernization hits you smack in the face." We agree.

As impressive as is the "what" of China's modernization, our fascination and research has always focused on the "how," especially over the last two decades. How China got to where it is today is amazing. If this were a history book, that would be our primary focus. However, this is a business book, written for business executives. Consequently, we focus on *where* China and its commercial enterprises are going and *how* they plan to compete and win along the way—their competitive strategy.

We say "their," but we really mean "its," and the change from plural to singular pronoun goes to the heart of one of the most common misperceptions foreign executives have about commercial China. Most Western executives, as they are trained to do, analyze the competitive strategy of suppliers, strategic partners, or commercial rivals with the individual company as the unit of analysis. Sadly, this approach has a fatal flaw because where a Western executive is trained to see an independent, multibillion-dollar enterprise, it is only the nose of a multitrillion-dollar beast. That monolith we label "Enterprise China." It consists not just of the company in focus but an entire ecosystem of companies tied together by the largest entity on the planet by employment and the second largest by revenues—the Chinese state, which includes the central, provincial, and municipal governments. But contrary to what most foreign executives imagine, the Chinese state is not working behind closed doors in smoke-filled rooms whispering its desires to commercial entities hoping that they will listen. No, because the state outright owns entities that account for 30 to 40% of the economy, it operates in the open. It is public about its intent of ensuring that no daylight comes between the vision, ambition, and strategy of the state and key commercial enterprises. However, Enterprise China extends far beyond this core cluster of state-owned enterprises (SOEs) and includes virtually all privately owned enterprises (POEs) of any significant size or importance. How, and the extent to which, this happens is a core part of the first third of the book.

Because most Western executives focus on individual enterprises, they also center their attention on the competitive strategy of that entity. However, just as there is an overarching Enterprise China monolith, there is an overarching vision and strategy that supersedes any individual Chinese business. Focusing on specific entity strategies is like looking at individual pieces but not seeing the picture of the overall puzzle. The good news is that the strategy for Enterprise China is not a state secret. It is not locked away in a vault. It has been laid out in public documents for all to see, but about which most foreign executives have only a passing awareness. In this sense Enterprise China's competitive strategy has been hiding in plain sight for nearly two decades. Consequently, the middle portion of the book is devoted to laying out Enterprise China's competitive strategy and the associated tactics.

Because this is a book written for executives, the final section focuses on the business implications of Enterprise China and its competitive strategy. Specifically, we ask and answer the question: What strategic options and actions can Western business executives take in competing *in* and *with* Enterprise China?

While there is no debating the impressive progress that China and its commercial enterprises have made, as all safe harbor statements stress, past performance is no guarantee of future success. Consequently, China's past may be prologue, but it is not prophesy, nor is it destiny. In 2019, we published a *Harvard Business Review* article that outlined many of the key factors that could derail Enterprise China. At the end of this book, we dive deeper into this topic.

We are neither in the camp that predicts that China will take over the world nor aligned with those that predict the coming collapse of the country. Rather, we take a pragmatic approach. Our perspective is that foreign executives ought to understand the nature of Enterprise China, should appreciate the elegance of its strategy, and acknowledge the focus and discipline of the Chinese. They would be wise to plan their own strategies accordingly and ought to take up a mantra of Navy Seals—assess and adapt. To best facilitate this, we lay out those factors that foreign executives should monitor as Enterprise China moves forward. We explain how those factors could help or hurt Enterprise China's strategy so that executives can adjust their own strategies as needed.

When we decided to write this book, it was in the middle of the COVID-19 pandemic, and the political tensions between China and the United Sates were high. Decoupling between the two was the talk of the time and persists in many circles. We are not ignorant of the importance of political relationships in the course of commerce, but we wanted to approach the topic of Enterprise China and its competitive strategy largely free of politics. We leave it to others to measure out blame or policy disagreements when it comes to ongoing or future tensions between China and the United States or any other country for that matter. Our goal is simple: Help executives make more informed and wise strategic choices for their companies relative to China. We hope our insights and recommendations will be relevant to executives regardless of whether they lead small, medium, or large companies or whether they have large investments and operations in China or none at all. We believe they are.

ACKNOWLEDGMENTS

We are grateful to many people who helped guide our thinking in preparing this book. These include those who participated in our research and who shared with us their rich experiences and challenged our thinking. We specifically recognize the guidance and input of Bob and Jenny Theleen, David Young, Doug Guthrie, Brian Hu, Dave Ulrich, John Nossiff, and Ali Jawad. We are also grateful to our editor, Daryl James, for his thoughtful comments. And finally, we express our deep gratitude to our families, who have put up with us over the many months we dedicated to composing this book. Their decades of support have been pivotal in shaping our worldviews and in allowing us to indulge in our fascination with China.

Chapter 1

A NEW TYPE
OF COMPETITOR

China has the world's attention. Most Western executives, whether their firms operate in China or not, can easily list key Chinese competitors. Many of these rival companies did not exist 30 years ago, but today they command respect—even if foreigners struggle to pronounce their names or simply refer to them by their initials, such as SAIC (Shanghai Automotive Industrial Company), ICBC (Industrial and Commercial Bank of China), or CNOOC (China National Offshore Oil Company). Unfortunately, the formidable Chinese foes that Western executives see do not capture the full picture of the challenges they face. Where a foreign executive sees an independent, individual multibillion-dollar Chinese company, it is merely the nose of a larger, multitrillion-dollar monolith. The real rival includes not just the individual companies on which Western executives typically focus their competitive analysis but an array of interconnected firms in a much larger ecosystem. More importantly, this monolith includes the largest entity on the planet by number of employees (386 million[1]) and the second largest by revenue ($1.3 trillion[2]). We're talking about the Chinese state, which includes national, regional, and municipal governments. We refer to this commercial totality as "Enterprise China."

Without taking this full picture into account, foreign executives can easily misunderstand their opportunities and challenges and miscalculate their responses. Consequently, we have two main objectives with this book. First, we provide a comprehensive review of Enterprise China with a focus on the competitive realities that Western companies face. Second, we lay out the strategies that Western firms might take as they compete *in* and *with* Enterprise China. To appreciate the challenges involved, foreign executives first must consider the distinction between Chinese enterprises and Enterprise China.

1

THE RISE OF CHINESE ENTERPRISES

As professors, we each took our first trips to China in June 1989. One of us traveled south to Shenzhen, and the other headed north to Beijing. Most readers will remember the momentous events of that month and year in China, when troops moved against protesters at Tiananmen Square. We certainly do. In the three decades that followed, our research, case study writing, and consulting on China have primarily focused on how Western firms compete in and with China. In the process, we also have directed and taught hundreds of executive development programs involving over 3,000 executives in which "Competing *in* and *with* China" was a central theme.

Competitive analysis was almost always a core topic in these programs. Typically, assessing Chinese competitors was a central element of that analysis. In starting these sessions, we regularly asked a simple question: "Who are your Chinese competitors?" Back in the 1990s, we invariably got one of three responses:

- I'm not sure.
- We don't really have any Chinese competitors.
- I can name a few, but we are not really worried about them. They aren't serious competition for us.

The story is different today. When we ask Western executives to name names, they typically have no problem identifying their key Chinese competitors, as well as those competitors' tier 1 customers and suppliers.

Domestic Strength: Growth as a Source and Market

What explains this change in response? The answer is as straightforward as it is profound: China has exploded as a supply source and as a market over the last 30 years. Because most readers are no doubt familiar with the story of China's growth, we will summarize it with just two charts.

The first shows China's fivefold increase as a supply source over the last 20 years (see Exhibit 1.1); China rocketed from No. 4 to No. 1 in the world. Today, it is at the top of the chart by a wide margin, with the United States a distant second.

Because China so strongly dominates global manufacturing, it is often referred to as the "world's factory." In some areas China is not just the top producer globally, its production is greater than all other countries combined. For example, in terms of steel production over the last 20 years, China has gone from producing about 16% of the global supply to 53%, or slightly more steel than the rest of the entire world combined. Likewise, China is not only the No. 1 producer of refrigerators in the world, but as with steel, it produces more than all other countries put together. In mobile phones, it is not even a close race. China produces roughly 65% of all the smartphones made on the planet. In terms of

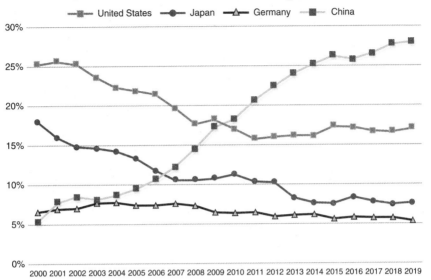

Share of Global Total Manufacturing Value Added

Exhibit 1.1 China's Rise as a Source
Source: World Bank.

televisions, more than 70% of all the televisions produced in the world are made in China. The same is true for air conditioners. And the list goes on. With this large and strong position in supply and manufacturing, it is little wonder that Western executives can name key Chinese companies, especially those in their upstream value chain.

The second chart illustrates how far China has come as a market (see Exhibit 1.2). The country has soared from No. 11 to No. 2 in the world as measured by its share of global GDP. Although the slope of the line representing China's rise as a market may not look steep, it represents a 900% increase over the past 30 years.

While China as an overall market is second only to the United States, it is No. 1 in several areas. For example, China is now the largest retail market in the world. Within retail, China is the largest e-commerce market in the world both in terms of total revenue and number of customers who purchase online. China is also the largest car market in the world. And it is the world's largest market for luxury goods such as designer handbags and Swiss watches. Again, the list goes on.

China's explosive growth as both a supply source and market have given birth to and nurtured a host of new, large, and strong Chinese companies. Again, most readers either know or can intuitively understand this dynamic, and consequently it needs little further explanation. However, a single chart provides a useful summary (see Exhibit 1.3). This chart shows the number of Chinese firms on

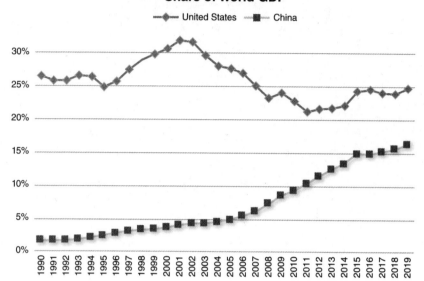

Exhibit 1.2 China's Rise as a Market
Source: World Bank.

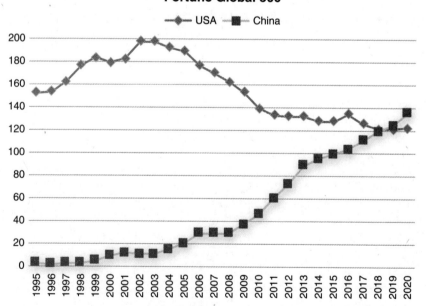

Exhibit 1.3 The Rise of Chinese Firms
Source: Fortune Global 500.

Fortune's list of Global 500 firms from 1995 through 2021, representing the largest 500 firms on the planet by revenue.

To appreciate the growth of large Chinese companies, consider that in 1995 when *Fortune* launched its first list of the top 500 global companies, China had only three firms on the entire list; 19 other countries had more. In 2021, China had three firms just in the top 10. With 135 Chinese firms on the total list, no other country had more, including the United States (122 firms), the second year in a row that China was No.1 and the United States was No.2.

As a consequence of China's size and scope as a source of supply and as a market, most large foreign multinational firms have at least some operations in China. Those operations may be primarily upstream or downstream, but many firms have operations in China across the entire value chain. For firms without much or any presence in China, they nevertheless have likely encountered Chinese competitors exporting products into their home markets or setting up shop next door.

Foreign Strength: Growth as an Exporter and Investor

The proposition that indigenous Chinese firms would have an inside track when it comes to competing on their home turf is easy to understand. How they have achieved that domestic strength and how they plan to elevate it will be the focus of an important part of this book.

However, as we will explain and examine, Chinese firms are not content with dominating domestically. Through exports and foreign direct investment (FDI) abroad, they plan not only to compete overseas but to lead globally. This is why firms with no presence in China, whether they are small, medium, or large, which are completely content to stay home and not engage in battles with Chinese firms, will nonetheless find themselves in a fight going forward—if they are not already struggling today. The next five charts help to illustrate the development of this competitive battlefield.

Export Strength

Most firms with no presence in China first encounter Chinese competitors via exports from China (see Exhibit 1.4). Given the significant rise in Chinese exports over the last 20 years, many firms already have felt the pain of losing market share because of Chinese exports appearing on their shores. For example, US firms have seen imports from China explode from $103 billion in 2000 to just over $500 billion in 2021. China's successful expansion via exports has enabled it to overtake historical export leaders such as Japan, Germany, and the United States. Today, China is the world's largest exporter.

Because international trade also has grown over the last 50 years, a better way to appreciate the success of Chinese exports is to view them from a relative perspective—that is, their share of total global exports (see Exhibit 1.5). Here the results are visually even more stunning. China's global share of exports has soared

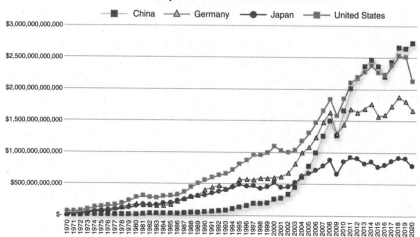

Exhibit 1.4 Goods and Services Export Value ($US)
Source: World Bank.

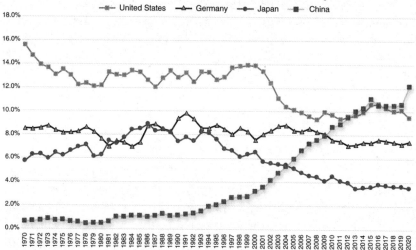

Exhibit 1.5 Share of Goods and Services Export Value
Source: World Bank.

1,665%, while those from Germany, Japan, and the United States have declined 12.5%, 39.0%, and 39.2% respectively. To put it bluntly, China's export gains have been the previous export champions' losses.

Books have been dedicated to explaining the dramatic rise of Chinese exports, so there is no need for us to do much more than hit on two highlights. The first driver of Chinese export success has been the country's abundant and cheap labor. All experienced executives understand this factor, though the key behind it and the strains on that source are typically less well understood, so we will take some space to highlight them here. The second driver of China's export success, improved infrastructure, is one that is often underappreciated by many outside the country. Consequently, we will devote a bit more space to this factor and illustrate it with some impressive numbers and charts.

Abundant and Cheap Labor. Few would debate that China's abundant and cheap labor has been a critical component of its export success. However, there is an element to this part of the story that typically goes underreported—internal migration. Many foreign executives underappreciate how vital internal migration has been in China, as the country has scrambled to staff its urban factories. In fact, during China's historic economic explosion, over 200 million Chinese migrated from low-paying, unproductive, rural farms to much higher-paying, productive urban factories. The potential of this cheap labor, which was larger than that of Japan, Germany, France, the United Kingdom, and Italy combined, would have gone uncaptured without this population shift. Had these 200 million workers stayed on their farms and not moved to urban factories, China's massive explosion of exports could not have happened.

Impressive Infrastructure. This migration could efficiently and effectively produce products for export only if the infrastructure required to (a) move raw materials and components into the country, (b) transport them from one subassembly location to another and ultimately to final assembly, and then (c) transfer finished products to ports for export was superior. Cheap and abundant labor with poor physical infrastructure would not have produced a winning combination. Any experienced executive understands this. What many Western executives might not realize is how much China has invested in infrastructure. To upgrade its physical infrastructure, the country has spent more on building and improving its roads, rails, and airports than the United States and Europe combined (see Exhibit 1.6).

This investment pattern continues unabated. Li Xiaopeng, China's minister of transport, announced in 2019 that during the previous year the country had invested the equivalent of US $460 billion in transportation fixed assets.[3] This included the development of an additional 8,000 kilometers of railway lines and 330,000 kilometers of roads, as well as five new civil transport airports. Morgan Stanley estimates that China on average will spend around $180 billion each year for the next 11 years—or $1.98 trillion in total.[4] That annual figure is almost double the past three-year average in China. In contrast, US public investment on infrastructure fell by nearly 11% from 2003 to 2017 when adjusted for inflation and the cost of infrastructure inputs. Today, China continues to invest more in physical infrastructure than the United States and Europe combined, even with the US's infrastructure bill passed in 2021.

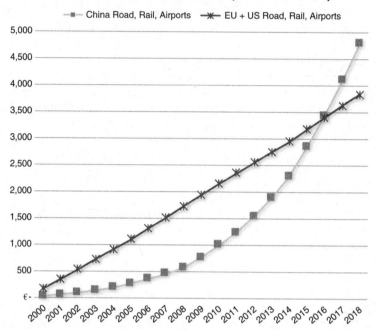

Exhibit 1.6 China's Cumulative Expenditure on Physical Infrastructure
Source: OECD.

Abundant and cheap labor that shifted rural farms to urban factories and aggressive investment in physical infrastructure have been key factors enabling Chinese firms to flood the world with exports. These were not the only factors, but they were pivotal and are often underappreciated. As a consequence of these exports, many wholly domestic firms across the planet that otherwise were content to mind their own business at home have nonetheless found Chinese exports eating away at their market shares and livelihoods.

Foreign Investment Strength
Exports were only the beginning of the disruption for firms that had no presence in China and no desire to compete with Chinese firms. The second major disruption for these "stay-at-home" companies was FDI by Chinese firms. Over the last 20 years, not only did the boom in China spur the formation of an astounding array of indigenous companies with sizable fortresses at home that facilitated exports abroad but also many decided they were big enough and strong enough to invest, expand, and set up overseas outposts. No doubt, the prospect of even greater international revenues drove Chinese firms' outward FDI. Exports make

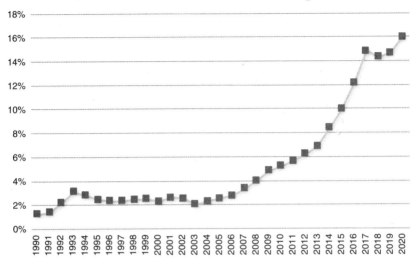

Exhibit 1.7 China's Expansion Overseas
Source: Adapted from UNCTAD World Investment Report 2020.

the most sense (and money) when they can be standardized and made the same regardless of where they are to be sold in the world. Any customization hurts the capture of economies of scale. However, not everyone everywhere wants the same thing. The more exports need customization in order to penetrate a foreign market, the more sense it makes to produce localized versions not in China but in, or close to, that market.

This is often what motivates firms, including Chinese firms, to move from exports to FDI.[5] Exhibit 1.7 illustrates the dramatic rise in Chinese firms' investments and accumulation of overseas assets (as measured by FDI outward stock). As a consequence of these overseas investments, even executives who thought they were safe from competitive confrontations with Chinese firms have found no reprieve or escape. Though China's increase in foreign assets is absolute and as a percentage of GDP (now 15%) is impressive, as a percentage of GDP it lags far behind Switzerland (230%), Germany (59%), France (66%), Japan (42%), and the United Sates (39%). Therefore, there is likely even greater outward Chinese FDI flows to come going forward.

EMBRACING THE CHALLENGE

China today is no longer just a source of cheap products or a distant market of 1.4 billion consumers. China has emerged as the world's factory and the world's second-largest market overall and the largest market in many sectors. As a consequence, it has attracted approximately 1 million foreign firms to set up some type of operations on its shores.[6] For these foreign firms, the competitive focus on China is ever present, and the understanding that the battle involves more than individual Chinese firms is growing. Many Western business leaders share a growing concern about falling behind the Chinese. Consider the letter that Intel CEO Bob Swan sent to then president-elect Joe Biden stating, "A national manufacturing strategy, including investment by the U.S. government in the domestic semiconductor industry, is critical to ensure American companies...lead the next generation of innovative technology [against the Chinese]."[7]

For firms with no presence in China whose executives may have hoped to avoid the confrontations by staying home, those hopes and dreams are fading fast. Today, Chinese exports reach into nearly every corner and crevice in the world. Where standardized exports are not enough, Chinese firms have invested vast sums to set up local operations to take the fight directly to their foreign rivals.

In the final analysis, executives of large or small, multinational or domestic companies cannot ignore or escape Enterprise China. However, a superficial or headline-driven understanding of its competitive strategy and tactics can cause foreign executives to miscalculate the size and scope of their challenges and opportunities. The purpose of this book is to fill that gap so that executives can avoid missteps.

THE RISE OF ENTERPRISE CHINA

Although the dramatic rise of Chinese firms on the *Fortune* Global 500 from 3 to 135 visually illustrates the amazing ascent of large and powerful individual Chinese companies, as we said at the outset, the real story isn't about individual "bigger, badder" Chinese companies at home or abroad. At best this is only half the picture. Competing against *Chinese enterprises* is not the same as competing against *Enterprise China*.

A Unique Framework for Analysis

Enterprise China necessitates a different framework for analysis. Instead of concentrating solely on individual companies, executives should focus on the entire monolith that includes the company *and* the government as one entity. In traditional competitive analysis, as taught in almost every MBA program in the West, executives concentrate on competitors, suppliers, and customers as individual actors. In these traditional models, the company is always in the foreground and the government remains in the background. Traditional competitive analysis does not ignore governments or pretend that they cannot influence business policy via licensing requirements, taxes, and other regulatory controls. But ultimately strategists focus on the company because they assume that it is free to make decisions within the guardrails of government regulation. This is the essence of free market capitalism, which governs most Western firms and their executives.

Domains of Control and State Influence

In the case of Enterprise China, however, the company and the state are both in the foreground. Decisions are coordinated, and companies take indirect cues and direct commands from the state. In the case of China's largest companies, state control and influence is direct and largely based on ownership—most often, complete ownership—which is why we refer to those entities as state-owned enterprises (SOEs). But the state's control and influence go beyond this. Ultimately, Enterprise China consists of three domains of control and influence.

Central SOEs

When foreign executives discuss Chinese SOEs, they often equate "state" with Beijing and the central government. This assessment has merit. The central government and the State-owned Asset Supervision Administration Commission of the State Council (SASAC) that owns central SOEs are important for at least two reasons. First, SASAC is not some minor department stuck off somewhere in the briar patch of China's gigantic bureaucracy. No, SASAC reports directly to the State Council of the People's Republic of China. Second, even though the number of firms directly owned by SASAC is small—just 96—their impact is huge. Of the 135 firms on the 2020 *Fortune* Global 500 list, 49 were owned via SASAC. Few have brand names and none of them advertise their ties to the state.

Provincial and Municipal SOEs

Nonetheless, it is a mistake to equate "state" ownership only with Beijing. The vast majority of China's 150,000 SOEs are owned by provincial and municipal governments.[8] These firms are generally smaller, but of the 135 Chinese firms on the 2020 *Fortune* Global 500 list, 33 were owned by provinces and municipalities.

To appreciate the breadth of these two other levels of governmental ownership and control, consider just a few facts. In terms of provinces, China has 23. The largest has a population about the same as the entire country of Japan. In terms of municipalities, China has 113 cities with populations exceeding 1 million. This is four times the number of cities of this size across all of Europe and the United States combined. Shanghai, for example, has 26 million people, which is more than the entire country of Australia. China's largest city, Chongqing, has more people than the population of Taiwan and almost twice that of the Netherlands.

Privately Owned Enterprises

Even when the government does not own the company, as in the case of privately owned enterprises (POEs), the government exerts significant influence and control through regulations and administrative guidance that is beyond what is typically the case in other countries. This is true whether POEs are publicly listed on stock exchanges or held by private individuals. The case of Alibaba, which we discuss later on and in Chapter 3, shows the extent of this influence.

Reasons for Concern: Why You Should Pay Attention

All this notwithstanding, we have more than once encountered experienced executives who at first were skeptical of the need to think about competition with Chinese enterprises in the context of "Enterprise China." Their retort often was something along the lines of the following:

> Sorry, but we've seen this movie before. We've seen Japan Inc. or Korea Inc. try to use industrial policy to benefit their own indigenous firms. To a lesser degree, countries such as Canada, France, and Brazil have also tried it. In these cases, some indigenous companies might have benefited from their government's helping hand, but eventually they had to stand on their own two feet. Some succeeded and others failed. In the end, things didn't turn out quite as the alarmists warned. In other words, the government was helpful to some domestic firms particularly in the early days, but the industrial policies and actions didn't fundamentally change the competitive game.

True enough. We have no argument with the contention that policy efforts in "Japan Inc." and elsewhere fell far short of predictions. However, we would argue that China is different and consequently, business executives should think differently about Enterprise China.

But what, you might ask, is so different? Why should we think differently about Enterprise China than we did about Japan Inc. or others in the past? It comes down to three factors. First, the level of integration and control between the Chinese state and Chinese commercial firms is something the world has never seen before. Second, the extent to which the state strategizes about this integration in commercial, and not just political, terms is also outside the scope of past examples. Third, the scale of economic power behind Enterprise China dwarfs Japan Inc., and all other comparisons, by a wide margin. With that, let's take a brief look at each of these three points of difference in more detail.

Layers of Integration

As we mentioned, most experienced executives will be at least somewhat familiar with how governments in many countries have used industrial policy to benefit their indigenous firms. However, China is unique. It is not simply formulating industrial policy and cajoling commercial firms to comply. Furthermore, China is not just closely connected to key commercial companies because government officials and corporate executives went to the same universities or belong to the same political party. As we mentioned, the central government owns and controls 96 firms, most of which are among the largest firms in China and typically the largest in their industries in China. When you add the firms owned by the provinces and municipalities, the more than 150,000 SOEs exert a tremendous influence on the Chinese economy. For example, a study by the World Bank in 2019 estimated that SOEs in China accounted for between 23% to 29% of China's GDP.[9]

To be clear, when we say "state-owned," we don't mean that the state holds small minority stakes in these firms. Rather, we mean that the Chinese government—whether at the national, provincial, or municipal level—has a direct equity stake or complete ownership of the company and consequently directs the affairs of the company.

When we say "directs," we do not mean that the state provides "administrative guidance" (a term some readers will recall from the days of Japan Inc.). Rather, we mean that it controls the company, including its financing, its strategy, and its mergers, acquisitions, or divestitures, as well as the appointment of its executives.

Taken together, this level of integration and resulting control of SOEs is far more than was ever the case in places like Japan or Korea. And it goes far beyond acceptable norms and practices in countries that have in the past relied on at least some state-owned corporations, including France, Sweden, Norway, Canada, and Brazil. Even compared to countries such as Russia, where at one time government ownership of commercial entities was relatively high, it never reached this level with roughly half the country's total working population being employed by the government or one of its SOEs, which is the case in China. In addition, in the case of Russia or other countries where the government did own sizable commercial assets, the SOE option was not embraced as a long-term solution. In these other cases, the governments eventually sold most or all of its equity in order to shift much needed capital into the state's coffers. In other cases where the government held controlling interests in large entities, it committed to divesting its holdings at an appropriate time in the future. Ownership was viewed as a transitory and not a permanent condition. This is not the case in China. These SOEs are "national champions" not just because they are some of the biggest companies in the nation but because they champion the interests of the nation, and the state's ownership and direction of these SOEs ensures this.

If this direct ownership were the full extent of what constitutes Enterprise China, it would be more than the modern world has ever seen and would deserve a book on its own. However, the integration of Chinese companies with the government goes beyond SOEs. In China's case, the government also largely controls "national champions" that it helped nurture and grow but which it does not own.

Alibaba is a case in point. While most outsiders have little knowledge of the state's role in Alibaba's growth, even the casual observer would have noticed the dramatic and profound control of the firm that the government asserted in late 2020 and early 2021. For context, in 2020 Alibaba was the second most valuable company in all of China, with a market cap at its peak of $665 billion. Its founder, Jack Ma, was the fourth richest person in the country with an estimated net worth of nearly $50 billion.[10] As part of Alibaba's ecosystem, Ma had developed Ant Financial. In 2020, Ant was set for an IPO, which was scheduled to bring in $35 billion (the largest IPO in history) and value Ant at about $315 billion out of the gate. At that level, Ant would have been worth more than Société Générale, Deutsche Bank, Credit Suisse, Barclays, ING, Santander, and Goldman Sachs combined. However, when Ma made comments about the government stifling innovation and the need for reforming the national financial system, the government was not happy and called him in for questioning. The government subsequently determined that important ownership stakes in Ant's IPO were "going to political families that represent a potential challenge to President Xi and his inner circle."[11] At that point the IPO was indefinitely halted. Alibaba was further fined $2.8 billion for breaking anti-monopoly rules in early 2021. Alibaba, Jack Ma, and anyone else with any savvy recognized that the Chinese government could and would exert control over POEs whenever it felt that they were straying outside the lines. To the CEOs of SOEs and POEs alike, the message was clear: the state is the boss, and don't forget it.

Our point here is that while state ownership bequeaths control, foreign executives should not interpret the lack of state ownership as bestowing freedom to commercial entities and signaling an absence of government control. Nor should foreign executives assume that because state ownership isn't evident, it does not exist. Indeed, Chinese state equity positions are notoriously difficult to determine. This is because most major shareholders of medium and large Chinese companies, including corporate investors, are themselves either fully or partly owned by government entities. It is safe to say that virtually every major company in China today has some level of either direct or indirect government ownership, and all are subject to state control.

Whether one agrees or disagrees with China's actions or ownership roles is beside the point. The point is that one could search far and wide to find a parallel case of government control of gigantic private firms such as Alibaba, and that search would come up empty, except in China. Thus, the high degree of state control over commercial enterprises is not limited to SOEs but extends to POEs and is without precedent.

Commercial Orientation

On top of this extraordinary level of state ownership and control is a level of commercial orientation relative to Enterprise China's competitive strategy that is also unique. Although we will explore this in greater detail in subsequent chapters, here it is helpful to lay out some basics. The good news is that it does not take cloak-and-dagger spy craft to uncover China's vision and strategy. Nor does it require relying on the opinions or the speculation of analysts or experts. Fortunately for all, Enterprise China's vision and strategy are hiding in plain sight (and have been for nearly two decades). The problem is that many Western executives haven't really focused on them, while others have dismissed them as *political* proclamations and therefore of little relevance to their own *commercial* interests. However, China's vision and strategy are as commercial as any company's vision and strategy in the West.

Vision. Enterprise China's "CEO," President Xi Jinping, recently rearticulated the country's strategic vision to the 19th Party Congress in October 2017. He stated that China would "become a global leader in terms of composite national strength and international influence." At first flush, this statement may not seem particularly "corporate" or, for that matter, profound. However, if you stop and consider the structure of China's vision relative to that of most commercial companies, the similarities are striking. For example, most corporate vision statements are some version of the following: "Our vision is to be become the global leader in X (insert the relevant industry or sector)." If you take President Xi's vision statement and make it a bit more direct, he is saying that China seeks to be one of the strongest nations on earth and one of the most influential. There is a clear co-mingling of economic and political objectives. If anything, Xi's vision is ambitious.

Strategy. Having an ambitious vision is one thing, achieving it is another. To achieve it you need a plan—a strategy for how you are going to compete and win along the way. Enterprise China has exactly that. In fact, it has articulated a three-part strategy, or what we label "strategic pillars." The first pillar is to reduce and effectively eliminate China's overdependency on foreign firms for key technologies and products. The second pillar is to ensure that indigenous firms dominate China's domestic market. The third is to win globally. Put simply, Enterprise China seeks to become a global leader in terms of national strength and international influence by reducing its external dependency, dominating domestically, and winning globally. For each of the strategic pillars there are three key tactics designed to achieve the strategic objectives. It would not take a communication executive in a Western multinational more than a few minutes to take these elements and create a nice graphic to put into a PowerPoint presentation for both internal and external consumption. In fact, it might look something like what we put together (see Exhibit 1.8).

Blueprints. As we mentioned, to get at China's competitive strategy, one need not silently slip into a secure government office and take clandestine photos of top-secret documents with a camera disguised as a pen. One need not comb through stacks of obscure papers and government documents and run them through a complex algorithm to decipher encrypted messages. No, China's competitive strategy is not a secret; it has been laid out in very public documents for nearly two decades. The three key publications that reveal the strategy include:

- National Medium- and Long-Term Science and Technology Development Plan (MLP): 2005–2015
- Made in China 2025 (MIC 2025): 2015 to 2025
- China Standards 2035: 2020–2035

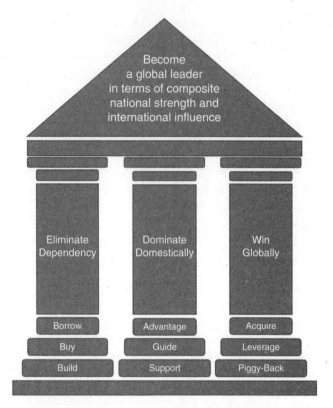

Exhibit 1.8 China's Vision and Competitive Strategy

Based on these and supporting initiatives, the essence and rationale of each of the three pillars in the competitive strategy are quite clear. In Chapters 2, 3, and 4 we dive deeply into each of the three strategic pillars, their rationales, and their accompanying tactics.

For those in the West who typically view governments through a strictly political lens, including the Chinese state in "Enterprise China," and looking at the whole from a competitive strategy, perspective may be an unfamiliar approach. After all, outside China, corporate and national political interests are often portrayed as at odds with each other. However, in China the two are one. The determinants of competitive strategy are not just the firm or its executives but the state.

Within the context of this three-part strategy, President Xi has increasingly used the phrase "Dual Circulation" as a shorthand for China's three-part competitive strategy. The first element of the dual circulation focuses on "internal circulation," which refers to the domestic cycle of development, production, and consumption. This increased internal circulation is predicated on reversing the country's foreign dependency and facilitating the domestic domination of indigenous firms.

The "external circulation" refers to the country's international activities, notably both continued exports from China to the world and the expansion of Chinese firms' value chains out into the world via FDI and setting standards for the world.

Scale of Power

Up to this point we have made the case that foreign executives should not just analyze their Chinese competitors but should view them within the context of "Enterprise China" because the level of integration between commercial enterprises and the state is unprecedented and because that integration has been deployed in a decidedly commercial context. The third reason that executives should include an analysis of Enterprise China in their competitive plans is because of the sheer scale and power that is being brought to bear. The resources at play are orders of magnitude more than has ever been witnessed before and, in most cases, far beyond what any individual company could muster on its own.

Business executives know that when it comes to businesses, money matters. Consider the largest company on the planet in 2021 in terms of sales revenue: Walmart. It took in more annual revenue ($559 billion in fiscal year 2021) than the GDP of 172 of the 193 member countries of the United Nations. Impressive. Yet neither Walmart nor any other company comes close to having the financial power of Enterprise China. For example, in 2020 China's SOEs generated about $9.7 trillion in revenue,[12] which is about 18 times the revenue of Walmart that same year ($519 billion). These firms accounted for 60% of all Chinese firm capitalization and 30% of China's total GDP. SOEs assets were nearly 60% of GDP, or about $8.6 trillion.[13] That's a lot of cash, but there's more—debt capital. SOEs have gained access to $13.2 trillion via debt, which is 92% of China's GDP (see Exhibit 1.9).

Of course, companies in other countries also have access to debt capital. However, consider that Chinese SOEs have had a debt-to-asset ratio of 1.5 and a debt-to-revenue ratio of 1.4. Non-state-owned firms in most industrialized countries would find it extremely hard if not impossible to secure debt capital greater than one third to half of their total assets, and Chinese firms have access at nearly three times that level. Even if a lender were free to charge any interest rate it desired, it is highly unlikely that a company in any Western country could secure debt that was 1.4 times its annual revenue. In short, the level of resources pumped into SOEs is in a category unlike elsewhere in the world in modern times.

Despite heavy indebtedness, Chinese SOEs do not pay high interest rates. One study found that on average Chinese SOEs pay interest rates that were 44% lower than POEs in China.[14] This is in part because most SOE debt come from bank loans, and all the largest banks in China are state-owned. Even if some of these bank executives thought lending at such high levels of indebtedness or at such low rates is unwise, if the government wants the loans to be made, they will be.

Finally, SOEs benefit by paying little or no dividends to the state. Although the state could theoretically be entitled to all of the SOEs' after-tax profits, the Chinese state has historically avoided seeking any dividend payments from SOEs.[15]

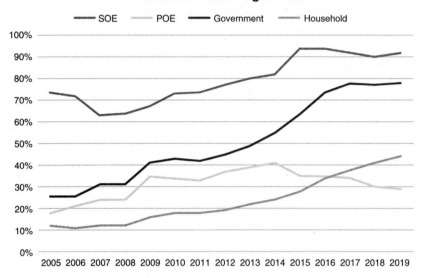

Exhibit 1.9 SOE Debt

Sources: Macquarie Group, National Bureau of Statistics of China; Ministry of Finance, People's Bank of China.

It's a pretty good model when the state pays the costs and the company keeps the profits.

Together, the massive subsidization of debt and the absolution of the need for dividend payments leads to a skewed system of incentives. For Chinese SOEs, as well as the countless number of POEs dependent on the state for funding and project approvals, protecting and promulgating Enterprise China is in their best long-term financial interests.

Removing the Blinders: Why Enterprise China Is Different

The idea that *any* government can support a long-term competitive strategy is foreign to most in the West, who are used to governments lurching from one policy to the next with the election of every new president or prime minister. To most business leaders in the West, the state is synonymous with bureaucracy, lethargy, and being an obstacle to economic progress. The idea that a government — whether Chinese or their own — could have a coherent and consistent strategy for commercial competitiveness and leadership and stick to it through thick and thin is inconceivable. Not so in China.

For at least three generations, Westerners have believed or at least hoped that economic prosperity would lead to greater economic liberty in China. After all, the pattern of capitalism leading to prosperity and prosperity leading to democracy has been observed across many nations and times. Consequently, supporting economic ties with China and promoting Chinese economic growth was akin to supporting eventual democracy with all the lasting and deep changes that would follow. Thus, foreign investment in Enterprise China was viewed by many in the West as an investment in one's own long-term institutional and philosophical interests.

What is shocking to a lot of business and political leaders in the West is that China has in many ways become the economic equal to the United States *without* changing its system. Authoritarianism has not derailed growth. In fact, the vast majority of Chinese (over 90% according to one study) believe that authoritarianism has been a key to China's success.[16] In another 2020 study by the University of California found that 88% of Chinese preferred their country's political system. In contrast, surveys in the United States typically show US government approval ratings in the sub-forty percent range.[17] Clearly, China has prospered on its own terms and, if anything, is now doubling down on what has worked so well.

Thus far, China's trajectory has largely been of China's making. It will not be easily deterred. The country's humiliating decline and subjugation to the United Kingdom, the United States, and later Japan in the 19th and 20th centuries have left an enduring mark on the proud Chinese,[18] something that we elaborate on in Chapter 2. Particularly shameful was the loss of Hong Kong to the British as the result of the opium wars in 1839. Many Chinese scholars refer to this era as the "century of humiliation."[19] Hoping that China will suddenly come to its "senses" and embrace US-style capitalism is a fool's game. China is bound and determined to prevail, to prove the West wrong, and to take its rightful place as the Middle Kingdom. And Enterprise China plays a central role in this plan.

STRUCTURE OF THE BOOK

While history and context are serious considerations, our focus is ultimately on the implications of Enterprise China for foreign business leaders and their companies. Our contentions and the reasons that we think every CEO of a moderately sized firm or larger should read this book are simple. Chinese competitors in China and outside China are now of a size and capability that they should not be underestimated. Furthermore, no matter their apparent competitive capabilities (or even lack thereof), the individual enterprises do not constitute the full competitive picture. The full picture requires pulling back the curtain and examining the additional force behind them—the Chinese state. The individual enterprises in China at best constitute only half of what is Enterprise China. In fact, in most cases, it is a mistake to think of the two as separate entities. They are one.

To formulate intelligent and successful long-term strategies to compete in and with their Chinese rivals, Western executives must take a comprehensive view of

Enterprise China. Without understanding not just what they see in their rivals' corporate strategies but what is behind, underneath, on top of, or in parallel with those strategies—the Chinese government's competitive strategy—Western executives are at great risk of incomplete at best and completely inadequate at worst assessments of the challenges in and with China. As a consequence, they are also at risk of miscalculating their competitive options and actions.

In our next three chapters we will take a close look at China's three strategic pillars. In Chapter 2, we take up the first strategic pillar—China's determination to rid itself of dependency on the West. In Chapter 3, we examine the second strategic pillar of ensuring that indigenous firms dominate the domestic China market. Chapter 4 explores the third strategic pillar of winning globally. In Chapter 5, we examine the strategic options for foreign firms with operations inside China, and in Chapter 6 we examine the options for firms without operations there. In Chapter 7, we explore and analyze what could cause Enterprise China's strategy to derail and not achieve its aims. In the final chapter, we pull together, round out the implications, and extrapolate forward.

Chapter 2

STRATEGIC PILLAR I: REVERSING DEPENDENCY

In Chapter 1 we highlighted China's vision and competitive strategy. As noted, to become one of the internally strongest and externally most influential nations on earth, China first seeks to reduce and eventually reverse its dependency on foreign firms (and countries) for key technologies and products. This pillar of the Enterprise China's strategy is not new. It was articulated nearly two decades ago in the National Medium- and Long-Term Science and Technology Development Plan (MLP). In this strategy document, Enterprise China explicitly names targeted sectors for reducing dependency and articulates goals and metrics by which progress would be measured.

Specifically, the MLP identifies a host of industries including energy, water and mineral resources, environment, agriculture, manufacturing, transportation, information and services, population and health, urbanization, public security, and national defense as key sectors in which China would reduce its external dependency. The main metric to measure progress would be local content. The initial goal was to increase domestic content to 30% in the targeted areas by 2020.[1]

In May 2015 China released its second competitive strategy installment— Made in China 2025. MIC 2025 is a continuation of the MLP but represents an important update of Enterprise China's competitive strategy. MIC 2025 modifies the targeted sectors and raises the local content goal from 30% to 40% by 2020. It also extends the time frame of this import substitution policy and adds the goal of reaching 70% local content in the 10 targeted sectors by 2025.

But how do you ensure that you achieve 70% local content and are only 30% dependent on external suppliers in key sectors? Setting the goal is certainly an important initial step, but anyone who has ever set a goal of losing "x" number of pounds knows that setting the goal alone does not ensure that you will lose the weight. You need a plan, a set of tactical actions. Enterprise China understands this and has laid out three key tactics for reducing its external dependency.

WHY REDUCE DEPENDENCY?

Before we dive into exactly *how* Enterprise China plans to reduce and even reverse its external dependency, it is worth examining *why* China has established this strategic pillar as part of its competitive strategy. To fully appreciate this *why* question, we need to briefly remind readers of some historical context.

Restore the Middle Kingdom

Although we feel no need to recount in detail China's long history, a few key points help put China's ambition and determination to reverse its dependency on foreign products and technologies into perspective. Scholars believe that China is the world's oldest continuous civilization, going back nearly 7,000 years. Across these millennia, China has been known by multiple names. Traditionally and most commonly, China has referred to itself as "Zhongguo," which is literally translated into English as the "Middle Kingdom." The Middle Kingdom was a reference to China's position between heaven and the rest of the world. The early Chinese also believed that their civilization was located in the middle of the entire earth and was surrounded by barbarians. This view of China as being distinct from the rest of the world was nurtured by the geography of the country.[2] The Himalayan mountains and Gobi desert to the south and west, the vast Mongolian and Siberian plains to the north, and the Pacific Ocean to the east all provided natural boundaries and protection.

In the premodern era, China had the world's strongest economy. Additionally, for nearly 900 years it was the world's undisputed technological leader.[3] The list of inventions from China is long and distinguished, including gunpowder, paper, iron and steel smelting, mechanical clocks, silk, porcelain, the compass, the umbrella, and the kite. While there are divergent theories as to why China subsequently fell behind Europe in science, technology, and productivity, most scholars point to the country's geographic isolation and its inward-looking political system as key contributors.[4]

Regardless, beginning in the 15th century and for nearly the next 500 years, China's isolation caused it to miss the Age of Enlightenment and the early part of the Industrial Revolution.[5] We refer to this period as the Great Isolation. To some extent this lag left China vulnerable to the economic and military power of other nations at the beginning of the 20th century. As a consequence, China suffered great humiliation in its subsequent economic and military subjugation at the hands of foreign countries, such as Japan.

China's resurgence, which began in the late 1970s, brought a renewed sense of national pride. Today, many Chinese have returned to the frequent use of "Zhongguo," or the Middle Kingdom, to describe their country. To them, it reflects the view that China was once a united and powerful nation and is now primed again to assume its historical and proper role as the center of the world. These feelings were encouraged by President Xi Jinping, who has routinely reminded his Chinese audiences of China's goal to take back its "rightful" position as the most powerful country in the world. One example of this is a speech that Xi made before China's 19th National Party Congress in 2017. "Now is time for the nation to take center stage in the world," he said.[6]

The country's ambition for economic and political hegemony has been aided by additional social forces that are often overlooked in the West. One important force was the dominant role of the Han Chinese within the country. The Han now constitute 90% of China's population and have become the most dominant, cohesive ethnic group in the world.[7] This in turn has led to a lack of ethnic diversity at the top of Chinese political and economic institutions. This lack of diversity is a unifying force within China but also contributes to an "us" versus "them" (foreign countries and companies) mindset. The predominant thinking in China is that if the nation is to return to its rightful place at the center of the world, it cannot be dependent on outsiders for products and technology that are critical to its prosperity and sovereignty.

One final historical element that helps explain China's first strategic pillar is its feeling that the West is in a self-inflicted decline. Chinese leaders believe the waning of the West is rooted in arrogance, the breakdown of social institutions, hypocrisy, and ignorance. Chinese Communist Party (CCP) speeches ahead of the centenary meetings in the summer of 2021 repeated time and again the same basic message: "The East is rising while the West is in decline."[8] For many in China, the country's superior growth compared to all other major countries in 2020—in spite of the COVID-19 pandemic—was proof of its superiority and the resiliency of the Chinese system and people.

Whether one agrees with these Chinese perspectives or not is not the point. Appreciating these feelings and recognizing how they drive Enterprise China's first strategic pillar is. Enterprise China wants not only to compete with the West but ultimately to prevail over it. This is not possible while being dependent on outsiders. As a consequence, China must reduce and ultimately reverse its external dependency.

Recalibrate Layers of Interdependency

The important point of all this is to appreciate how deep and fundamental is Enterprise China's desire and determination to remove its excessive external dependencies in key sectors. While countries and individuals can disagree on what constitutes "excessive," in today's global world, some level of interdependence across national security, commercial and consumer products, and technologies is inevitable. Put differently, *complete* independence is virtually impossible. Some degree of trade among countries is inescapable. After all, even the Hermit Kingdom of North Korea still imports a smattering of Western goods.

It shouldn't be surprising that essentially all countries depend on foreign sources for *some* of their products and technologies. But in the case of China, this is a very large number. At an aggregate level in 2021, China imported nearly $2.7 trillion in goods and services (see Exhibit 2.1), up 1,184% since 2002.

In absolute terms, this can make it seem as though China has heavily depended on imports for a long time. However, when considered as a percent of GDP, its imports have declined since 2002 and are only up 29% since 1985. In addition, as measured against GDP, China's imports are similar to the United States and Japan, and China is far less dependent on imports in general as compared to Germany (see Exhibit 2.2).

If China's imports are not that out of line with those of other countries, why is it so set on reducing its external dependency and implementing local content goals that, if achieved, would result in substantial import substitution? Although we covered the historical context to this question already, it is worth repeating. China fell behind the world once; it has no interest in falling behind again. Perhaps more importantly, China's period of relative decline opened the door for economic and military subjugation. China has zero tolerance for that possibility ever again. Consequently, China is highly motivated to ensure it reduces its external dependency and consequently is in better position to control its own destiny.

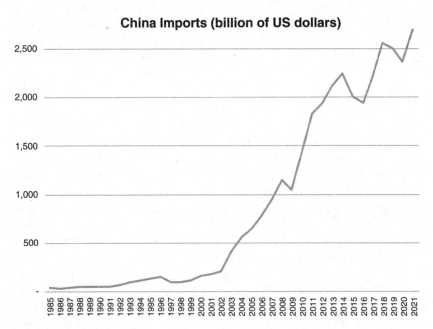

Exhibit 2.1 Imports into China
Source: World Bank.

Imports as a Percentage of GDP

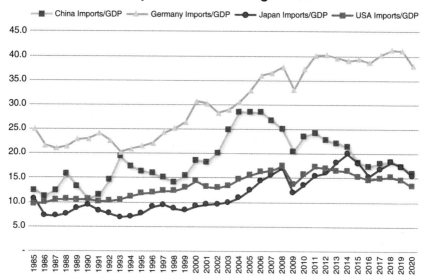

Exhibit 2.2 Imports as a Percentage of GDP
Source: World Bank.

While some may believe that national pride is the singular motivation for the country's first strategic pillar, we argue that there are additional motivations. In the following sections, we examine the top three.

Capture Technology Multiplier Effects

Many years ago, Michael Boskin, an economic advisor to the first President Bush, memorably quipped, "Potato chips, computer chips, what's the difference? A hundred dollars of one or a hundred dollars of the other is still a hundred dollars." Chinese government officials understand the flaw in this thinking. In today's world, microchips are much more important than potato chips. Therefore, China's competitive strategy focuses on reducing dependency not across the board but in technology-intensive industries. Chinese officials seem little concerned about foreign involvement in industries such as beverages, luxury watches, or apparel within its borders. These are not the industries targeted under MIC 2025. Nor are Chinese officials overly vexed by soaring food imports. In fact, China's growing appetite for higher quality food led to a fourfold increase in food imports in one decade (2007 to 2017) to $105 billion.[9] Instead, Enterprise China's external dependency concern is focused primarily on high-value-added, technology-intensive industries.

China's focus on technology is rooted in the belief that one technology can accelerate the development of other technologies, and that these in turn can improve the overall competitiveness of industries, which in turn bring prosperity and strength to the country. There is ample evidence to support this contention. Research has shown that innovations have multiplier effects that can accelerate the development of related technologies.[10] For example, a strength in manufacturing semiconductors can positively affect progress in 5G. And the converse is also true. Being a laggard in key technologies makes it more difficult to catch up in other industries. For example, a weakness in power generation and distribution can inhibit the development of high-speed electric trains. Because technology fuels key industries today, it makes sense for China to pay particular attention to its level of technological dependency.

Almost two-thirds of China's technology-intensive imports come from just three countries: the United States (31%), Japan (21%), and Germany (10%).[11] It should come as no surprise that the United States tops the list of sources of technology. The US leadership in technology is manifest in several key industries. In the fields of biotechnology and pharmaceuticals, the United States has 12 of the top 20 firms in terms of market capitalization. With just two firms, Switzerland is No. 2 on the list. In semiconductor wafers, the United States is home to four of the world's top eight companies. Other industries where US companies control more than 50% of global market capitalization include software, IT services, tech hardware, health care equipment, and energy.[12] In nanotechnology, scientists from US research institutions published 4,688 nanotechnology-related patents in 2019 versus 1,105 for South Korea, 918 for Japan, and just 825 for China.[13] In other industries, Japan is No. 1, ahead of the United States. For example, in photonics, of the top ten major companies in the world in terms of market growth, five are Japanese and only three are American.[14] In machine tools and equipment, Germany leads the pack. In 2019, German companies controlled 16% of the global machinery trade, making Germany the world's No. 1 supplier, exporting 80% of the machine tools it produced. Out of 31 different machine equipment sectors, German companies held the No. 1 or No. 2 market position in 21 of these sectors.[15]

In sum, the first reason that China seeks to reduce its external dependency in key sectors is because those sectors are critical to future national strength. How can China be among the strongest countries in the world if it is not among the best in the most important technologies? How can it be among the best if it is buying 70% of key technologies and products from the likes of the United States, Germany, and Japan? Enterprise China's answer: it can't.

Move Up the Value Stack

Related to this first rationale is a highly connected second rationale. If China were to continue to import technology at the high end of the value stack from the United States, Japan, Germany, and others, China could easily be relegated to lower-end value activities, such as putting semiconductor chips into products rather than producing the semiconductors. Apart from the multiplier effects of leading in high technology, if China were relegated to only lower-value and labor-intensive activities toward the bottom of the value stack, this would dampen China's future domestic prosperity and global leadership. You do not need a PhD in economics to understand why this is the case. You don't generate the greatest revenue by doing the least value-adding activities. To be relegated to low-value activities would generate lower prosperity and fewer national leadership opportunities, which in turn would violate China's vision. Nearly 20 years of consistent statements by Chinese leaders makes it clear that this violation is simply not acceptable.

Mitigate Supply Disruption Risks

A third rationale for seeking to reduce its external dependency is the risk of supply disruption. For example, if you were 90% dependent on external suppliers of semiconductor chips and there is a significant supply disruption, the Chinese factories that make the washers and dryers, refrigerators, air conditioners, automobiles, and so on that require those chips for both internal consumption and export would grind to a halt.

Any experienced executive understands the negative impact of supply disruptions. No one wants them. However, most experienced executives also would point out that supply portfolio diversification is a common means of mitigating supply disruption risks. By diversifying your external suppliers, if one supplier in Japan suffers a massive disruption due to a tsunami and the resulting meltdown of a nuclear power plant, for example, you could rely on alternative suppliers in your diversified portfolio from places such as India or Singapore, which were not affected by the tsunami. Mitigating supply disruption risk does not require making the inputs yourself. Consequently, it's worth asking: Why can't China mitigate its supply disruption risk by diversifying its external supply portfolio? Why does it believe that mitigating this risk requires massive increases in local content and the related import substitution?

Before Enterprise China could answer this question, an experienced executive might also quickly point out that this risk mitigation approach not only helps you hedge against unanticipated supply disruptions, but it helps you keep a single supplier from gaining too much power and leveraging that power into higher prices. In fact, in combination, these two benefits of a diverse supply portfolio are exactly why many companies and their executives use this risk mitigation strategy and are reasonably comfortable *not* making 70% of what they need in-house but sourcing it from external suppliers. Why doesn't Enterprise China simply take up this tried-and-true supply risk mitigation strategy?

TO TRUST OR NOT TO TRUST; THAT IS THE QUESTION

Quite frankly, the cost-benefit analysis of dependency comes down to trust. The more you trust your diversified portfolio of external suppliers, the more comfortable you are with mitigating your supply disruption risk by diversifying your supply portfolio. However, the less you trust your diversified portfolio of external suppliers, the greater your incentive to bring things in-house. But this may come off as too quick or simplistic an answer, so let's walk through it all with a concrete, practical example—semiconductors.

In 2019, China accounted for just over 50% of all semiconductor demand globally. This demand was generated both by China's internal consumption and by what it incorporated into products that it shipped overseas as exports. To meet this combined demand, in 2020 China imported about $378 billion in semiconductors.[16] It produced only about $21 billion—6% of the value of its imports.

Looking forward, some estimate that by 2025 the global semiconductor market will be $800 billion. If China retains its share of this total demand, it will need approximately $400 billion in semiconductors via a combination of local production and imports. The MIC 2025 strategy calls for China to produce 70% of its need domestically, which would equate to about $280 billion. This is more than a tenfold increase in five years from where it was in 2020. Whether China can do this is a separate question—one that is related to strategy execution rather than formulation, which we will address in Chapter 7. But let's continue an examination of the scenario.

What if, in 2025, China failed to meet its objective and was still importing over 90% of its needed semiconductors as was the case in 2020? If you were the head of Enterprise China and semiconductors went into an innumerable array of products consumed within China and incorporated into products exported from China, how worried would you be about your dependency on external suppliers? How much more worried would you be if over 60% of your chips came from Taiwan? You might get fairly nervous about your level of external dependency.

But you also might say:

> *Hey, wait a minute. If I'm Enterprise China and I control 50% of the global demand for semiconductors, why should I get overly anxious? Why do I need to produce 70% of my semiconductors at home versus offshore? Why can't I leverage my huge demand advantage over suppliers, such as Intel, Qualcomm, or SK Hynix, to ensure both reliable delivery and good prices? Yes, I'm dependent on them for chips, but they are dependent upon me for demand—for an important portion of their revenue.*

This is quite a reasonable question to ask. Why couldn't China just continue to leverage its demand advantage going forward as it has in the past? After all, for the past 20 years, China achieved its current position of generating half the world's semiconductor demand by importing, not making, the chips it has needed. If China had insisted on consuming or exporting chips primarily made in China, could it have reached the position of making up 50% of global semiconductor demand? It seems unlikely because it simply would not have been able to generate sufficient supply locally. So why should China feel it must reverse its dependency in semiconductors when it has such a strong demand position? This same question would apply to a whole host of sectors where China is the largest source of demand and in many cases generates more demand than the rest of the world combined. Why would it formulate this strategic pillar of reducing dependency and stick to it for nearly two decades instead of diversifying its external supply and leveraging its demand advantage to ensure both reliable and competitively priced supply?

In this light, the answer of trust appears to be much more palatable and powerful. After all, what happens to the robustness of the traditional diversified supply portfolio risk mitigation strategy if you have doubts regarding *all* the external suppliers in the diversified portfolio? The answer is obvious. You set up a strategic pillar of producing onshore 40% by 2020 of what you need in aerospace, biotech, information technology, smart manufacturing, maritime engineering, advanced rail, electric vehicles, electrical equipment, new materials, biomedicine, agricultural machinery and equipment, pharmaceuticals, and robotics manufacturing, and raise that goal to 70% by 2025.

HOW WILL CHINA REDUCE DEPENDENCIES?

If you are going to reduce your external dependency from 90% to 30%, you need a plan—a set of tactics—for how to achieve such a monumental reduction. Enterprise China has articulated a three-part plan for cutting its dependencies: borrow, buy, and build. With a solid understanding of why China is so intent on reducing its dependencies and producing 70% of what it needs in key sectors onshore and having that substitute for imports from offshore, we can now more effectively examine each of the import substitution tactics in some detail. As we will examine in greater detail in Chapter 5, these tactics matter because they have important competitive implications for foreign firms, especially those in the 10 key sectors targeted by Enterprise China.

Borrow from External Players

For more than 15 years, Enterprise China's first avenue of action for reducing dependency has been to borrow, or what officially is often labeled as "extraction." This involves lifting targeted technology from external players on which Enterprise China is overly dependent. Enterprise China has leveraged mandatory joint ventures (JVs), as well as licensing and other regulatory requirements in pursuit of the tactic of extraction.

JVs have been a particularly important extraction vehicle. MIC 2025 specifically noted that the central government would "encourage the overseas transfer of high-end equipment, advanced technology" and "transform[ing] the utilization of foreign capital to emphasize joint ventures." An investigation by the US Trade Representative (USTR) into the extraction of targeted technology via JVs concluded that "the Chinese government uses foreign ownership restrictions, such as formal and informal JV requirements, and other foreign investment restrictions to require or pressure technology transfer from US companies to Chinese entities." Clearly the USTR didn't like this, but Enterprise China was doing exactly what it set out to do—extract targeted technologies via JVs in order to reduce its dependencies on foreign firms.

Limit Foreign Ownership through JVs

In the 1980s and 1990s, virtually all foreign direct investments (FDIs) in China were through JVs. In 1988, only 10% of FDI in China was wholly owned. Although the percentage of wholly owned foreign operations in China has increased over time, JVs are still frequently encouraged and even required by the Chinese government. As of 2020, China still imposed foreign ownership caps on 33 industries,[17] including nonelectric automobiles, telecommunication services, banking, agriculture, hospitality, and chemicals. The ownership caps effectively require some type of joint ownership. The extraction of foreign technologies has been and continues to be the primary motivation for these ownership limits and mandatory JVs.

Foreign companies frequently acquiesce to state pressure to form JVs because of their eagerness to access China's vast and growing market. Unfortunately, many foreign executives fail to link this tactic to Enterprise China's strategic pillar of reducing external dependency. Alternatively, perhaps they thought that Enterprise China would not be successful in borrowing knowledge and technology from them in the pursuit of this first strategic pillar. In either case, the intent of JVs in Enterprise China's ambitions to reduce dependencies is clear. It was, and continues to be, to extract knowledge and technology that can be used to produce key products onshore and thereby over time substitute for the imports coming from offshore.

In the minds of many foreign executives, the best JVs in China are long-lived. In the minds of many Chinese, the best JVs in China are the ones that can be milked and then exited quickly. Even when foreign executives worried about the potential seeping of information and technology out of the JV and into their partner's main organization, research by Aaron Friedberg at Princeton has shown that they often underestimated the ability of their Chinese partners to quickly absorb their technical skills.[18]

Extract through Joint Ventures

Even the best-managed foreign firms face daunting challenges in tip-toeing through the JV minefield in China. Despite some reductions of FDI restrictions, numerous sources report that Chinese pressure to transfer technology has become more implicit, often carried out "behind closed doors."[19] This is the case not only for US firms but European firms as well. In a report to the European Directorate-General for Trade, attorneys representing European plaintiffs reported that "Chinese measures and practices no longer spell out the most controversial requirements in black and white. Verbal instructions and requests to 'volunteer' one's technology are today's rules of the road."[20] This is particularly true when the partner is a SOE. A 2013 study by the US Chamber of Commerce found that 43% of the foreign companies in advanced technology industries reported "de facto transfer requirements as a condition for market access" to China.[21] And in a 2017 submission to the US Trade Representative, the US Chamber of Commerce reported that:

> *Especially in instances where the Chinese partner is a state-owned or state-directed company, foreign companies have limited leverage in the negotiation if they wish to access the market. Although this type of technology transfer may not be explicitly mandated in a Chinese law or regulation, it is often an unwritten rule for market access.*

A case in point is the aviation industry. China became the world's largest aviation market in 2020. China's state-owned airlines (China Southern, Air China, China Eastern, etc.) purchase the vast majority of commercial aircraft in the country, including spare and replacement parts. Because of this huge purchasing power, China has required foreign firms to form JVs with local manufacturers for production in China rather than simply importing planes and parts. All partnership agreements include strong provisions for technology transfers. According to a study by RAND Corporation:

> *Chinese aviation industry leaders have made no secret of their desire to trade market access for technology; joint ventures are their vehicle of choice to acquire advanced foreign technologies . . . . Such joint ventures are designed to help Chinese firms acquire technologies, managerial know-how, and production experience.*[22]

Beyond direct or indirect pressure to transfer technology, JV regulations in China typically limit technology protection to just 10 years. After this period, Chinese licensees must be granted the right to use the foreign technology in perpetuity. Foreign companies have also complained about the direct misappropriation of their technologies by joint venture partners. US companies including Corning, DuPont, American Superconductor Corporation, Eli Lilly, and General Motors have sued their Chinese JV partners for essentially stealing proprietary technology not governed by their operating agreements.

A 2017 statement by the National Association of Manufacturers captures the concern of foreign companies that rely on JVs in China:

> *This tilting of the playing field leaves manufacturers with untenable choices: they must either transfer their technology to the new China-based joint venture, or they must cede the world's fastest-growing market to foreign competitors, thus harming both their short-term growth and their long-term competitiveness.*[23]

A case in point is American Superconductor Corporation (AMSC), a leader in software to control wind turbines. To sell into the Chinese market, AMSC partnered with Sinovel, a Chinese maker of the wind turbine hardware. After several years, AMSC discovered that Sinovel paid a Serbian engineer, Dejan Karabasevic, who was working at AMSC's Austrian development facility, $1.7 million for AMSC's full source code. Karabasevic was convicted for his deeds and served a year in an Austrian prison. However, having acquired the source code, Sinovel dissolved all its business with AMSC. Subsequently, the US government filed a criminal case charging Sinovel, two Chinese Sinovel executives, and Karabasevic with conspiracy to commit trade secret theft. The case was successful, and the company and individuals were convicted in 2018, though the Chinese executives were never extradited to the United States to serve their sentences. Though a moral victory, the financial consequences were tremendous. AMSC estimated that 20% of the wind turbines deployed in China in 2019 illegally used its software.

Over time and under pressure, Enterprise China has allowed a greater percentage of FDI to come through wholly foreign owned entities rather than JVs. This form of FDI increased from 10% in 1988 to 70% in 2017.[24] Nonetheless, the stock of JVs in China has remained high. Research published by Deloitte in 2020 shows that 90% of international JVs in China that were under the age of 15 years were still in operation; nearly 70% of JV under 25 years old were still legally operating.[25] This was largely due to the complexity and difficulty of converting existing JVs to wholly owned status as well as barriers in exiting China. Thus, even though the explicit rules requiring JVs have diminished over time, JVs as a means of "borrowing" have remained an effective force.

Leverage Regulatory Mechanisms

In addition to utilizing JVs, the state has turned to other regulatory mechanisms to extract knowledge and technology in order to reduce its dependency on foreign firms. The USTR concluded that "the Chinese government uses its administrative licensing and approvals processes to force technology transfer in exchange for the numerous administrative approvals needed to establish and operate a business in China."[26] Similarly, the US-China Economic and Security Review Commission concluded in 2019 that as "part of China's licensing documentation procedures, commercial firms are required to provide detailed product and process information to Chinese government agencies at the local and central levels . . . that is typically not required in other markets."[27] This method of extraction did not just target US firms. A survey in 2019 by the European Chamber of Commerce found that one in four European firms felt compelled to hand over technology in exchange for market access—more than double the sentiment just two years prior. In other cases, technologies that have been shared with the government because of regulatory mandates have been subsequently transferred to Chinese companies so that they can develop products or services to compete with the original foreign provider of the technology.[28]

One of the regulatory means of extraction has been to require foreign companies to train the employees of Chinese license holders in applying the technology beyond its narrow design parameters. This not only includes teaching them how to operate proprietary equipment but has often been extended to include such things as providing access to proprietary cloud computing technologies and systems.[29] Other foreign JV partners have complained of requirements that Chinese enterprises be granted licensing rights on nonmarket-based terms.[30]

Use Nefarious Means

Sometimes the extraction mechanisms have been more in the shadows and have involved illegal or other nefarious means. In 2019, China was the world's leading source of pirated and counterfeit goods.[31] It has been estimated that between 2017 and 2019, 80% of counterfeit goods seized in the United States were made in either China or Hong Kong. This is a clear indication of the failure of the Chinese state to take decisive actions to shut down the manufacture and trade of pirated goods.[32] But it goes far beyond selling fake Nike shoes and New York Yankees hats. It involves increasingly complex parts and finished goods in virtually every industry in the economy, including aircraft and automobile parts, pharmaceuticals, advanced electronics, toys, apparel, and even food.

Many in China view the theft of foreign IP (intellectual property), including copyrights, patents, and trade secrets, as appropriate given the country's ideological conflict with the West. The United States, in particular, is considered a dangerous adversary that is hostile to the CCP. One Chinese scholar has called the US threat "Westernization" subversion.[33] Consequently, IP theft is often condoned in private if not in public statements. In a 2019 study, nearly 20% of CFOs of North American firms reported that Chinese firms had stolen intellectual property from them over the past year.[34]

A 2020 Harvard University, Kennedy School study ranked China as a "most comprehensive cyber power," second only to the United States. And China was No. 1 in the world for its "intent" to use its cyber capabilities for national objectives.[35] Key to China's cyber prowess is the role of the People's Liberation Army and the Ministry of State Security. Their targets are a mixture of foreign governments, technology laboratories, and business institutions. Technologies and market intelligence are frequently shared with Chinese SOEs and even publicly traded Chinese companies. It has been reported that companies such as Huawei and ZTE have gained significant advantages from these state incursions in their efforts to expand in Africa[36] as well as other locations.

China's cyber intrusions have targeted a wide range of industries. These include the global oil and gas industries, petrochemicals, telecommunications, health care, real estate, and defense industries.[37] In August 2020, US prosecutors charged five Chinese hackers with illegally accessing and stealing the intellectual property from more than 100 US companies. The hackers were alleged to have ties to the Chinese state intelligence community. In announcing the charges, Deputy Attorney General Jeffrey Rosen said, "Regrettably, the Chinese Communist Party has chosen a different path of making China safe for cybercriminals so long as they attack computers outside China and steal intellectual property helpful to China."[38] The defendants were also linked to cyberattacks in Japan, India, Brazil, Singapore, Taiwan, and South Korea among other countries.

Other Chinese groups have targeted global pharmaceutical companies including Bayer, Merck, and GlaxoSmithKline. Operating under the code name "Dragonfly," the hackers targeted the intellectual property of these companies in an effort to bolster the Chinese domestic pharmaceutical industry, which had been targeted under MIC 2025. In a report on the cyber intrusions, IT security company SCADAfence reported:

> Faced by an ageing demographic and rising cancer rates on mainland China, the Chinese communist party is set on bolstering its domestic pharmaceutical industry by 2025. Years of siphoning off intellectual property from Western pharmaceutical companies may now be paying off as mainland Chinese manufacturers are reported to be developing cancer drugs that will dramatically undercut the prices charged by Western companies, who have had to bear the cost of years of innovative and cutting-edge research.[39]

Many cyber intrusions go undetected for years. A 2014 indictment of "members of the People's Liberation Army" of China by the US Justice Department charged the defendants with committing computer fraud over the period of 2006 to 2014. The charges alleged that the "conspirators stole trade secrets that would be particularly beneficial to Chinese companies at the time they were stolen."[40] Companies targeted in the cyber fraud include US Steel, Alcoa, Westinghouse Electrical Company, SolarWorld, and the United Steelworkers.

Chinese efforts to "borrow" technology from foreign sources shows no signs of slowing down. In September 2020, US FBI director Christopher Wray testified before Congress that Chinese hackers were "actively targeting US companies involved in COVID-19 research . . . whether it's vaccines, treatments, testing technology, etc."[41] Then in early 2021, the US National Counterintelligence and

Security Center (NCSC) warned that the Chinese government had targeted US health data, more particularly DNA information, from an unsuspecting US public. Their approach included legal and illegal means and picked up speed during the COVID-19 crisis. The focus of their efforts was a Chinese biotech company, BGI, which offered COVID-19 testing kits and labs in a number of countries. But rather than focus exclusively on COVID-19 testing, the NCSC asserted that the DNA results were more broadly targeted because "the PRC understands the collection and analysis of large genomic datasets from diverse populations helps foster new medical discoveries and cures that can have substantial commercial value and advance its artificial intelligence and precision medicine industries."[42] According to the NCSC, the ultimate goal for the Chinese was to use broad swaths of DNA information from diverse populations to outpace Western companies in pharmaceutical development and innovation.

Questions arise as to the identity of the instigators of these intrusions. Are the hackers sponsored solely by state actors who then share their information with Chinese businesses? Or are the cyber intrusions driven by the companies themselves? According to the US Trade Representative:

> The U.S. government has evidence that the Chinese government provides competitive intelligence through cyber intrusions to Chinese state-owned enterprises through a process that includes a formal request and feedback loop, as well as a mechanism for information exchange via a classified communication system . . . . China uses the intelligence resources at its disposal to further the commercial interests of Chinese state-owned enterprises to the detriment of their foreign partners and competitors.[43]

It is the norm of economically advanced countries to prohibit and criminalize cyber intrusions, including the theft of data and intellectual property. While China has occasionally spoken out against cyber theft, its enforcement actions leave much to be desired. In contrast, strong links between the Chinese state intelligence community and SOEs are often interpreted as an endorsement of cyberespionage. Certainly, perpetrators of cybercrimes can be found throughout the world. But China's pattern of cyber intrusion is in a class that is unique. Commenting on the difference between China's approach to cyber activities with those of other countries, the USTR asserted the following:

> Claims that there is no meaningful distinction between the Chinese government's cyber activities and that of other countries, including the United States, are not valid. China's cyber intrusions are unique from those of Western market economies because the intrusions occur within the framework of China's extensive state-driven economic development model, which has no parallel in Western market economies. Not only does the United States not rely on extensive industrial policy tools to identify specific commercial sectors and commercial

technologies for development, the United States does not have national champions and state-owned enterprises to implement such policies.[44]

Given complaints by foreign firms regarding these extraction methods, why don't foreign firms do more to oppose them? According to surveys conducted by the US Chamber of Commerce, many foreign companies feel that they have no recourse in dealing with the misappropriation of their technology.[45] This finding is echoed by the US China Business Council, which reported that US companies "fear that they will face retaliation or the loss of business opportunities if they come forward to complain about China's unfair trade practices."[46] Others have argued that US laws need to be changed to allow companies to counterattack against Chinese hackers, thus providing a deterrence and give US companies a new competitive tool.[47]

Acquire Foreign Firms

In addition to extraction, Enterprise China has also sought to reduce its dependency by buying foreign firms that own the technology that China deems important to its self-reliance. MIC 2025 specifically notes that the central government would "support enterprises to perform mergers, equity investment and venture capital investment overseas" to achieve this objective.

The year after MIC 2025 was announced, Chinese acquisitions of US firms soared 533% to $57 billion. This spectacular increase did not go unnoticed in the United States, and in the following year, the Committee on Foreign Investment in the United States (CFIUS), along with other US government agencies, started to scrutinize and block acquisitions due to national security concerns. The level of deals subsequently plummeted to under $10 billion in 2017 and totaled only $2.9 billion in 2019.

In addition to full acquisitions, MIC 2025 called for state-backed venture capital (VC) investments as a means of acquiring insights into key technologies. Like M&A investments, the year after MIC 2025 was announced, Chinese VC funding soared from $3.3 billion in 2015 to $11.5 billion in 2016. However, unlike M&A activity, which quickly declined, VC funding continued at high levels until mid-2018 when the United States passed a law that allowed US agencies to review potential investments by Chinese VC funds and required Chinese VC funds to disclose their funding sources. With this new law, Chinese VC investments plummeted to less than $5 billion in 2019.

In support of outbound investments, Chinese firms, particularly SOEs, as well as those closely aligned with the state, receive subsidized financing to facilitate foreign acquisitions. In investigating the use of acquisitions, the US Trade Representative concluded that:

The Chinese government directs and unfairly facilitates the systematic investment in, and acquisition of, U.S. companies and assets by Chinese companies, to obtain cutting-edge technologies and intellectual property (IP) and generate large-scale technology transfer in industries deemed important by state industrial plans.[48]

The story of Chinese rail equipment giant CRRC provides a valuable illustration of how acquisitions, combined with broader state assistance, have helped propel Chinese firms forward. CRRC was formed in 2015 through the merger of two other giant rail companies: China North Locomotive and Rolling Stock Corporation (CSR), and China South Locomotive and CNR. Both were state-owned corporations organized in 2008 and 2009, respectively. A primary objective of the merger was to create an entity with the scale necessary to "increase international competitiveness" and "realize the Go Out strategy" set by the Chinese state.[49] Previously, CSR and CNR had invested heavily in technology partnerships with US firms such as GE and Electro-Motive Diesel, as well as Canada's Dynix, Australia's Delkor Rail, and Germany's E&M.

Once formed, CRRC soon became one of the most heavily subsidized companies in China. State funds were used to support exports, and within just a few years the company had signed sales contracts for rail equipment in 105 countries. No other company in the global industry had grown internationally so rapidly as CRRC. At the same time, R&D facilities were built through JVs with leading technical centers and universities in the United States, the United Kingdom, and Germany. CRRC then undertook a series of acquisitions including Cideon Engineering, based in Germany and Switzerland, and Vossioh Locomotives, based in Germany. The company also attempted (but failed) to purchase Skoda Transportation for €2 billion. Skoda was a major exporter of rolling stock to the European Union and the United States. As a show of support for CRRC and to curry favor with the Chinese state, China CEFC Energy Company (at the time one of the 10 largest public companies in China), together with the Beijing Municipal Road and Bridge Group, purchased 80% of the Czech company TSS Cargo in 2016. TSS Cargo was the largest Czech railway operator and would no doubt become a major customer for CRRC. (As an aside, CEFC would go on to declare bankruptcy in 2020 after revelations of a web of fake deals designed to secure bank loans. Most believe that CEFC would have been saved had it been an SOE.)

Along the way, CRRC was helped by other connections to the state. Executives at CRRC (and, before it, CNR and CSR) held leadership positions not just in their firms but also in the CCP. CRRC's chairman of the board, Liu Hualong, also served as the CCP's party secretary. And Vice Chairman Xi Guohua served as the deputy party secretary.[50] CRRC also partnered with state-owned companies including China Aerospace Science and Technology Corporation, China Insurance Investment Fund, Industrial and Commercial Bank of China (ICBC), Shanghai Pudong Development Bank, and the Beijing Municipal Government in providing US $15 billion to fund the "National Innovation Fund" designed to nurture "military-civil fusion industries." CRRC joined other partnerships with

Chinese technology companies to fund and develop new energy automobiles, unmanned vehicles, and new materials. The company also launched a partnership with Huawei to develop "intelligent public transportation products."[51] Additionally, CRRC also had investment links with BeiDou, China's satellite systems company, as well as Shandong Tianhua, a major manufacturer of silicon carbide materials, an area of focus in the state's MIC 2025 plans. Welcome to Enterprise China!

Build Internal Capabilities

China recognizes that to reduce its dependency and gain greater self-sufficiency, it cannot rely only on borrowing or buying key technology; it must also build or develop next-generation technologies and their supporting industries internally. This is no small undertaking. To focus Enterprise China's efforts on key industries and to ensure that efforts are fully coordinated, the government has deployed what is referred to as the National Strategic Emerging Industries Development Plan (SEI Plan).

Target Key Sectors

The SEI Plan houses the state's initiatives to nurture strategically emerging industries and to ensure they become fully developed. The SEI Plan is updated every five years, consistent with national economic planning. The country's 12th five-year SEI Plan, launched in 2010, focused on the development of seven emerging industries such as energy conservation and environmental protection, information technology, new materials, and new energy vehicles.[52] It also recommended fiscal and taxation policy that nurtured certain Chinese companies into becoming what were called "backbone enterprises" — in essence, national and global champions.[53]

The 13th five-year SEI Plan, covering the years 2016 to 2020, promoted such initiatives as the Internet of Things, cloud computing, big data, biotechnology, and artificial intelligence.[54] The plan worked by using the "coordinated development of the supply chain and the innovation chain as a means of cultivating new formats and new models, develop distinctive industrial clusters, and promote regional economic transformations to form a new pattern of innovative economic agglomeration and development." The goal was to double the value added of strategic emerging industries from 8% to 15% of the Chinese economy over the five years of the 13th five-year plan.

China's 14th five-year SEI Plan, covering the years 2021 to 2025, narrowed the industries that were targeted. These included 5G mobile networks, intelligent and new energy vehicles, industrial robotics, vaccines, and semiconductor manufacturing. The plan included the sponsorship of the Ministry of Science and Technology, Ministry of Industry and Information Technology, and Ministry of Finance, which together vowed to build complete strategic ecosystems through state planning and state investment.[55] In announcing these initiatives, the government indicated that the plan was "designed to help China avoid being 'strangled' by its dependence on imports for key technologies and components and instead relying on its own technological breakthroughs."[56]

Support Localized Research and Development

A key component of the SEI Plan is directing state funding of R&D activities, especially involving but not strictly limited to SOEs. Since the 1990s, tens of thousands of government laboratories have been effectively relocated to SOEs.[57] Consequently, compared to other countries, the proportion of government-to-corporate expenditures on R&D in China is now among the lowest in the world. This is shown in Exhibit 2.3 below.

It isn't that the Chinese government doesn't heavily support R&D, it's just that the country is increasingly housing technology development within SOEs. While Chinese companies dominate R&D spending, the Chinese government, academia, and industry work together as partners in ways that other countries do not seem able to replicate. This can provide synergies and speed the translation of core research into industrial applications. Case in point: in 2016, China launched the Micius satellite designed to use photon beams sent in a quantum state that achieves absolutely secure communications based on quantum key distribution (a method that uses quantum properties to exchange cryptographic keys in such a way that is provable and guarantees security).[58] The efforts were part of a much bigger quantum science laboratory established in Eastern China and funded with a $10 billion budget. The effort is designed to secure the Chinese government *and* industrial leadership in quantum communications and encryption.[59]

Country	Business (%)	Government (%)
Japan	79.1	14.6
China	76.6	20.2
Germany	66.0	27.9
USA	62.4	23
UK	54.8	25.9
Italy	54.6	32.7
Canada	41.1	33.1

Exhibit 2.3 R&D Financed by Business and Government (2018)
Source: OECD Main Science and Technology Indicators.

Between 1991 and 2018, total Chinese expenditures on R&D, including projects carried out by businesses, government, and academic research centers, increased a staggering 35-fold. That year, China's spending on R&D represented 25% of the world's total investment in R&D, greater than Japan, Germany, South Korea, and France combined.[60] Clearly, China is serious about building its technological base and owes much of its success to its rapidly expanding homegrown capacity.

Our analysis suggests that China has set aside over half a trillion dollars in various funds targeting MIC 2025 initiatives and projects. For example, it set up a $31 billion fund to support the development of indigenous semiconductor capabilities. Some of the other large funds include the Special Constructive Fund ($270 billion), the Shaanix MIC2025 Fund ($117 billion), the MIIT and China Development Bank ($45 billion), and Gansu MIC 2025 Fund ($37 billion). As we learned from the CRRC case, funding often comes from equity infusions or outright loans from other SOEs, often operating in industries that are only tangentially related. This is Enterprise China at its finest.

Acquire Talent

Money matters, but when it comes to innovation and development, having the right, bright, innovative people matters as much or more. Funding research and development is critical to achieving technological leadership. But every country interested in innovation also needs world-class scientists and administrators to put the money to good use. To upgrade its workforce, China has invested heavily in advancing its efforts to both grow and poach talent.

Grow Domestic Talent. Between 2000 and 2019, the number of college graduates in China increased from 1 million to over 8 million people. But where Chinese universities really made progress was in their science, technology, engineering, and math (STEM) programs. Between 2000 and 2016, the number of STEM graduates increased 12-fold, from about 400,000 to 4.7 million.[61] Today, China has more STEM graduates than India, the United States, Japan, Germany, France, Italy, the United Kingdom, and Canada combined. In 2019, the United States graduated 55,703 students with doctoral degrees.[62] In 2018, China had an estimated 389,518 students in doctoral programs.[63]

Poach Overseas Talent. China also has moved aggressively to recruit the world's top scientists. The initiative, called the "Thousand Talents Plan," is sponsored by none other than the CCP. It targets scientist around the world at leading universities, research centers, and corporate R&D and design facilities. To advance these efforts, the country has set up a network of 600 talent recruitment stations worldwide.[64] According to a report published by the Australian Strategic Policy Institute, these recruitment stations are located in countries including the United States, Germany, Australia, the United Kingdom, and Japan. Between

2008 and 2016, "China's talent-recruitment programs drew in almost 60,000 overseas professionals." The initiative is not limited to hiring foreign scientists to work in China; it also includes collaborative efforts and consulting projects that involve, according to the report, "grey areas including undisclosed conflicts of interest and external consulting work, to illegal actions including cyber espionage and theft."[65]

The influx of scientists combined with massive government and corporate expenditures on R&D has had a significant impact on China's advancements in technology. In 2015, China topped the United States for the first time in the number of scientific papers published. By 2020, China produced 19.9% of all academic papers, with the United States coming in second with 18.3%. Germany ranked third with a 4.4% share.[66]

Assessing Enterprise China's Progress

China is making progress in its shift from technology follower to leader in a growing number of industries. One important advantage is afforded by the state, which has given preferential access for Chinese SOEs and some POEs to Internet-generated data for the 800 million Chinese consumers who are online. The reams of data provided, combined with cybersecurity laws that tilt in favor of Chinese companies, gives Chinese domestic firms a leg up when it comes to data-centered innovations. This has spurred innovations in such fields as digital platforms and associated markets including small money–based transactions, as well as the development of apps and related technologies that help facilitate consumer interactions—for example ridesharing and automated convenience stores.[67]

Enterprise China has also made great progress carving out leadership positions in fields such as facial recognition and unmanned aircraft. Both are built on the integration of artificial intelligence, camera technologies, data processing, and analytics. In 2021, China accounted for more than half the world's facial recognition business, with Chinese companies fanning out to countries such as Uganda, Mongolia, Singapore, Ecuador, Germany, and the United Arab Emirates. While the United States and Japan have considerable acumen with related technologies, regulatory barriers and social norms are major barriers. Likewise, China is now the global leader in unmanned aircraft. In 2021, Shenzhen-based DJI controlled about 70% of the world's drone market. The company began operations in 2006 and by 2021 had offices in the United States, Germany, the Netherlands, Japan, South Korea, Beijing, Shanghai, and Hong Kong. Its drones packed state-of-the-art rotor stabilization controllers, camera platforms, and 3D mapping applications. No doubt close ties with the state and tight connections to a supportive technology ecosystem were central to the company's—and country's—leadership role.

COMPREHENSIVE EFFORT TO REVERSE DEPENDENCY

As we highlighted, reducing external dependency is the first pillar in Enterprise China's competitive strategy. China's motivation for reducing its dependency is straightforward. Dependency is a threat or at least a risk to the country's control over its destiny. However, China has made it clear that it does not view all dependencies equally. It is most concerned about those technology areas that it deems critical to both its future national prosperity and security.

Given the interdependencies between the state and Chinese corporations, foreigners sometimes struggle to connect the dots and fully comprehend Enterprise China's drive to eliminate dependency. Enterprise China's borrow, buy, and build tactics are somewhat opaque and rarely deployed in a sequential fashion. A picture of Enterprise China squeezing every benefit out of borrow before moving on to buy and from there to internal build is inaccurate. In reality, the tactics can be, and often are, used simultaneously, although one may receive greater attention than others at a particular point in time. Because of the time lags and often checkerboard deployment of the three tactics, many foreign observers may be drawn to the here and now of what their Chinese competitors are doing today, while missing the long-term efforts of Enterprise China to free itself of dependency on the West over time.

LCD Displays: Case Study

A good example of the sometimes bumpy journey from dependence to independence can be found in the production of LCD displays. For more than a decade, the industry has been dominated globally by Samsung and LG. To displace these two Korean giants, the Chinese state first decided to subsidize two local firms, BOE Technology Group and China Star Optoelectronics Technology (CSOT) so they could undercut the costs of both LG and Samsung in interface devices. With state support, both companies then aggressively moved to poach Korean engineers who had been working for LG and Samsung as well as key suppliers. Their goal was to "borrow," or extract, key technologies and later re-innovate and develop new technologies from a Chinese base. Along the path, both LG and Samsung shifted their focus from LCD to OLED technology. BOE then adapted its game plan and decided to become a major supplier of OLED screens to Apple, thus pushing LG from its position as the company's No. 2 supplier. With state support and encouragement, BOE also began to supply OLED panels to Chinese manufacturer Huawei. This in turn allowed for greater economies of scale, which in turn was used to support more research, or "build" activities, while also lowering unit costs. For its part, CSOT bought 11% of a related Japanese technology company, JOLED, for approximately US $205 million.[68] CSOT subsequently committed to setting up the world's most technologically advanced production facility for OLED panels in Guangzhou with mass production starting in 2022.

As this example illustrates, all three tactics were utilized but not necessarily in a rigid sequence. To reiterate our key point, it can make sense to move through the borrow, buy, and build tactic in sequence. However, Enterprise China's emphasis is on the utility of the tactics in whatever sequence will serve the strategic objective of reducing external dependency.

The IDAR Model

Whether it's with LCDs, rail equipment, or semiconductors, the paths to shaking off dependence are in many ways idiosyncratic to each industry. However, when viewed from a broader Enterprise China perspective, several common steps are evident. Here, it is helpful to combine interrelated components within a larger concept of what can be referred to as IDAR, or *I*ntroducing, *D*igesting, *A*bsorbing, and *R*e-innovating. This strategy is reviewed at length in a "Special 301 Report" conducted by the US Trade Representative's Office.[69]

Introducing: The goal is to introduce Chinese companies to foreign technologies. Among other options, these may include technology transfer agreements, the encouragement of inbound investment for foreign technology companies, and the establishment of foreign R&D centers.

Digesting: In this stage of the technology acquisition process, the state works with local companies to facilitate institutional learning and the dissemination of technology within and across Chinese industries. This includes analyzing what is useful and what can be applied to research and commercial enterprises within China.

Absorbing: The next stage in the technology acquisition process includes institutionalizing foreign technologies within Chinese enterprises. This typically involves embedding the new technology in locally developed products and services. To facilitate this step, the state provides targeted financial assistance and facilitates the creation of supportive local ecosystems. Through government supported technology centers and "national technology transfer centers," the objective is to ensure that newly acquired technologies become deeply imbedded and widely used.

Re-innovating: This final stage includes the transformation of Chinese enterprise from fast adopters of foreign technologies to the champions of innovation. It is only at this point when Chinese companies can assume their leadership position on the world stage. They are now in a position of strength from which they can subsequently set the standards to which foreign firms adhere. With this strength comes the ability to maximize value creation, helping Enterprise China to move from strength to strength.

CONCLUSION

Companies that focus too heavily on the separate and individual actions of Chinese companies at specific points in time may miss the broader and longer-term objective of Enterprise China to eliminate external dependency. They may also miss Enterprise China's resolve to stick to a long-term plan for global leadership. Speaking at the opening of the 2008 Beijing Olympics, a younger Xi Jinping alluded to China's path: "No force can shake the status of our great motherland . . . No force can stop the advance of the Chinese people and the Chinese nation."[70] As we will address in later chapters, executives in foreign firms not only must understand the extent of China's resolve to eliminate its over-dependency on foreign firms for key products and technologies, but they must also fully appreciate the implications of this first pillar in China's three-prong strategy for their company.

Clearly Enterprise China is committed to reducing and even reversing its external dependencies, particularly in technology-sensitive industries. Raising local content requirements while borrowing, buying, and building technology and products on which Enterprise China feels it has excessive external dependencies is a critical first component of its competitive strategy. However, if you play the long-game of three-dimensional chess, you would likely not stop with just this first strategic pillar. Reducing or even reversing dependency is a nice first step, but alone it might not ensure the actualization of China's vision of being among the strongest and most influential nations on earth. You might need an additional step. Chapter 3 covers that next step and Enterprise China's second strategic pillar of dominating domestically.

Chapter 3

STRATEGIC PILLAR II: DOMINATING DOMESTICALLY

The second pillar in China's competitive strategy is to dominate domestically. Although we commented on this in Chapter 1, in this chapter we dive deeper. In doing so, we address three key questions. First, what does dominating domestically look like? Second, why is it necessary? Third, how does Enterprise China plan to achieve it? As with the first pillar, we do not have to guess or speculate in finding the answers to these questions. Enterprise China has provided clear guidance.

WHAT DOES DOMINATE DOMESTICALLY LOOK LIKE?

The phrase "dominate domestically" could mean any number of things. It could mean that indigenous Chinese companies needed to be either No. 1 or No. 2 in every industry. It could mean that indigenous Chinese firms must have the best technology or must have unique technology that foreign firms would have to buy in order to compete in China. While it could mean these things or more, Enterprise China has operationalized it quite simply: market share.

To dominate, indigenous Chinese firms need to control a high share of the domestic Chinese market. It is that simple. But what is the threshold at which domination is achieved? For the targeted sectors, MIC 2025 in general articulates that the targeted market share is roughly 70%. However, in some segments, this number is higher. For example, in the case of electric vehicles and energy equipment, MIC 2025 envisions indigenous Chinese companies capturing 80% and 90% domestic market shares, respectively.

If Enterprise China is intent on seeing indigenous firms dominate with 70% or greater market share, why would foreign firms even bother to break into or stay in the Chinese domestic market? The reality is that the "leftover" market (i.e., 10%–30% of the total) in absolute terms may still be quite large and attractive for foreign firms to pursue. However, in that pursuit, they need to understand exactly how Enterprise China plans to dominate. This has important implications for how foreign firms can successfully compete *in* China or what might cause them to fail. In addition, and as strange as it may seem, how Enterprise China plans to dominate domestically has important implications for foreign firms competing *with* China even if they have no presence in China today and don't plan to have one tomorrow. However, we should not get ahead of ourselves. We will cover the implications in later chapters, but for this chapter, we focus on why Enterprise China wants to dominate domestically, why it is necessary, and how it plans to achieve it.

WHY DOMINATE DOMESTICALLY?

At first blush, you might think that every country would want its indigenous firms to dominate its domestic market. But that is not necessarily the case and has not been the reality during most of China's explosive growth from the 1980s through the early 2000s. Specifically, between 1980 and 2005, China's economy soared 1,096% without indigenous firms dominating key sectors of the economy.

Singapore is a shining example of a country that grew and prospered without policies that sought to facilitate indigenous firms dominating the domestic market. Specifically, between 1980 and 2005, Singapore's economy soared 719% without indigenous firms playing leading roles in its economy. It grew another 140% between 2005 and 2019—or a total of 1,865% between 1980 and 2019—while showing relative indifference to the "nationality" of locally operating entities. In fact, one could argue that Singapore would not have the size, strength, or breadth of the economy, tax revenue, or jobs that it has today without the large number of foreign firms operating there. Let's briefly examine two examples.

The first example is banking. Arguably, banking is a critical sector in virtually every country. Consequently, essentially all countries regulate the banking industry inside their sovereign borders. Interestingly, even though Singapore is consistently ranked as the fourth most important banking center in the world, there are only six local banks and 117 foreign banks operating there. While the six local banks are strong in certain areas, taking the entire sector of banking in Singapore, international firms, not domestic firms, dominate. Given this, it is worth asking the question: Would Singapore be the financial powerhouse it is today if it insisted on local firms dominating its banking segment? It seems highly unlikely. By allowing foreign firms in and providing a level playing field for competition between local and foreign firms, Singapore enjoys the employment and tax revenue generated by a thriving overall banking industry. It also enjoys the

spillover benefits that come from a strong banking segment in attracting and supporting other industries.

One could argue that banking, especially corporate banking, by its nature is
more international than domestic. Therefore, the dominance of foreign banks
in Singapore is not the fairest example. OK. Let's take the hotel industry as the
second example then. By its nature the hotel industry is quite local in every
country including Singapore because foreign visitors who stay overnight in a
country must arrange for local, domestic accommodations. Singapore attracts
nearly 19 million overnight international visitors each year.[1] However, Singapore does not insist that indigenous hotels dominate this important segment of
the domestic market. In fact, only 45% of all the hotels in Singapore are owned
by domestic companies; 55% are international brands.[2] But the number of hotel brands and their domestic or international nature doesn't tell the full story.
Singapore has a total of 63,741 total hotel rooms, and 88% (56,092) of them are
owned by the international hotel brands operating in Singapore, and only 22%
belong to indigenous owners. Would Singapore be the destination powerhouse it
is if it insisted on local firms dominating its domestic hotel segment? Here too, it
seems highly unlikely.

So why does Enterprise China insist on indigenous firms dominating its
domestic market? To examine this in more depth, let's return to the example of
semiconductors—a targeted sector by Enterprise China. As we noted in Chapter 2,
China generates just over 50% of the world's demand for semiconductors and
achieved that position without indigenous Chinese firms dominating China's
domestic chip market. In fact, China imports nearly 90% of the chips it needs.
We raised the question in Chapter 2 but revive it here again: Could China have
reached such a high level of global demand if it had insisted on producing within
China 70% of the semiconductor chips the country needed for both internal consumption and global export? The answer again seems that it would be unlikely.
Given this and given the commanding demand position that China enjoys in
semiconductors, the legitimacy of questioning why Enterprise China insists on
indigenous firms dominating the domestic market is even clearer.

There are three fundamental rationales behind this strategic pillar. First, dominating domestically supports the overall vision of domestic strength and international influence. Second, dominating domestically reinforces the first strategic
pillar of reducing dependency on foreign firms and countries. Third, dominating
domestically facilitates China's third strategic pillar of competing globally. In the
following sections we walk through each of these rationales in more detail.

Support the Overall Vision

To control its destiny in terms of domestic strength and international influence,
Enterprise China believes it has little choice but to dominate its home market. If it does not dominate its domestic market, especially in key areas, it risks

permanently relegating its firms and their employees to peripheral or low-value-added activities, while allowing foreign firms to provide the high-value activities and jobs.

This is a point we raised in Chapter 2. In this chapter, we will examine it in more depth by looking at the example of high-speed trains. Suppose foreign rail equipment manufacturing firms, such as Alstom, were to dominate the domestic market in China. Why would this be so bad? Enterprise China sees several reasons for why it would be.

First, if the high-paying engineering work to design or fabricate the trains were done outside of China and Chinese workers were left doing lower-value tasks such as assembling the trains in China, the country and its workers would be denied the economic value of those higher-value activities. OK. But what is so wrong with that? From Enterprise China's perspective, low-value activities and jobs do not lead to world-beating national strength. How can China be among the strongest nations in the world if it does not dominate its own critical markets at the highest end of the value stack? How can China be as strong as Germany, France, or Japan if engineers in those countries are the ones designing the train's wheels and suspension systems that create the lowest level of friction and the smoothest ride at high speed, while maintaining the optimal contact with the track, while China is simply installing the suspension and wheels on the train after they arrive in China? Enterprise China believes it can't. To support the central vision of national strength, indigenous firms must dominate domestically—at least in key sectors.

However, as we already noted, Singapore is a prosperous country. Yet foreign firms, not domestic, dominate many sectors of its economy. Singapore doesn't seem to care if a high-paying job for a local Singaporean is with an indigenous Singaporean company or a foreign firm operating locally. Regardless of what type of company people work for in Singapore—foreign or domestic—they still pay taxes to the Singaporean government; they still spend their money in Singapore on housing, food, clothing, entertainment, and so on. Additionally, what does it matter if the corporate taxes paid to the Singaporean government are paid by a homegrown or international entity? Given all this, why couldn't China go the way of Singapore in some key sectors and still gain prosperity and national strength?

In Chapter 2, we highlighted how external dependency, risk, control, and trust were key drivers of Enterprise China's first strategic pillar. They are at the heart of the matter for this second strategic pillar as well. In terms of the second strategic pillar, what is the risk to China if Alstom dominates the high-speed train segment in China? What is the risk if the high-level design and engineering work is done in France or Germany and not in China?

Certainly, one factor is the risk that much of the economic contribution of this high-value work would be made outside China, not inside. But there is more. For example, what is the risk to the country generally and the domestic rail industry specifically if Alstom holds back some its most advanced technology?

And a related question: How much influence could China exert on Alstom if the company located its highest-value-adding activities offshore, outside China? Put more generally, for a national government, which firms are easier to influence and control, foreign or domestic? The answer is obvious and true in virtually every country around the world, including China. Influencing and controlling domestic firms is much easier for the Chinese government than influencing and controlling international firms operating within its domestic borders. As an extension, the government more easily can influence and control home nationals versus foreign nationals living in China.

Why is this the case? One reason is because most domestic firms have more to lose from a confrontation with the government than foreign firms. This is true because domestic firms almost always have more invested in their home country than foreign firms have invested in that country. Those investments include not just factories, equipment, and property, but personal relationships involving leaders and employees.

Let's take the example of Coca-Cola and Nestlé in the United States to illustrate the dynamics. Both companies have large international operations, including in beverages. The United States is the largest beverage market for both companies. Consequently, both have significant investments in factories, distribution capabilities, employees, advertising, and more in the United States. However, for Coca-Cola the United States is home, and the company simply has comparatively more at stake in the United States than does Nestlé. This is true whether we look at the tangible side of the ledger (e.g., its headquarters, production facilities, bottling operations, and distribution networks) or the intangible side of the ledger (e.g., leaders, employees, corporate culture, and brands). To be clear, because Nestlé has significant investments in the United States, it does not want to walk away from the US market. But if push came to shove, Nestlé could more easily reduce its presence or walk away from the United States than Coca-Cola could.

This is the situation for most domestic firms compared to international firms, especially those whose home country is economically large. If an international firm has too many difficulties or basic incompatibilities with doing business in a particular foreign market, it can scale back or pack up and go home. While it is possible for domestic firms to do the same, it is much more costly on every front, particularly if they have to give up their home base. With more to lose from leaving, governments naturally have more leverage over domestic firms.

If we return to banking in Singapore, this is certainly the case. It is much more costly for a domestic bank such as DBS to leave Singapore than for HSBC. Nonetheless, if HSBC and all the 116 other foreign banks decided to leave Singapore, the country would get disproportionately hurt by the moves because of its dependence on those banks. But Singapore doesn't seem too worried about HSBC or any of the other foreign banks getting upset, packing up, and leaving. Why not? How does Singapore mitigate this risk? Singapore mitigates this risk by adopting laws, rules, and regulations that conform rather than conflict with dominant standards globally. Consequently, why would HSBC leave? It would not find materially better laws, rules, or regulations someplace else. As a result, the risks are low that HSBC or any of the other of the 116 foreign banks that dominate Singapore would become bad actors in the country or leave it.

This is not the case for China. Many aspects of Chinese laws, rules, and regulations are relatively unique, both in content and process. Therefore, the risk that foreign firms could decide to leave because they could enjoy better or more favorable laws, rules, and regulations elsewhere is real. If an important group of foreign firms dominated a particular sector in China and decided independently but in aggregate to scale back or leave, China would disproportionately suffer. Consequently, from Enterprise China's perspective, allowing foreign firms to dominate important segments of the domestic economy represents nontrivial risks—risks that are much easier to manage if those segments are dominated by indigenous firms. This dynamic is true whether the government owns the entities or not. However, if the government also happens to own the entities, then its control is assured.

As we discussed in Chapter 2, if you also don't fully trust foreign firms, the risks we've just examined get bigger, and the benefits of having domestic firms that the state can more easily influence and control grow as well. From this perspective, given China's vision of being one of the strongest nations in the world, the strategic pillar of having indigenous firms dominate the domestic market is a no-brainer.

Reinforce Strategic Pillar 1

Dominating China's home market with indigenous firms also reinforces Enterprise China's first strategic pillar of reducing dependency on foreign firms and countries. A simple example illustrates this rationale. Here we cycle back to semiconductors and take the case of US-based Qualcomm.

As noted already, China generates over 50% of the global demand for semiconductors. Some of this demand comes from the fact that over 60% of all smartphones in the world are made in China. Qualcomm is a major supplier to various industries, but chips for smartphones accounts for about 70% of Qualcomm's total revenue. Of these sales, China (including Hong Kong) accounted for about 60% of its total revenue, worth about $14 billion in 2020. The vast majority of its sales in China were via exports *to* the country rather than from products produced *in* the country.

As we discussed in Chapter 2, China's first strategic pillar is to reduce its dependency on foreign companies such as Qualcomm and their key technologies. Therefore, Enterprise China seeks to have 70% of the semiconductors it needs produced in China. If Enterprise China continues to push toward its 70% domestic content objective by 2025, what is Qualcomm to do? If China pushes hard enough, Qualcomm faces three options.

- **Option 1:** Qualcomm could decide to forgo its revenue from China and keep its product and process IP out of China. Given that 60% of Qualcomm's revenue comes from China, choosing Option 1 and walking away would be difficult. The impact on the company's stock price would undoubtedly be grave.
- **Option 2:** Qualcomm could continue to sell to China but move important portions of its production into China. Clearly this option includes IP and other risks for Qualcomm.
- **Option 3:** Qualcomm could try to maintain the status quo by leveraging its key supply position. After all, Qualcomm chips are not commodities that Chinese smartphone manufacturers can just buy anywhere from any company or can start making themselves tomorrow. Consequently, Chinese customer firms would struggle to replace the functionality that Qualcomm chips provide.

However, suppose China was willing to endure some pain in switching to other suppliers if Qualcomm refused to relocate some of its production onshore in China. Suppose further that this action—or threat of action—by China were to force Qualcomm to embrace option 2. Qualcomm would move 70% of its offshore production capabilities that previously had supplied imports to China into China (i.e., direct import substitution). Let's further assume that China were to allow Qualcomm to set up a wholly owned operation rather than force it into a JV. Further suppose that Qualcomm were to work hard to guard its IP in China. Finally, suppose that all of Qualcomm's efforts were to go well, allowing the company to sell as much or more in China producing there as it did before when it was exporting to China.

Given this successful move by Qualcomm, suppose that Intel and other chip makers were to follow Qualcomm's lead and move previously offshore production onshore. Where would this leave Enterprise China? China would have achieved its import substitution and local content objectives, but it would still be dependent on foreign firms for key technology and products. The risk would be less because the dependency would have moved from offshore to onshore, but it would not have been eliminated and certainly not reversed.

If foreign firms moved production onshore in China and China remained dependent on them, these foreign firms theoretically could shut down their Chinese operations or redirect critical inputs to production sites in other countries. You might reasonably respond: "Yes, it is theoretically possible, but why would they?" If 25% to 60% of their chip revenue were to come from China, their economic self-interests simply would not allow them to shut down or otherwise diminish their operations there. Therefore, the potential supply disruption risk is just that—possible but not probable.

This is all true enough. But for Enterprise China the key question is not whether foreign chip firms *would* shut down, move, or reduce their operations in

China but whether they *could*. The answer to this question is, "Yes, they could." What is important about this question and its answer is that the less you trust outsiders, the more this question and its answer matters. The less you trust foreign firms, their executives, and their home country governments, the more insurance you need to mitigate the downside risk. That insurance policy in this case is to dominate the domestic market with indigenous firms. These firms can be trusted more or certainly can more easily be controlled, especially if you own them. And they can be guided to produce custom-designed products just in time for their Chinese buyers. This is in part why MIC 2025 set not just domestic content targets but market share targets as well. Market share targets help ensure that China's external dependency is reduced and eventually reversed by having indigenous firms dominate domestically.

Reinforce Strategic Pillar 3

Thus far we have explained that Enterprise China seeks to have indigenous firms dominate domestically to strengthen the country and to add insurance to its ability to reduce its external dependency. In addition to these two reasons, there is a third. Having indigenous firms dominate domestically facilitates Enterprise China's third strategic pillar—it helps Chinese firms win globally. As already described, China seeks not only to be among the strongest nations *in* the world but to exercise leading influence *on* the world. But how exactly does dominating at home help firms compete abroad? A key explanation is that Chinese firms that dominate domestically can create profit sanctuaries at home to help fund their expansion, competitiveness, and ultimate influence abroad.

A profit sanctuary is an area in which a company makes protected profits that it can use to fund or subsidize activities in other areas—in this case global expansion, presence, and position. Enterprise China's ambition to win globally and influence the world more broadly would be difficult to achieve only from a base in China. How can China influence the world with no presence around the globe? In Chapter 4, we explore more fully what winning globally looks like, why Enterprise China feels that it is a competitive imperative, and how it plans to achieve this third strategic pillar. But for now, our point is that to compete globally and be among the most influential countries internationally, Enterprise China is convinced it needs a wide presence and strong position across the planet.

We make a big deal of understanding the rationales behind Enterprise China's second strategic pillar of dominating domestically because if foreign executives understand the rationales, they can better anticipate how diligent and consistent Enterprise China is likely to be in pursuing this objective. Based on our experience and understanding of these rationales, we believe Enterprise China is completely serious about pursuing its second strategic pillar and is well on its way to achieving it. We will examine the specific tactics it has employed, but first we need to describe a key choice China made regarding its fundamental approach to dominating domestically.

PATHS TO DOMESTIC DOMINATION

To dominate domestically Enterprise China had two fundamentally different paths it could have taken. Under both alternatives, China could have made conditions difficult for foreign firms domestically while enabling indigenous firms to dominate. Alternative 1 would involve the development of *many* indigenous firms in a given segment. No one indigenous firm would have a large share. Instead, many domestic firms would dominate in aggregate but not individually. Alternative 2 would involve *few* indigenous firms in a given segment. Only one or two firms would have been allowed to have a large share of the market. In that sense, a few indigenous Chinese firms would dominate individually *and* in aggregate.

Both options would have been viable, but whether Enterprise China should have chosen alternative 1 or alternative 2 is now a moot question. It made the choice years ago. It chose alternative 2. Since then, Enterprise China has been building big national champions to dominate their respective sectors. This building process has accelerated over the past five years.

Advantages of Concentrating Competitors

Enterprise China chose alternative 2—focusing on fewer versus more competitors—for two fundamental reasons. First, having only one firm or a few firms dominate each segment of the domestic market enables much more focused monitoring and control by the state. Second, having only one firm or a few firms dominate each market segment enables larger and more focused profit sanctuaries from which to take on the rest of the world.

Facilitate Monitoring and Controlling

A theme that we have raised in terms of Enterprise China's competitive strategy is that it always prefers greater rather than less control. The fundamental belief is that the greater the degree of control, the more likely is the achievement of the targeted outcome. To control firms, you need to monitor them. You need to know what they are doing and not doing. The more firms you have to monitor, the more difficult the control task. The more difficult the control task, the more likely that the result could deviate from the intended outcome.

Following this line of logic, monitoring a handful of firms that control 85% of a particular sector is easier than monitoring 100 firms that together command the same share. Consequently, if you want greater control over firms, controlling fewer rather than more firms is easier. As we have stated numerous times, this is even more true if the government is the owner of the large, dominant national champions. Consequently, Enterprise China has generally sought to establish a few national champions to dominate key segments of the domestic market.

Concentrate to Strengthen Profit Sanctuaries

As sound as this rationale is, a second compelling reason exists for having few rather than many indigenous firms dominate the domestic market. That second reason relates to profit sanctuaries. Because the costs of international expansion and global competitiveness are high, Enterprise China needs those domestic profit sanctuaries concentrated rather than dispersed.

Although most readers are likely to accept the statement that global expansion is expensive, a short example adds richness to this intuitive idea. Let's take oil and gas as an illustrative sector. Excluding Chinese firms, our research finds that the largest 10 oil and gas firms in the world generate over $2 trillion in revenue, the majority of which is produced outside each firm's home country. ExxonMobil is a typical example with investments in more than 100 countries. Those operations and their assets are listed on its balance sheet at over $330 billion. More than half those assets are outside its home market in the United States. ExxonMobil has proven reserves around the world of about 7.9 billion barrels of oil. Of this total, about 60% of reserves are scattered around the world and only 40% are in the United States. Over the last 20 years, ExxonMobil has allocated $411 billion to capital expenditures to build up its asset base and oil reserves. Given that most of its assets and reserves have been outside its home market, the assumption seems safe that more than half of ExxonMobil's past capital expenditures (over $200 billion) have been made outside the United States. With this in mind, building up a global presence similar to ExxonMobil is no small task for Enterprise China. In fact, it is likely so large that it would prove too formidable for even an army of small companies to achieve.

Rather, it makes more sense to have a few large companies, or even just one, take up this challenge. But suppose that China could direct an army of small companies to expand globally to take on the likes of ExxonMobil by sending some to tackle South America, others to take on Western Europe, and others to go after Africa, and so on. Theoretically, Enterprise China could achieve a global presence by coordinating a battalion of smaller oil and gas companies. Unfortunately, physical presence is necessary but not sufficient to win globally. Because international oil companies have been in different parts of the world in many cases for over 100 years, much of the "easy oil" already has been found and extracted. What remains are oil reserves in remote places with difficult geological structures, such as the deep ocean or the frigid Arctic. These reserves require significant technology and ability to find, drill, and extract. Consequently, finding, tapping into, and extracting this oil takes not just global presence but significant investment to develop the required technology and human capital.

These large investments and capital expenditures, as well as technical expertise, most assuredly exceed the limits of what any small company could profitably tackle. Not only would a small company simply not have the absolute resources necessary, but even if it could access the capital required, it would have a more limited revenue base across which to amortize the development costs. Amortizing the large technological development costs across a small revenue base would leave the firm with significantly higher costs per barrel of oil than a large, global competitor such as ExxonMobil. The only way to have similar technological investments *and* margins is to have a similarly large revenue base across which the development costs could be amortized. China understands these basic economic realities, and therefore, has sought to have fewer and larger firms dominate its domestic oil and gas market.

Unsurprisingly, just two firms, China Petroleum and Chemical Corporation (Sinopec) and China National Petroleum Company (PetroChina), dominate the Chinese domestic market. These two firms accounted for 83% of the total domestic natural gas supply (168 billion cubic meters) in 2020. In addition, they accounted for 59% of the total gas imports into the country (just over 140 billion cubic meters).[3] However, they didn't just dominate the domestic market; they were large firms by any standard. For example, in 2020 Sinopec was ranked as the second largest firm in the world (*Fortune* Global 500) with $407 billion in revenue. Only Walmart was bigger. It was the largest company across all industries in China and was the largest oil and gas company in the world. PetroChina was equally impressive. On the *Fortune* Global 500 list, it was No. 4 with $379 billion in revenue. It was the third largest firm in China and the second largest oil and gas company in the world, comfortably ahead of No. 3 Royal Dutch Shell ($352 billion).

In sum, Enterprise China seeks to have indigenous firms dominate the domestic market primarily by having a few big "supertankers" capture a commanding share of the market rather than have a flotilla of smaller boats dominate. The large firms are often referred to as "national champions," a term we have used previously.[4] Most of these national champions are SOEs. Their ownership structure and state control mean that they are not only the champions *in* the nation but they are champions *of* the nation.

THREE TACTICS TO DOMINATE DOMESTICALLY

Even after determining that having a few firms dominate domestically was the better path than having many, there are many possible means by which Enterprise China could ensure that a few firms dominated domestically. Here Enterprise China consistently leveraged and continues to leverage three core tactics: create an advantage for SOE national champions, guide SIEs (state-influenced enterprises) national champions, and support unique ecosystems.

Create Advantages for SOE National Champions

Enterprise China invests in national champions for three main reasons. These firms provide concentrated targets for state control, they help support a reduction in external dependency, and they provide domestic profit sanctuaries to fund global expansion. State ownership makes all of these things easier.

In talking about national SOE champions, we want to reiterate that ownership by the state can happen at all three major levels of government: national, provincial, and municipal. As examples, China's largest company by revenue, Sinopec, is centrally owned by SASAC. Datong Coal Mining Group, one of the largest coal mining firms in the world, is owned by the Shanxi provincial government. Multibillion-dollar Shanghai Jiushi (Group) Co. is owned by the Shanghai Municipal People's Government.

While governments in all countries have a hand in their country's industrial policy, most have shied away from a visible ownership hand in shaping the companies within the industries targeted by government policies. This is not the case for China. In fact, the SASAC announced in 2006 that SOEs would secure "absolute control" over seven strategic industries: defense, electrical power, petroleum and petrochemicals, telecommunications, coal, civil aviation, and shipping. It also announced that SOEs would continue to play a key role in other industries, including machinery, automobiles, information technology, construction, steel, and nonferrous metals.

To advantage SOEs and achieve the size necessary for domestic domination by a few firms, the government has employed two major mechanisms: favored treatment and mergers. Both are important, but mergers, especially megamergers since 2015, have had an especially important impact on achieving the size necessary for domestic domination by a few firms. Therefore, in the following sections, we examine favored treatment but devote more space to examining what China has done relative to M&As.

Give Favored Treatment

Several scholars have studied the treatment of SOEs compared to POEs and foreign firms in China and found that the government has consistently provided favored treatment to SOEs.[5] That favored treatment has included easier access to capital, lower interest rates, preferred commerce with other SOEs, and easier licensing. While all of these points of preference matter, arguably access to capital is among the most important.

To appreciate the level of access to capital (specifically debt) that SOEs have enjoyed compared to POEs, as we noted in Chapter 1, SOEs have debt levels that are over 90% of GDP but account for roughly 30% of GDP. In contrast POEs have debt levels of only 30% of GDP but account for 70% of GDP. In 2018 senior government officials made public speeches in which they stated that POEs account for 60% of China's GDP.[6] Logically, this suggests then that SOEs contributed 40%. This softens the advantage for SOEs in terms of their debt levels relative to economic activity, but the point of advantage remains. Importantly, as we noted in Chapter 1, POE debt as a percentage of GDP has declined from 41% in 2014 to 29% in 2019, while SOE debt as a percentage of GDP has soared from 63% in 2007 to 92% in 2019 (see Exhibit 3.1).

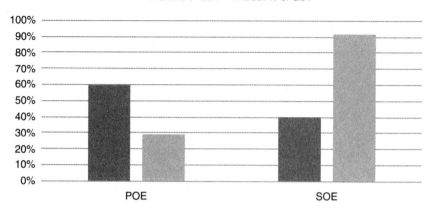

Exhibit 3.1   POE and SOE Share of GDP and Debt

Sources: Macquarie Group; China Ministry of Finance.

This large, disproportionate share of debt by SOEs suggests that they have privileged access to debt capital. This is easy to understand given that the majority of the debt is bank loans and the fact that all the large banks in China are also SOEs. In essence, it is state-owned banks that are funding SOEs. Nonetheless, this large SOE debt as a percentage of GDP might not be problematic per se if SOEs could easily service that debt from growing revenue and increasing profit. Unfortunately, the serviceability of China's SOE debt is worsening, not getting better (see Exhibit 3.2). To examine this, we looked at debt relative to revenue and profit. The level of debt relative to both revenue and profits has been steadily increasing since 2007. Alarmingly, the level of debt SOEs carried in 2019 was 2.4 times annual revenue and nearly 42 times the amount of these firms' profits.

Clearly access to funds via debt allows SOEs to grow their asset base, whether that be through capital expenditures or mergers and acquisitions. In general, SOEs have grown their asset base in line with their increase in debt (see Exhibit 3.3). Put more directly, the increase in SOE debt has directly funded their increase in assets.

Unfortunately, the lack of full reporting of financial results by SOEs makes perfect attribution of the increase in asset growth due to capital expenditures or M&As difficult to determine. Nonetheless, the explosion of asset growth since 2007 corresponds with a significant increase in M&A activity in SOEs, which we examine in the next section.

Promote SOE Mergers

As mentioned, our analysis, and that carried out by others, suggests that SOEs as national champions have grown in important measure due to domestic mergers

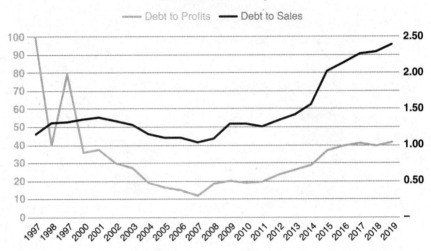

Exhibit 3.2 SOE Debt-to-Sales and -Profits Ratios

Source: China Ministry of Finance.

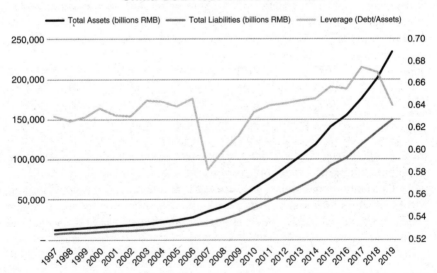

Exhibit 3.3 Debt-to-Asset Ratio and Growth

Source: China Ministry of Finance.

since 1997 and due to megamergers since 2015. Much of the reduction in the total number of SOEs has been a function of these mergers. However, it is worthwhile to note that a small reduction in the number of SOEs has been due to the government allowing some to go out of business.[7] The total number of SOEs shrunk from 262,000 in 1997 to 150,000 in 2018 (43% reduction). At the same time, the average asset size per firm increased by 2,624% (see Exhibit 3.4). Quite simply, as the number of SOEs shrunk dramatically, the average size of SOEs increased significantly. Put in the context of a growing economy, SOE assets relative to GDP increased from a low of 126% in 2006 to a high of 237% in 2019. All this suggests that the reduction in the number of SOEs was largely a function of mergers.

This overall pattern has been especially true for central SOEs under the jurisdiction of SASAC. When the SASAC was established in 2003, it controlled 196 firms. By 2018 that number had shrunk to 96 (a 51% reduction). However, the average size increased by 1,327% (see Exhibit 3.5).

We highlight these changes in central SOEs because they tend to be significantly larger than those under provincial or municipal ownership, as illustrated in Exhibit 3.6, which shows how many times larger central SOEs have been than all other SOEs. In line with China's choice to dominate domestically with only a few firms in each segment, central SOEs have been a primary category for national champions. For example, in 2003, the average total asset per central SOE was 42 *billion* RMB compared to 136 *million* RMB for all SOEs across China— meaning that central SOEs were on average 308 times as big SOEs owned by

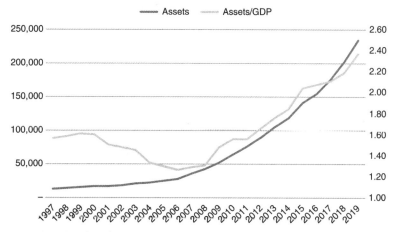

SOE Assets and China GDP ($B)

Exhibit 3.4 China SOE Total Assets and GDP
Source: China Ministry of Finance.

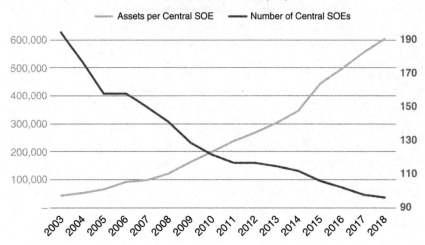

Exhibit 3.5   Central SOE Numbers and Size
Source: China Ministry of Finance.

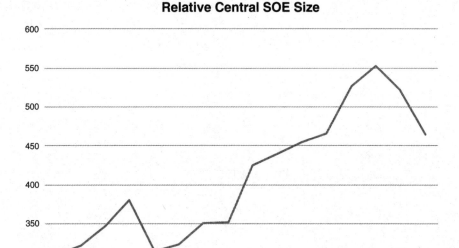

Exhibit 3.6   Central SOE Relative Size
Source: China Ministry of Finance.

provincial and municipal governments. This difference grew over time, though it declined in 2017 and 2018. Nonetheless, in 2018, the average central SOE asset size was 466 times larger than the average SOE (604 billion RMB compared to only 1.3 billion RMB).

Given the large size of SOEs in general, and of central SOEs in particular, at first blush, it may seem like an overreach for the government to seek such a commanding hand over the tiller of national champions across a large number of sectors in the economy. However, except for the scale, in many ways the task is no different than the CEO of a large commercial company in the United States, Germany, or Japan controlling the divisions and subsidiaries that constitute the depth and breadth of the total global enterprise in order to align them with the corporation's overall vision. Likewise, just as corporate CEOs might restructure and combine units to capture economies of scale, reduce redundancies, and achieve sufficient mass to influence competitive dynamics, so too has China's leadership restructured and combined entities to ensure domestic domination by indigenous firms—particularly the ones it owns.

This combination via megamergers has been most evident in the last decade. Following we highlight some of the more influential megamergers.

CNR and CSR Merger. As we discussed in Chapter 2, CNR and CSR merged in 2015 to create China Railway Rolling Stock Corporation (CRRC), the largest train manufacturer in the world. CRRC has a virtual monopoly domestically. Its revenue is larger than its main rivals Siemens, Alstom, and Bombardier combined! While CRRC basically controls all the domestic market, it also has a 30% global market share.[8] In one of its first overseas efforts after the merger, CRRC outbid six competitors to build the cars for Boston's new subway system. CRRC's winning bid of $566 million was slightly more than half that of Bombardier's $1 billion proposal.

Sinotrans, CSC Holdings, and China Merchant Group (CMG). In 2015 the merger of Sinotrans (a transportation and logistics firm), CSC Holdings, and China Merchant Group (a Hong Kong–based transportation, finance, and real estate company) created an integrated logistics, energy transportation, and port giant with total assets of about $110 billion. With this leap forward, it became the largest shipping and logistics firm by a wide margin, not just in China but in the world, moving ahead of the Danish A.P. Moller-Maersk, with its $63.2 billion in total assets.

State Nuclear Power Tech Corp. and China Power Investment. In 2015 the Chinese government approved the merger of State Nuclear Power Tech Corp. and China Power Investment. The combined entity, State Power Investment Corp. (SPIC), had total assets of $112 billion. The merger was driven largely to begin consolidating the nuclear power providers in China to three, including China National Nuclear Power Corp. and China General Nuclear Power Group for a combined installed capacity of about 58 gigawatts.[9] Although France's Areva (total assets $29 billion) was the world's leading nuclear power plant maker at the time with over 90 reactors installed worldwide, in 2018 the French government had to recapitalize the company and in the process it sold its reactors' business subsidiary (now Framatome), also sold its nuclear propulsion and research reactors (now Techniatome), and incorporated the remaining nuclear cycle business into a wholly owned enterprise of the French government, which was renamed Orano.

China National Cotton Reserves Corp. (CNCRC) and China Grain Reserves Corp (Sinograin). In 2017 China approved a merger between CNCRC and Sinograin, with combined assets of approximately $219 billion. The new Sinograin instantly became by far the largest agricultural products company in China and the world. In fact, globally, its assets were greater than its five largest competitors combined (Cargill, $60 billion; Wilmar International, $47 billion; Archer Daniels Midland, $44 billion; Olam International, $26 billion; Louis Dreyfus Company, $19 billion).

Baosteel and Wuhan Iron and Steel. In 2016 Baoshan Iron and Steel Group (Baosteel) and Wuhan Iron and Steel merged to form the new Baowu Steel Group. Its combined annual production capacity was around 60 million metric tons; it had total assets of $106 billion and a workforce of 228,000 people, making it the dominant domestic player and putting it in second place globally behind ArcelorMittal. However, in 2020 Baowu Steel passed ArcelorMittal, which produced about 78 metric tons at the time, and became the largest steel company on the planet with 115 metric tons.

Shenhua Group and Guodian. In 2017 Shenhua Group (China's largest coal miner) and Guodian Group (one the country's largest power generation companies) merged to form China Energy Investment Corp. (CEIC). The new entity became the dominant player in China and world's largest power company (total assets of $271 billion and installed capacity 225 gigawatts), dwarfing international competitors such as Electricité de France (EDF) with 132 GW, Korea Electrical Power Corp. with 90 GW, Enel with 85 GW, and Tokyo Electric Power with 64 GW. CEIC became not only the market leader in China but also became the largest developer of alternative energy power generation globally.

CSIC (China Shipbuilding Industry Corporation) and CSSC (China State Shipbuilding Corporation Limited). In 2019 CSIC and CSSC, the two largest shipbuilders in the country, were merged with the combined entity retaining the CSSC name (China State Shipbuilding Corporation). With total assets of $112 billion and 310,000 employees, CSSC became the dominant shipbuilder in China by far. In the process it also became the largest in the world—twice as big at the No. 2 player, itself the result of a merger. In 2019, Korea Shipbuilding & Offshore Engineering ($21 billion in total assets), a shipbuilding holding company of Hyundai Heavy Industries, announced its intention to acquire Daewoo Shipbuilding and Marine Engineering ($10 billion in total assets). This merger ran into approval headaches in various jurisdictions, especially Europe, but with the transfer of its LNG shipbuilding technology to medium-sized shipbuilders including STX Offshore & Shipbuilding and Hanjin Heavy Industries, the likelihood of the merger's approval increased. By January 2022, the European Commission had not yet completed its review of the merger. However, even if the merger receives final approval, CSSC would not only dominate China but would still capture 48.8% of all new ship orders globally.[10]

China Electronics Technology Group and China Putian Information Industry Group. In 2021 China Electronics Technology Group and China Putian Information Industry Group (Potevio) agreed to a merger, which would make Potevio a wholly owned subsidiary of CETG. The combined entity would employ 220,000 people and generate over $50 billion in revenue across a wide variety of products including defense radar, wireless communications, security, semiconductors, electric vehicle recharging equipment, smart city software, and more. The combined entity would have a total of 15 publicly traded companies across three stock exchanges (Shanghai, Shenzhen, and Hong Kong).

SinoChem and ChemChina. In 2021 the two largest chemical companies in China merged to form Sinochem Holdings. The new entity dwarfs all other players in China and is the world's largest chemical company with combined revenue of $150 billion, 220,000 employees, and assets worth $245 billion. The next two largest global chemical companies (BASF and Dow) had only $102 billion in revenue combined.

The growing share of the Chinese economy that SOEs take in general and the rise of SOE national champions, especially facilitated by megamergers, highlight Enterprise China's determination to build national champions that the state owns and controls in order to dominate the domestic market. In the process many of these national champions have not only become by far the largest firms in their sectors in China, but often they have become the largest firms in their sectors globally, often dwarfing their next largest international competitors. We will examine this issue in more depth in Chapter 4 and the implications more fully in Chapters 5 and 6.

Guide SIE National Champions

Despite the emphasis on SOE national champions, Enterprise China has also looked to POEs as national champions. In some cases, the government has facilitated (at the best) or allowed (at the least) these POEs to become large and dominant in their respective markets. In all cases, the government has either exercised control or signaled that it would exercise control over these firms to ensure that they keep in step with the government's objectives. We refer to these firms as SIEs.

Arguably the development of national champion SIEs has happened most prominently among Internet companies. Despite their more recent emergence and short organizational histories when compared to industrial firms or long-established service firms such as banking, the Chinese government has nonetheless been quite conscious of the overall context of digitalization and the Internet that has given birth to these firms. Consequently, the government did not just let the Internet go where it may in the country and did not just allow companies to emerge in unintended ways. Instead, the state has used a visible hand in shaping the context of the Internet in China and from time to time has extended (or thrust) that visible hand of influence in the direction of specific firms.

Install the Great Firewall

The most important influence the state extended on the general context and development of the Internet in China was a multiyear initiative commonly referred to as the Great Firewall. Nearly 16 years after the first email was sent in the United States, China delivered its first email in September 1987. The message was: "Across the Great Wall we can reach every corner in the world."[11] Despite this message, the Internet was not allowed to reach out at will beyond the Great Wall or come freely over the wall into China. For roughly the first decade of the Internet in China, it was only open to Chinese government use. Public use did not come until 1995. Even then, the government did not allow the unfettered use of the Internet. In 1997 the Ministry of Public Security set out regulations to control the Internet. Key sections (articles 4–6) are captured here:

> Individuals are prohibited from using the Internet to: harm national security; disclose state secrets; or injure the interests of the state or society. Users are prohibited from using the Internet to create, replicate, retrieve, or transmit information that incites resistance to the PRC Constitution, laws, or administrative regulations; promoting the overthrow of the government or socialist system; undermining national unification; distorting the truth, spreading rumors, or destroying social order; or providing sexually suggestive material or encouraging gambling, violence, or murder. Users are prohibited from engaging in activities that harm the security of computer information networks and from using networks or changing network resources without prior approval.

Soon afterward, the state initiated "Golden Shield," a software initiative that allowed the government to monitor data sent and received and block IP addresses and domain names. Other initiatives came later. Collectively, these efforts have been described as the "Great Firewall."

State Council Order 292, issued in September 2000, required Internet service providers in China, both foreign and domestic, to ensure that the information sent out through their services adhered to Chinese law. In 2002 the government required foreign firms to sign a pledge that they would "patriotically" observe Chinese law. More than 100 companies, including Yahoo!, signed the pledge.

Target the Beneficiaries

After the Internet was used to organize protests (Falun Gong, 1999) and disseminate information about embarrassing incidents, such as a train crash in which the train was buried rather than the crash investigated (Wenzhuo, 2011), China tightened its grip on foreign Internet players—blocking many, including the following:

- 2009: Facebook
- 2009: Twitter
- 2009: YouTube
- 2010: Google
- 2011: Instagram
- 2012: Gmail, Google Maps
- 2017: WhatsApp
- 2017: Pinterest
- 2018: Twitch
- 2018: Reddit

While the Great Firewall kept foreign Internet companies at bay or blocked them completely, homegrown companies were allowed to flourish. Some of the larger players include e-commerce retailers Alibaba and JD.com (vs. Amazon), search engine Baidu (vs. Google), Weibo (vs. Twitter), Tencent QQ (vs. Facebook), WeChat (vs. WhatsApp), and Tudou and Youku (vs. YouTube).

The dominance of these players has been impressive. For example, in 2020 Alibaba accounted for about 53% of all e-commerce in China, and in the same year China accounted for about half of the world's e-commerce sales. By comparison, Amazon had a 40% share of US e-commerce in 2020. AliExpress, Alibaba's business-to-consumer platform, had over 150 million buyers in 2020. Its largest one-day sales volume was just over $74 billion. That *one day's* worth of sales would rank it ahead of Nissan Motor's *annual* revenue, as well as 375 of the Global *Fortune* 500 companies' annual revenues. In terms of mobile payment, in 2020 China accounted for 83% of all global mobile payments. Alipay from Alibaba and WeChat from Tencent controlled over 90% of all mobile payments in China. WeChat had over 1 billion users, and Alipay had nearly 900 million users in 2020. Baidu accounted for over 80% of all searches in China. QQ instant messaging service had over 700 million users. The dominating position of these players has simply left little if any room for foreign competition.

In pointing out the benefits of the Chinese government's restrictions to homegrown Internet companies and services, we do not want to imply that these companies did not work hard or were just given their success. This is not the case. Companies such as Alibaba recognized opportunities and made smart choices for how to compete and win those opportunities. Nonetheless, not having to compete with unfettered foreign behemoths and having government support has had significant benefits for these indigenous Chinese companies. For example, many of the organizations that used Alibaba's early business-to-business e-commerce site were government entities.[12] The use of Alibaba's platforms by government entities continues today.

Make Clear the Boundaries

As we highlighted in Chapter 1 with the example of Alibaba, SIE national champions are nonetheless subject to direct and powerful influence by the state. In Alibaba's case, the state was not happy with Jack Ma's comments about the state nor the potential financial beneficiaries of Ant's initial public offering. Consequently, the anticipated largest IPO in history was scrapped in 2021. But Ant is not the only case of the Chinese government exerting significant control. Didi provides an even more recent illustration.

At its beginning in 2012, Didi was only one among more than a dozen ride-sharing start-ups in China. Many had witnessed the explosive growth of Uber, which was started in 2009 in the United States, and thought the market opportunity in China was much greater, not just because of the larger population but because of the high level of urbanization and low level of car ownership in China compared to the United States. Cheng Wei, the founder and CEO of Didi, previously had worked at Alibaba but wanted to run his own show. The name "Didi" essentially stood for "honk honk taxi," and the name reflected Cheng's model for Didi, which was more Hailo than Uber. Hailo was a UK-based start-up that focused on London's black cabs. Modeling itself after Hailo more than Uber made sense because China had many more taxis than car service companies and cars, which was the segment that Uber initially targeted. Rather than recruiting private drivers, Didi focused on getting its app into the hands of taxi drivers who already had smartphones.

As the competition among the early rideshare start-ups ensued, it soon came down to two indigenous Chinese firms—Didi and Kuaidi. Not accidently each was affiliated with one of the already strong Internet-based companies in China. Didi gained the backing of Tencent, and Kuaidi had Alibaba's support.

The competition between the two was ferocious. The story goes that at one point in the fight, Didi technicians were working nonstop to fix some technical glitches, and a Didi engineer worked so long without a break that he had to have his contact lenses surgically removed.[13] In the midst of this most intensive competitive period, Pony Ma, the founder of Tencent, loaned Didi some engineers and space. This helped Didi keep pace with and move somewhat ahead of Kuaidi.

However, a major change in Didi's trajectory happened in 2014, when Tencent let its WeChat users send small financial gifts during the traditional New Year gift-giving period via its payment app. With this success, Tencent realized that if Didi customers could use WeChat's mobile payment app on their smartphones to pay for their Didi rides, the convenience would be irresistible. They were right. Soon afterward, Alibaba responded with a similar service for Kuaidi via Alipay. Ridership soared, as did the intensity of competition between the two companies.

Recognizing that a continued war was only going to leave each side bloodied, bruised, and potentially on financial life support, they reached a truce, and in 2015 Kuaidi and Didi merged. Because Didi had more ride volume, it took a controlling stake in the merged entity (60%) with Cheng set up as the CEO.

While this was going on in the foreground, Uber was gaining in the background. It was advancing in large part because it had a better app that was easier and more reliable to use. However, it initially used Google Maps, which didn't work in China as well as Baidu Maps. This left drivers sometimes struggling with directions. Although Uber's technology seamlessly interfaced with customer's credit cards, making it so that customers did not need to do anything regarding payment at the end of the ride, it had no equivalent to either Alipay or WeChat. This mattered because many Chinese did not own credit cards. As a consequence of these and other missteps, Uber's progress in China was not as fast as the company initially had hoped.

Still, Didi was wary of Uber in China. In an effort to keep Uber from focusing too strongly on China, Didi invested $100 million in Lyft, Uber's main rival back in the United States. As Didi gained in China, Apple recognized the opportunity and in 2016 invested $1 billion in Didi. Within 30 days, Uber raised $3.5 billion from Saudi Arabia's Public Investment Fund. A funding arms race emerged. But given how much both companies were losing in China, they recognized that their competition likely would end in mutual financial destruction. This caused both firms to think about an armistice.

Fortunately for Didi, by this point, its early work with taxi drivers gave it the edge over Uber in China. Seeing the writing on the wall, Uber bowed out of China in late 2016 by selling its business there to Didi for a 20% stake in the company.

From that point on, Didi went from strength to strength. On June 30, 2021, Didi Global launched its initial public offering in the United States, raising $4.4 billion and valuing the company at $68.5 billion (incidentally, giving Uber a handsome return on the money it had invested in China before bowing out). The Chinese authorities, of course, knew of this impending IPO. Everyone did. However, within days of Didi's IPO, the Cyberspace Administration of China (CAC) opened an investigation into the company's violations of national security, cybersecurity, and data security laws. It contended that Didi was "illegally collecting and using personal information." CAC banned Didi's ride-hailing platform from China app stores. Didi's stock took a quick 20% hit. By August 20, 2021, the stock had dropped from a high of $16.40 to a low of $7.47—a decline of 54%. That equated to a market cap loss of $43 billion.

In the wake of this, key questions circulated:

- Did CAC really believe that by listing in the United States, Didi would be obliged to share passenger information with US agencies contrary to

Chinese law *or* was it simply worried that Chinese platform companies such as Didi could become too influential in society and wanted to ensure that the Chinese government—not private companies—had control over such data?

- Was CAC signaling to Didi and all Chinese companies that international funding from foreign listings did not increase their independence from the regulatory control of China or China's willingness and ability to hurt the shareholders of those companies if the government did not feel that the companies were properly listening to and complying with government wishes?

The correct answers to these questions are hard to prove with any certainty, but the subsequent announcement in early December 2021 by Didi that it would delist from the New York Stock Exchange leans in the direction of the government signaling its ability and willingness to be *large and in charge* and that public listing even overseas cannot insulate a company from the heavy hand of the state.

Support Unique Ecosystems

Up to this point, we have argued that to ensure indigenous firms dominated the domestic market, Enterprise China has built up a small number of large national champions in targeted sectors. These national champions tend to be SOEs. But because the Chinese government can and is willing to take bold steps to influence and control companies it doesn't own, we also have described an important set of SIEs that have become national champions—even if reluctantly for some.

However, how Enterprise China achieves the second strategic pillar of dominating domestically cannot be fully or properly understood simply by looking at individual companies in isolation. China has sought to ensure domestic domination by indigenous firms by also fostering ecosystems that are unique to China and hard for outsiders to penetrate.

Reasons for Support

Enterprise China has supported unique ecosystems for fundamentally two reasons. First, unique ecosystems facilitate Chinese firms' dominance of the domestic environment. Chinese firms know the territory, the players, the rules of engagement, and so on, and the more those elements are part of an integrated, domestic ecosystem, the more the insiders can leverage that knowledge against outsiders in securing more business and greater profits. Second, to the extent that Chinese ecosystems are unique, foreign firms often must make specific and significant investments in China to break into them. This extra investment prevents foreign firms from simply (a) leveraging their past investments and existing capabilities, (b) amortizing those expenses across the added revenue gained from China, and (c) expanding their margins and capturing greater profits. Thus, unique ecosystems not only help Enterprise China generate and capture domestic profits for indigenous firms but they also raise the cost of doing business *in* China and thereby lower the profits that foreign firms can extract *from* China. Alibaba is an exemplar of the types of ecosystems in China that foreign firms may find difficult to penetrate.

Alibaba started as an e-commerce platform in 1999 but quickly sought to build a larger ecosystem. Ming Zeng, chairman of the Academic Council of the Alibaba Group, commented:

> We realized ... that we were truly building an ecosystem: a community of organisms (businesses and consumers of many types) interacting with one another and the environment (the online platform and the larger off-line physical elements). Our strategic imperative was to make sure that the platform provided all the resources, or access to the resources, that an online business would need to succeed, and hence supported the evolution of the ecosystem.[14]

The ecosystem at first was focused on linking buyers and sellers. Once established, data on buyers and sellers, as well as the transactions plus improvements in technology, allowed Alibaba to expand into digitally enabled advertising, marketing, product recommenders, logistics, and finance (see Exhibit 3.7).

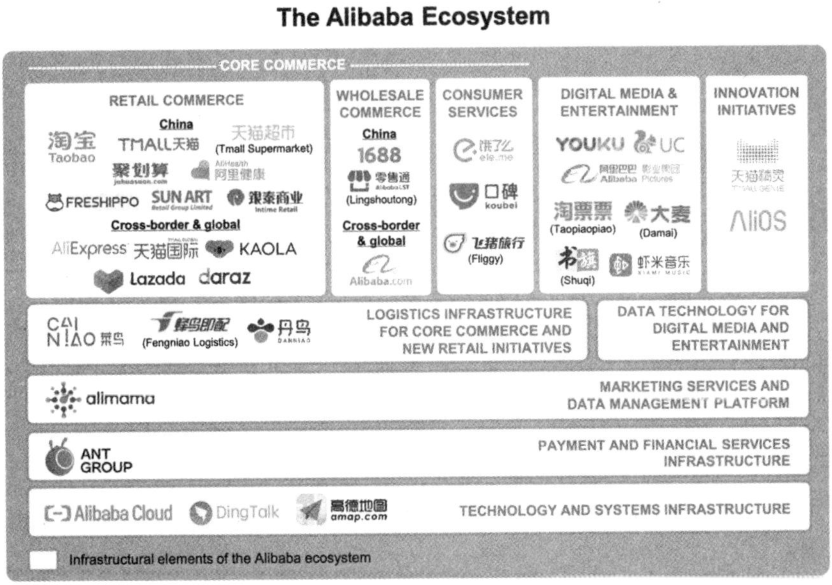

The Alibaba Ecosystem

Exhibit 3.7 Alibaba's Ecosystem
Source: Alibaba May 2021.

Alibaba's ecosystem is vast and covers e-commerce (B2B and B2C), logistics, marketing, advertising, data management, financial services, and IT infrastructure. But the ecosystem also extends beyond the companies that Alibaba owns or controls. It collaborates with hundreds more companies in each of its key domains.

Alibaba was adept at finding areas of need in China that were underserved and then utilizing all its relevant capabilities to fill the need. For example, most Chinese banks would not bother with loans of less than $1 million. Yet many small businesses needed loans much smaller than that. Ecosystem member Ant Microloans targeted those businesses. Because these small businesses lacked traditional credit histories, banks were reluctant to loan to them. Alibaba realized that it could analyze the mountains of data it had on small business transactions to estimate small business loan risk. In the next seven years, Ant loaned $13.4 billion to nearly 3 million small and midsize enterprises and now can process the average loan request in minutes, not months, with a default rate of about 1%.[15] As Ant made more loans, it compared performing loans to nonperforming loans to gain even greater insights that helped vet subsequent applicants and determine loan amounts, interest rates, and payment terms. As Ant's artificial intelligence–enabled decisions get better, so too will its revenue and profit from just this one area of ecosystem application.

Ant Financials' capabilities can extend to the simplest things, such as renting a ride-share bicycle. Instead of going to a rental location and leaving a deposit and then paying for the rental by cash or credit card, a prospective rider with Ant can (a) see available bikes, (b) use the app to scan a QR code on the bicycle, (c) have the system check the renter's credit history through Sesame Credit (potentially avoiding the need for a deposit), (d) see if the renter has money available via AliPay, (e) assuming all looks good, open the lock on the bicycle, and (f) when the bike is returned, automatically lock it and complete the transaction. As Chairman Zeng notes:

> In ecosystems with many interconnected players, business decisions require complex coordination. Taobao's recommendation engines, for example, need to work with the inventory management systems of sellers and with the consumer-profiling systems of various social media platforms. Its transaction systems need to work with discount offers and loyalty programs, as well as feed into our logistics network.[16]

Like so many other ecosystems, communication standards and application programming interfaces (APIs) are critical for everything to work together within Alibaba's ecosystem. This is in large part why in 2020 Enterprise China launched Standards 2035, which we will examine in greater detail in Chapter 4. Chairman Zeng also noted that "figuring out the right incentive structures to persuade companies to share the data they have is an important and ongoing challenge."[17]

Difficulty Breaking In

How does a foreign firm break into this sort of ecosystem, especially when the ecosystem in one sense is getting tighter and tighter and more and more integrated? For example, in 2016, Alibaba introduced an AI-powered chatbot. It wasn't a typical chatbot that matches customer queries to a repository of answers. It "trained" with experienced representatives of Alibaba's Taobao merchants who know their products, policies, and delivery systems. Alibaba used machine learning to improve the chatbot's ability to both figure out what the customer's problem really was and offer solutions and actions for the customer to take. The more and longer a firm is in Alibaba's ecosystem, the better the chatbot could perform for the merchant. As an example, Senma, an apparel company, saw its bot-enabled sales soar 26 times higher than its top human salesperson. Such is the power of Alibaba's ecosystem.

CONCLUSION

Enterprise China is well on its way to dominating domestically in targeted sectors. Areas remain, of course, where it lags behind its objectives. Semiconductor manufacturing is just one example. However, the last decade has demonstrated Enterprise China's determination to press forward. It has made progress on its first strategic pillar of reducing its external dependency. It is working hard to ensure that national champions dominate key sectors. It has already achieved this in notable areas such as oil and gas, steel, chemicals, high-speed trains, and many others.

No doubt some readers are already wondering whether Enterprise China can continue to move forward at the same speed or whether it will falter. In Chapter 7, we will examine in more detail the factors that CEOs should watch to better determine whether China will succeed or stumble in fully implementing its competitive strategy. However, before we get there, we need to examine closely its third competitive strategy pillar—winning globally.

Chapter 4

STRATEGIC PILLAR III: WINNING GLOBALLY

In the previous chapter, we discussed China's second strategic pillar, which is to dominate domestically. In this chapter, we focus on China's third strategic pillar—to compete and win globally. Winning at home is one thing; winning in the home markets of your competitors is quite another. If this weren't enough, China is determined to win in the technology-intensive industries central to the Fourth Industrial Revolution. The focus adds weight to an already heavy lift, considering that many of the toughest foreign competitors have significant head starts on China in the targeted sectors and sophisticated operations already in place.

Despite these challenges, Enterprise China recognizes that in a globally connected world continued prosperity at home is at least partially dependent on competitiveness abroad. This focus is supported by the fear that unless China can be competitive, it risks repeating the "great isolation" that the country suffered from the mid-15th century to the mid-20th century. Losing out on the nascent high-tech industries that will drive prosperity over the coming decades would trap China in the role of low-end manufacturer of commoditized products with few opportunities to move up the value stack. Enterprise China recognizes that increasing prosperity and strength at home depends on winning abroad.

On top of this, domestic strength and international influence are key to ensuring that China never suffers economic, military, or political subjugation again. We can hardly emphasize enough China's determination to avoid this type of humiliation again and its desire instead to regain what the Chinese believe is their rightful place in the center of the world. To this claim, some contend that if the military and economic subjugation were such an anathema to China, why was its global response so muted at the turn of the 20th century with no major resurgence until the last few decades? To this we can only say that "that was then, this is now." Even if China wanted to assert itself on the world stage 100 years ago after its subjugation and humiliation, it simply did not have the military, political, and economic power to demand a starring role. Deng Xiaoping captured this reality well with his oft-quoted saying: "Hide your strength, bide your time."[1] Deng's dictum has now gone into retirement.

For those who hope or predict that China will again turn so inward that it backs away from asserting itself on the world stage, we see essentially zero chance of this. China is committed to assuming its central place as a star on the world stage, competing for top billing against the likes of the United States, Germany, Japan, France, and the United Kingdom. This means competing *and* winning. And what does winning globally look like? Certainly, it means that Enterprise China would like to see Chinese companies as global leaders in revenue and market share. But it goes further than this. Competing and winning means that in key areas the rest of the world would ultimately become dependent on Enterprise China. This would be no small achievement, one requiring an aggressive strategy that leverages the combined and coordinated efforts of the state and commercial enterprises.

How does Enterprise China plan to compete and win globally? How will it win so well that it flips the dependency relationship in its favor? As with the other two strategic pillars, we need not guess at the answer. China has answered the question for us and laid out its tactics. As a consequence, we only need to examine those tactics closely and consider their implications.

These tactics include three key elements. First, Enterprise China seeks to gain competitive presence in the world by acquiring foreign companies—not just for their technology and products but also to gain advantage from their established positions in their home markets and other markets around the world. Second, Enterprise China seeks to secure its global competitiveness by controlling important international standards. This is the essence of Standards 2035, which we mentioned earlier but will examine in greater detail in this chapter. Third and finally, Enterprise China seeks to gain global competitiveness by piggybacking on the state's foreign policy initiatives—primarily through the "Belt and Road" initiative that we discuss later in this chapter. To the extent that China can successfully enact all three of these tactics, it has the potential, and we would say ambition, to win in global markets and go from being dependent on foreign companies and countries to having them depend on China.

In the next sections we discuss all three tactics separately. However, at the outset we acknowledge that while each tactic is treated separately, they interact and are in many ways interdependent.

ACQUIRE INTERNATIONAL PRESENCE AND POSITION

In Chapter 2 we discussed Enterprise China's commitment to using acquisitions to reduce its dependency on foreign firms and countries for key technologies and products. This is consistent with MIC 2025, which was designed to "foster second-tier companies that are leaders in design and innovation."[2] The focus of international acquisitions relative to global competitiveness is primarily to help Enterprise China expand internationally and leapfrog its way to global presence and strength. However, before we get too deep into the topic, it is important to describe three basic kinds of foreign acquisitions and the motivations behind each.

Types of Foreign Acquisitions

The first type of foreign acquisition focuses on acquiring strong, local players. These players have commanding positions in their home market but not much elsewhere. Typically, these home markets are larger in size rather than smaller. For Chinese firms, these acquisitions provide a quick means of moving up the local experience curve in terms of customers, competitors, suppliers, workers, regulators, and so on in a key foreign market.

For example, in 2012 Chinese conglomerate Dalian Wanda Group bought AMC Entertainment for $2.6 billion, including debt. In 2012, AMC was the largest owner and operator of movie screens and theaters in the United States—the largest movie market in the world at the time. AMC had 5,000 screens across 239 theaters in the United States and eight theaters in Canada. In total, AMC took in just over $2 billion in annual revenue. With this one sweeping acquisition, Wanda, which was the largest theater operator in China, became the No. 1 theater operator in the United States. Given the difficulty of finding attractive, new theater locations, getting building permits and approvals, funding construction costs, and understanding the changing tastes of US moviegoers in terms of preferred seats and concessions, Wanda likely would have needed decades to get to the same spot that AMC already occupied. However, Wanda's expansion in the United States did not stop with AMC. Wanda used AMC to then buy US rival Carmike Cinemas in 2017 for $1.1 billion, which had just under 3,000 screens across 276 theaters.

Informed readers will know that the AMC acquisition by Wanda subsequently suffered due to the COVID-19 pandemic, which caused many movie theaters, including AMC, to close their doors for over a year. The ensuing financial difficulties forced Wanda to give up its majority shareholding of the company in March 2021. Despite this setback, in the eight years leading up to this, Wanda gained valuable knowledge and experience in the US movie market that otherwise would have taken decades to acquire.

The second type of foreign acquisition targets significant regional players. To some extent acquiring these foreign firms affords similar advantages to local players, but they also provide a shortcut to the acquirer in achieving regional-level economies of scale and scope. For example, China's Sany Heavy Industry Co. announced the acquisition of German concrete pump maker Putzmeister Holding for €360 million ($473 million) in 2012. Although Putzmeister had global sales of $750 million in 2011, the majority of its revenue came from Europe, where it was the No. 1 maker and seller of concrete pumps and pumping trucks. With this purchase, Sany went from being No. 1 in China to No. 1 in Europe as well.

The third category of acquisitions focuses on global players. Global players typically provide both presence and strong position not only in the target's home market but also around the world. Were Chinese firms to try and build such a global presence and position on their own, it might literally take decades. Clearly, the greater the geographic scope of the target, the greater the global presence that the acquisition can bestow. Strength in position can come from a variety of sources including brand, technology, customer relations, and R&D capabilities. International acquisitions can also be a means of sidestepping mounting trade barriers for Chinese firms by shifting production out of China and into other countries, while at the same time currying favor with local customers. Major Chinese investments in the tire industries in countries as diverse as Algeria, Thailand, and Serbia are an example of such efforts to circumvent increasingly expensive tariffs.[3]

A decade ago, Chinese firms had a reputation for overestimating their ability to make global takeovers work and overpaying for them. As we will describe later in this chapter, roughly half of announced Chinese acquisitions never get completed. In the early 2000s, high profile failures included TCL's targeting of Thomson Electronics of France, SAIC's pursuit of SsangYong Motor Company of Korea, and Ping An's takeover of financial services giant Fortis.[4]

One of the largest global acquisitions was of Swiss-based Syngenta, a firm created in 2000 through the merger of the agrichemical businesses of Novartis and AstraZeneca. These firms had both been in operation for decades before they merged. The deal created the largest agrichemical business in the world with presence in over 100 countries. The China National Chemical Corporation (ChemChina) acquired Syngenta in 2015 for $46 billion. The acquisition instantly gave ChemChina a global presence and added more than $15 billion in revenue. As we mentioned in Chapter 3, ChemChina merged with SinoChem in 2021, and the agricultural businesses of the two firms were combined with those gained in the Syngenta acquisition to form the Syngenta Group in June 2021. At the time, it was widely anticipated that the Syngenta Group would be spun off and listed publicly. The IPO would value Syngenta at about $60 billion, raising $10 billion for the parent firm, while still leaving it with over 70% control of the new public company.[5]

Another example of using acquisitions to expand globally is Lenovo. The company began its life in 1984 as New Technology Developer, which changed its name to Legend Holdings in 1988. Initially, Legend focused on reselling branded computers in China. In 1990 it began to sell its own computers in China, owing to the fact that it had created a "Chinese-language motherboard that would enable consumers to use [PC] technology in their own language."[6] Legend became the undisputed market leader in the PC industry in China by 1996. The company then changed its name to Lenovo in 2003, with *Le* from Legend and *novo* from the Latin word for "new" or, by extension, "innovation." Lenovo vaulted onto the world stage in May 2005, when it acquired IBM's personal computer business for $1.25 billion and an additional $500 million in debt. The acquisition immediately quadrupled the size of Lenovo and made it the world's third largest PC maker by volume, with sales in over 100 countries. By 2014 Lenovo was the largest PC maker globally, passing both Dell and Hewlett Packard.

Lenovo further expanded its global reach in 2014 with the purchase of Motorola Mobility from Google for $2.91 billion and IBM's x86 server business for $2.3 billion. While the purchases gave Lenovo an instant global presence in mobile phones and servers, neither acquisition engendered the global growth and success that the PC acquisition had. In fact, after the acquisitions, Lenovo slipped from third to fourth in servers with around a 5% market share and fell out of the top 10 among smartphone makers with only about a 2% global market share. Nonetheless, the acquisitions were designed to catapult Lenovo up the curve and provide global presence and competitiveness that otherwise would have taken decades to achieve organically.

Today these global acquisitions are not confined to large Chinese enterprises. For example, in early 2022 Liesheng, a medium-sized consumer electronics manufacturing and design company based in Guangdong province announced it was acquiring Suunto, the 85-year-old Finnish maker of hiking, diving, and outdoor sports watches and instruments. One out of every two dive computers in the world is a Suunto product and its sports watches are typically ranked amongst the best in the world. Interestingly, Liesheng purchased Suunto from Amer Sports, which was owned by Anta, based in Fujian, China. Anta had purchased Amer Sports, and with it Suunto, in its efforts to build a global business of well-established sports apparel and equipment brands. In addition to its strong global brand, Liesheng was interested in the opportunity to add to and extract technical value from Suunto. At this point the acquisition aspect of Enterprise China's third pillar includes not just the largest SOEs but medium-sized POEs and is far enough along that Chinese firms are increasingly buying foreign assets from each other. We expect this trend to continue.

Foreign M&A—the Numbers

To better understand how Enterprise China has used and is using foreign acquisitions to enhance global competitiveness, we examined its acquisitions over the past 25 years at several different levels. First, we reviewed the total number of foreign acquisitions completed. We focused on those completed rather than announced because our research and that of others has shown that less than half of the announced get completed.[7] Second, we examined the total value of these acquisitions. Third, we reviewed the average value of each one. Across all this analysis, we wanted to determine if movements in foreign acquisitions by Chinese firms corresponded to key announced strategies (i.e., the MLP and MIC 2025).

As we expected, we found that the number of international M&A deals by Chinese companies increased significantly after the MLP (see Exhibit 4.1). For example, Chinese companies completed more than twice as many international M&A deals in the five years after the MLP than they had in the 10 years before it. The number of deals continued at a similar pace through 2015. However, after the announcement of MIC 2025 in 2015, foreign acquisitions rocketed and nearly doubled in 2016.

The magnitude of the increase in M&A deals caught the United States and other countries' attention and engendered greater scrutiny and opposition thereafter to proposed acquisitions by Chinese firms. Uncharacteristically, the surge caught the Chinese government somewhat off guard. The rush to consummate M&A deals took a dramatic bite out of China's foreign exchange reserves, and consequently, the government reimposed capital controls.[8] The combination of greater foreign government scrutiny and Chinese government capital controls subsequently pushed the total number of deals down from 2017 through 2020. Even with this decline, the post-MIC 2025 period averaged 273 transactions compared to the MLP period of 124 deals per year.

Number of International M&As by Chinese Firms

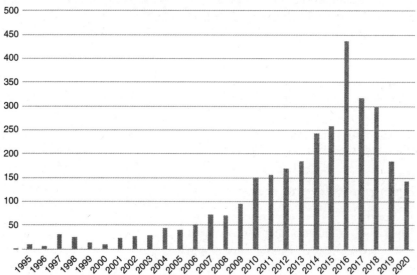

Exhibit 4.1   Number of International M&As by Chinese Firms

Source: Adapted from UNCTAD World Investment Report 2020.

As one would expect, the total net value of Chinese acquisitions moved up in close concert with the total number of deals (correlation of 0.91). The value of the deals in the five years after the MLP was roughly equivalent to the value in the previous 10 years (see Exhibit 4.2). Between 1990 and 2004, Chinese companies spent an average of $831 million per year on foreign acquisitions. After the MLP, this number exploded to an average of $27.4 billion per year. As with the number of deals, the total value of China's international acquisitions soared after the publication of MIC 2025. The post-MIC 2025 period averaged $64.7 billion per year, even with the decline in total value that came after 2016.

The data clearly show that both the absolute number and the value of China's foreign acquisitions increased after the release of the MLP and MIC 2025 strategic plans. The magnitudes of those increases are stunning. Still, we wondered if perhaps this boat of China's foreign acquisitions rose simply with a rising global tide of M&A activity. To test this, we examined whether China's share of all cross-border M&As also increased over these two periods. What we observed was that indeed China's foreign acquisitions rose significantly faster than overall global cross-border M&As. Specifically, China's share of cross-border M&As soared from around 1% in 2005 to a stratospheric 20% in 2013. This was followed by a two-year dip and then another spike in 2016 that took China's share to nearly 19%. Unsurprisingly, as the number of deals and value of Chinese foreign acquisitions declined after 2016, so too did China's global share of cross-border deals.

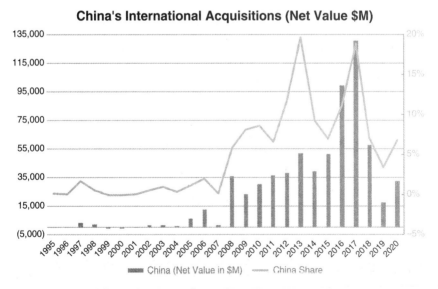

China's International Acquisitions (Net Value $M)

Exhibit 4.2 China's International Acquisition Value
Source: Adapted from UNCTAD World Investment Report 2020.

Finally, we were interested to see if the average size of Chinese foreign acquisitions increased as the number and value of deals went up. What we found surprised us. We expected that the average acquisition size would increase over time as Chinese firms gained experience with foreign acquisitions. What we found was a bit more complicated. First, as we expected, the average size of acquisitions increased dramatically with the introduction of the MLP. Specifically, in the 15 years before the MLP, the average deal size was $52 million. In the 15 years after, the average deal size was $225 million — 15 times larger. However, the deal size did not move up over time between the post-MLP and post-MIC 2025 periods. The average deal size from 2005 to 2014 was essentially the same as from 2015 to 2020 ($225 million).

In addition to examining the average deal size, we looked at the magnitude of variation of deal size over time. We expected that the variation would be lower with the guidance of the MLP and the MIC 2025 compared to the years before these strategic blueprints were announced. The data, in fact, confirmed this expectation. Specifically, from 1990 through 2004, the average variation was over two-and-a-half times greater than the average deal size during that period. While there was variation in deal size from 2005 through 2020, the magnitude of that variation was significantly less than the earlier period. Specifically, the average variation in deal size from 2005 to 2020 was only half as large as the average deal or three times less than the pre-MLP and MIC 2025 periods (see Exhibit 4.3), meaning that the variation after the MLP and MIC 2025 was about three times less than before.

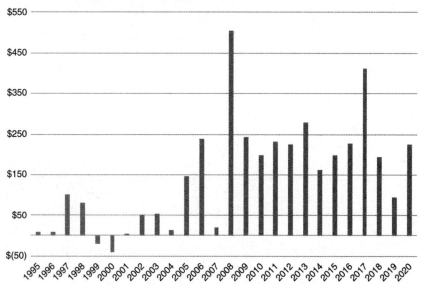

Average Chinese Deal Value (million of US dollars)

Exhibit 4.3 Average Chinese Foreign M&A Deal Value
Source: Adapted from UNCTAD World Investment Report 2020.

Strong State Support of International Acquisitions

The data clearly support the notion that Chinese firms increased their foreign acquisitions after the announcements of Enterprise China's formal strategy plans. However, the degree of state involvement extended beyond simply the announcement of these strategic plans. In fact, Chinese companies have had relatively little autonomy when executing their international expansion plans. This is also true today. Chinese overseas acquisitions were and are approved by the state, and in many cases, the state actively promotes certain acquisitions. A 2017 European Commission report states that most Chinese "overseas acquisitions have the direct backing of the state."[9] Separately, the Mercator Institute for China Studies, a leading German think tank, concluded in a 2016 report that "China pursues an outbound industrial policy with government capital and highly opaque investor networks to facilitate high-tech acquisitions abroad."[10]

State support for foreign investment by Chinese firms is central to what is referred to as its "Going Out" strategy.[11] Under this strategy, Chinese firms are encouraged to engage in international M&As through access to capital at below-market rates and reductions in bureaucratic and regulatory obstacles including exchange controls. A European Union Chamber of Commerce in China study finds that continued government "controls may actually motivate more Chinese companies to look for ways to align their investment plans with government priorities outlined in [MIC 2025], since presenting investments to the authorities that support their priorities … can be expected to achieve a higher rate of approval."[12]

Meeting Funding Challenges

One obstacle for many international acquisitions is funding. In the case of Enterprise China, state-owned banks have played and continue to play a central role in funding international M&As. In 2010 the size of China's banking sector surpassed the US banking sector. Chinese banks hit another milestone in 2016. They overtook the Eurozone's banking sector in size. Assets managed by China's banking sector reached $35 trillion in 2018, more than three times the size of the country's entire GDP. Our analysis of the top 10 banks in China—all state controlled—found total assets of $21.3 trillion versus $16.5 trillion for the top 10 banks in the United States.[13] Aggregate profits for the top 10 Chinese banks were $188.9 billion, more than double the aggregate profit of the top 10 US banks. In 2021, the three largest banks in the world were all Chinese.

By 2020 nearly 97% of all assets held by Chinese banks were loans made to Chinese entities. In comparison, US banks split their loans across domestic and international customers. Consequently, Enterprise China has access to vast supplies of capital through state-controlled and directed financial institutions. Here,

Chinese SOE debt—the kind used to fund international acquisitions—is owned by the state, which controls the country's money supply. Consequently, the supply of funds to Enterprise China is, at least in theory, only limited to the extent that international currencies, such as the US dollar, drains the state's foreign currency reserves beyond the government's point of comfort.

Another source of funds for Enterprise China has been through public listing of shares. A variety of both SOEs and POEs have listed their shares and become publicly traded, whether on a local exchange (now including Hong Kong) or on one of the major US exchanges. While there are schemes that allow Chinese companies to list on the European exchanges, their overseas efforts have focused principally on the United States. Overseas listings give Chinese firms access to additional funding sources to support international acquisitions and advancements in overall competitiveness. They also provide considerable prestige and credibility to Chinese firms operating within China, as well as abroad.

According to the US-China Economic and Security Review Commission, in October 2020 there were 217 Chinese companies listed on the three largest US exchanges with a total market capitalization of $2.2 trillion. Included in the mix were many Enterprise China companies with partial or minor state holdings, as well as eight national-level Chinese SOEs.[14] The amount of money raised on these exchanges dwarfs inward FDI flows. These funds help cover foreign acquisitions without putting strains on China's foreign currency reserves. In essence Enterprise China uses foreign equity exchanges to facilitate overseas expansion via other peoples' money.

Expanding Outward FDI

China's outward FDI was not limited to M&A activities but included investments in expanding existing operations, as well as greenfield projects. China's overall outward FDI exploded with the publication of the MLP in 2005 and surged again with the announcement of MIC 2025 (see Exhibit 4.4). China's outward FDI flow peaked in 2016 at $196 billion and has declined every year thereafter to $117 billion in 2019. In 2020 FDI jumped back to $132.9 billion, largely due to a bump in China's investment in Belt and Road initiatives, which we discuss more fully next. This recent growth in Chinese FDI flows is all the more impressive given that global FDI collapsed in 2020, falling a staggering 42% due to COVID-19-related obstacles and recessionary fears. By the end of 2020 the stock of Chinese FDI continued to grow and reached nearly $2.6 trillion.[15]

Obviously, foreign M&A activity is a component of overall outward FDI. Our analysis found that from 2005 through 2020, foreign M&As accounted for an average of 43% of all outward Chinese FDI. This is consistent with other

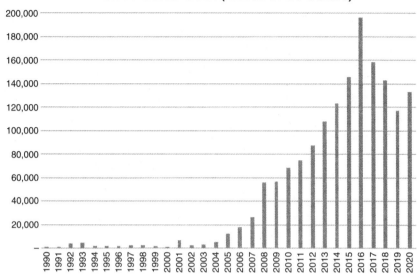

Exhibit 4.4   China's Outward FDI Flows
Source: World Bank.

research, such as an EY study showing that Chinese companies engaged in 591 international M&A deals in 2019 worth nearly $69 billion,[16] representing about one half of China's FDI that year.

LEVERAGE DOMESTIC STANDARDS FOR GLOBAL LEADERSHIP

In Chapter 1 we briefly discussed China's inclusion of Standards 2035 in its blueprint for achieving global leadership. Released in fall 2020, China Standards 2035 is designed to encourage Chinese technology companies to set global standards for their respective sectors. Setting global standards is most important in the emerging industries that are at the heart of MIC 2025, including 5G, electric vehicles, and artificial intelligence. Enterprise China understands that to compete with the best in the world, Chinese firms cannot just follow, imitate, and produce more cheaply. They must raise the bar for everyone, and this means setting the standards for products, services, and technologies. Werner von Siemens, the 19th-century German founder of the Siemens conglomerate, well captured the value of setting standards when he said, "He who owns the standards, owns the market."[17]

The Impact of Standards

This statement is truer today than ever. Standards are a necessary precursor to global trade; they are key to the interoperability of products and services. Standards govern items such as these:

- Width of train tracks;
- Size of light bulb sockets;
- Safety protocols in nuclear power plants;
- Frequencies used by mobile phones and Bluetooth devices;
- Size and shapes of connecting plugs and other electrical interfaces;
- Testing protocols for verifying pharmaceutical safety and effectiveness;
- Measurement of power output for electrical and gasoline engines;
- Classification of fibers used in clothing;
- Vibration frequency ranges for lithium-ion batteries in automobiles; and
- Interoperability of avionics and related devices in civil aircraft.

The list is nearly endless. In some cases—the size of light bulb sockets, for example—the standards have long been established and are rarely the subject of debate. In other cases, mostly in the nascent industries with high degrees of embedded technology that are at the center of MIC 2025, many standards are in flux and the implications are enormous. If Enterprise China can set and own the standard in these industries, the world will beat a path to its door.

Central Message of Standards 2035

The central message of China Standards 2035 can be roughly translated as "We will lead, and you will follow." Leading is aspirational with practical benefits. The underlying belief is that firms that are the best at innovating are also the ones more likely to set the standards. Likewise, they are the most likely to capture the lion's share of value creation. Google's Android operating system is a case in point. In 2021, it set the standard for 73% of mobile phones, with every company using the operating system, paying Google a licensing fee.

Although China Standards 2035 is about leading in stand-alone product design and functionality, it goes far beyond individual products. At its core, standards define interoperability—including how different components of hardware physically fit together and how hardware and software work together. Standards shape the entire playing field, which includes the broad ecosystem of technology suppliers, manufacturers, software designers, distributors, installers, and data management firms. And this is where Enterprise China, with its layers of interconnected stakeholders, shines. Enterprise China is an ideal vehicle for propagating global standards, and in return, it is a key benefactor of those global standards.

Standards 2035 is a signal to the rest of the world that China is committed to pivoting from being the world's factory to becoming the world's innovator. Rather than decoupling China from the rest of the world, China Standards 2035 captures China's continued commitment to global engagement. It envisions a future where Enterprise China, including entire supporting ecosystems, controls the key technology levers at the center of the global economy. As such, Standards 2035 should be viewed as an integrative force; it is not a tool of decoupling.

To Chinese firms in targeted industries, Standards 2035 provides a directive that they should double their efforts to dominate their industries globally—not necessarily in terms of total market share but in terms of their technology prowess. Over time, size and scale will become less important than technological leadership for Chinese companies. Shifting these objectives has important implications for how and where Chinese companies invest for the future.

Standards Cannot Be Imposed But Can Be Leveraged

China Standards 2035 is audacious because Enterprise China recognizes that it cannot unilaterally impose its standards on the rest of the world. Although it can dictate standards at home and can even force foreign firms operating in China to play by those rules, its direct standards authority stops at its borders. Standards outside China are set through a competitive and iterative process that involves private *non-Chinese* companies outside Enterprise China's direct reach. Often industry associations facilitate the codification of standards through either convention based on agreed-upon best practices or a formal agreement among members.[18]

Enterprise China recognizes that it cannot dictate standards to the world, but it hopes to dictate standards at home and leverage the size of its home market to persuade foreign companies to follow China's lead elsewhere. For example, if foreign CEOs completely ignore China's domestic standards, they could be blocked from that market. China is big enough in virtually every sector that not being allowed to play in that market would be a nontrivial negative outcome. On the other hand, if foreign CEOs bet heavily on the "China standard's horse," and the horse fails to win the global race, they could be left with a ticket that only has value in China, while needing to buy a new ticket to bet on the winning horse outside China. The longer they wait to buy this "x-China" ticket, the more expensive it becomes. In fact, if they wait too long, the ticket window might close, and they would be out of the global race.

The Example of 5G Standards

A good example of an industry singled out for attention under Standards 2035 is telecommunications and more particularly 5G. This new technology is 100 times faster than the 4G technology it replaces. Without question, 5G will play a central role in ushering in the Internet of Things, linking billions of sensors, machines, databases, and smart devices. Winning in 5G and related technologies has the potential to generate trillions of dollars of business for Enterprise China.

Previous generations were different. China had to follow the lead of Europe for 2G. Japan had the winning standards for 3G. Americans largely won the race for 4G standards. China is determined to win in 5G, and it now seems clear that the country has taken an early lead.[19] According to a 2018 Deloitte study, China had a total of approximately 1.9 million wireless 5G sites in the country, compared to approximately 200,000 in the United States. Looking at the competition another way, China had 5.3 sites for every 10 square miles compared to 0.4 sites for the United States.[20] Analysts point to a combination of factors that contribute to China's head start. Not only is China's domestic market massive, but the state's role in targeting 5G growth has been pivotal.

The state controls all of the country's three largest mobile operators (China Mobile, China Telecom, and China Unicom) and has pushed them to aggressively support 5G throughout the country. At the same time, it has nurtured equipment companies such as Huawei and has helped channel software companies such as Baidu to create apps that work on Chinese 5G networks. In short, Enterprise China has created a symbiotic ecosystem involving all key pieces of the 5G puzzle.[21]

China has been eager to leverage its domestic strengths in 5G for global leadership. It has worked tirelessly to influence international standards-setting bodies to ensure that Chinese 5G technology is used as the benchmark for the rest of the world.[22] In 2014 China effectively lobbied for the election of one of its former officials, Zhao Houlin, as Secretary General of the International Telecommunication Union (ITU). This UN agency acts as an independent arbiter that establishes the rules and standards at the center of the global telecommunications industry. Under rules that require a simple majority vote that give the same power to Zambia as the United States or Japan, Zhao was then reelected to the post four years later. Once in office, he shamelessly supported Chinese technology standards. He also has publicly defended Chinese telecom giant Huawei against US accusations of spying. "I would encourage Huawei to be given equal opportunities to bid for business," Zhao said. Speaking more broadly on another occasion, he provided a general endorsement of all Chinese telecommunication's capabilities. "Nowadays in the discussion of relevant ITU standards, China's technical strength is already in the first echelon and the international community expects China to play a greater role in the UN system," he said.[23]

One key beneficiary of this has been Chinese technology giant Huawei. The private company rose to global prominence at an impressive rate. The company's first customer was the PLA, which provided a series of rich contracts that helped jump-start operations. To fund expansion, Huawei then received an enormous $30 billion line of credit from the state through the China

Development Bank.[24] In just 10 years (by 2019), Huawei was able to move from zero market share to nearly 40% in the 4G mobile network infrastructure in Europe.[25] In 2019 Huawei controlled 29% of the global telecom equipment market. In Asia-Pacific, the company controlled 43% of the market, and in Latin America it was 34%.[26]

Observers cite two other factors that have been critical to Huawei's domestic *and* global success. First, the company spends heavily on R&D—nearly $20 billion per year. Up to half of its employees work in R&D-related functions. Second, more than any company in the 5G world, Huawei has fully committed to vertical integration. Its ability to define the technology and make the equipment (from switches to mobile devices) gives it a powerful technology advantage in terms of speed to market and interoperability.

In 2020 Huawei had 194,000 employees and operations in 170 countries.[27] Under President's Trump regime, Huawei was actively targeted as a Trojan horse and tool of the Chinese state. While the company has vigorously disputed these claims, its rise to prominence is viewed in the United States, Australia, Japan, and Europe as a major strategic threat both in terms of lost commercial leadership and also in terms of security.

Risks Go Both Ways

The risks go both ways when a single country tries to control standards in emerging technologies. To succeed, China has focused on nascent industries for which standards are not yet entrenched or remain in a state of flux. This reduces its risk of being boxed out of global markets. Also, China seems intent on applying its considerable political skills and clout to convince others to follow its lead. However, as much as Enterprise China might want to succeed in this effort, the path and process will be difficult. Naomi Wilson, writing for the Council on Foreign Relations, sums up the challenge: "The notion that the Chinese government is going to swindle the world's best engineers into adopting voluntary standards that will shape the technological landscape in China's favor, and continue to do so with every technological change, is a significant reach."[28]

If Enterprise China is not careful, it risks overplaying its hand. Politics and gamesmanship are central to China's efforts at leading globally on standards. Yet if not managed well, Enterprise China may embrace standards that are not supported by a large coalition of foreign enterprises. This would result in two competing sets of standards, with resulting products and services that are incompatible. Such an outcome would severely limit China's exports. While some modest differences in approach and design are possible, most companies—both within China and outside China—likely would prefer compatible technologies. Consequently, while Enterprise China's commitment to controlling standards is clear, the path ahead may be a bit bumpy.

PIGGYBACK ON FOREIGN POLICY INITIATIVES

The third element in China's strategic pillar of competing globally is to piggyback on the country's foreign policy initiatives. While other countries intentionally differentiate between government and commercial interests, Enterprise China operates as an extension of the state. Chinese firms not only have advanced warning of state initiatives but they also have a seat at the policy table, because as noted previously, many of the top executives at China's SOEs also have or have had political appointments. The contributions of Enterprise China to foreign policy initiatives include helping craft bespoke regulatory and financial initiatives at the macro and micro levels of individual Chinese firms.

Most CEOs of foreign firms are unfamiliar with the depth and breadth of Chinese business-government relationships. Many are also philosophically uncomfortable with the idea of both parties joining hands in a coordinated manner. These relationships run counter to their education and personal experiences. In many cases, Western CEOs view all governments as adversaries to be avoided, outsmarted, or blocked. But not so in China, where the mindset is nearly the polar opposite.

Belt and Road Initiative

Perhaps the best example of the symbiotic relationship between Enterprise China and the State is the Belt and Road Initiative (BRI). In many ways, the BRI is also an important tool in the adoption of China Standards 2035 and a key driver of many of Enterprise China's more recent M&A activities.[29] Sometimes referred to as the new Silk Road, the BRI was launched in 2013 by President Xi Jinping and targets infrastructure development projects from East Asia to Europe.[30] The "belts" part of the initiative refers to railroads designed to connect China with Europe, the Middle East, and central and Southeast Asia. "Roads" refer to highways, maritime routes, and ports throughout mostly the Indian Ocean region and the Middle East.[31]

BRI projects are designed to expand local economic development and link foreign markets to those of China. As such, the BRI appeals to countries eager to integrate their economies more fully with global markets and more particularly with China's manufacturing enterprises.[32] At the same time, BRI expands the use of Chinese renminbi as a currency of exchange, thereby providing new business opportunities and sales channels for Chinese companies without tapping into valuable foreign exchange reserves, and thus extending the influence of the Chinese state.

As of 2020, more than 60 countries have signed BRI development contracts or are in advanced discussions for these Chinese-sponsored projects (see Exhibit 4.5 for the top 10 countries).[33] Africa is a prime target of BRI projects, in part because the continent lags in infrastructure—from electrical generation to airports.

Country	Construction total ($ billion)
Pakistan	41.5
Saudi Arabia	35.3
Nigeria	32.6
Indonesia	29.0
UAE	26.9
Malaysia	25.8
Algeria	23.7
Ethiopia	23.1
Iran	22.2
Bangladesh	21.4

Exhibit 4.5   Top 10 Countries for Chinese Construction Activity (2005–2019)
Source: AEI.

Sector	Construction total ($ billion)
Power	335.4
Transportation	249.9
Real estate	90.7
Metals	35.9
Agriculture	16.5

Exhibit 4.6   Top 5 Construction Activity by Sector (2005–2019)
Source: AEI.

Examples of BRI projects on the continent include the Maputo-Katembe bridge in Mozambique, the Abuja-Kaduna railway line in Nigeria, and the Cherchell Ring Expressway in Algeria. Other projects in south and central Asia include the Magampura Mahinda Rajapaksa Port in Sri Lanka, the East Coast Rail Link project in Malaysia, and the China-Pakistan Economic Corridor project.

If we look at announced BRI-related construction contracts, it is easy to see that power generation and transport (primarily road and rail) dominate (see Exhibit 4.6). Not surprisingly, large SOEs have undertaken virtually all of the announced construction projects that had an individual project value in excess of $100 million.

Asian Infrastructure Investment Bank

BRI projects are enticing for resource-starved countries. The Chinese provide the funding, technical skills, and much of the trained labor. Funding is typically channeled through the Asian Infrastructure Investment Bank (AIIB), set up by Beijing in 2015. The AIIB serves as a competitor to the World Bank, which is viewed by the Chinese as being too bureaucratic and too dominated by US, European, and Japanese interests. The AIIB is intended to be less bureaucratic and more entrepreneurial and provide a greater voice for China. Since its founding, membership in the AIIB has grown to include over 100 member countries including the United Kingdom, France, Russia, Switzerland, and Germany. Still, China retains veto rights for decisions that require three-quarters approval.[34]

China has used the AIIB to fund the bulk of its BRI projects. Through this, and the BRI more specifically, China's political influence has grown significantly. It also has resulted in dozens of new bilateral government-to-government agreements[35] and generated a vast array of new business opportunities for Chinese companies. According to a McKinsey study, China has become the largest funder of infrastructure projects in Africa, financially backing around one fifth of all projects and constructing one third of them.[36] The McKinsey report estimates that in 2017 there were more than 10,000 Chinese-owned firms operating in Africa.

Growing Controversies

While the infrastructure development projects bring economic benefits to the recipient countries, BRI has not been without significant controversy. Many recipient countries have complained of being saddled with debts that they have little ability to repay.[37] Others are critical of the flood of Chinese workers who crowd out local workers who otherwise would benefit from the giant projects that are being rolled out. The chorus of complaints is growing. In Malaysia, former prime minister Mahathir Mohamad voiced his concern about what he calls "a new version of colonialism." He went on to cancel nearly $23 billion of BRI projects. Sri Lanka, for its part, defaulted on Chinese loans and ceded control over one its major seaports to China for a 99-year period.[38]

For their part, the United States and other Western nations have remained skeptical of the BRI and its long-term objectives. The US Economic and Security Review Commission, in its report to Congress, makes the following observation:

> The Chinese government's Belt and Road Initiative (BRI) is both a blueprint and a testbed for establishing a Sinocentric world order. The initiative has no membership protocols or formal rules but is based on informal agreements and a network of bilateral deals with China as the hub and other countries as the spokes. This framework lets Beijing act arbitrarily and dictate terms as the stronger party.[39]

MOVE FROM DOMESTIC TO GLOBAL LEADERSHIP

Thus far, we have touched on three key means by which Enterprise China has sought to compete globally. However, we have noted that in many ways the second and third strategic pillars are interdependent. In this section, we use the high-speed rail industry as an example of how Enterprise China moves from domestic domination to global leadership. While we have touched on rails in other chapters, our focus has been on the tactics deployed by Enterprise China. Now we are able to more fully review the full strategy behind Enterprise China's move from being a global non-entity to becoming the world's leader in the rail industry in less than two decades.

Beginning in 2003, China began to pursue a long-term plan to create an internationally competitive high-speed railway system. The ambition was audacious given the poor level of rail capability that China had in 2004. Phase one involved creating 74,500 miles of new high-speed track designed to link major population and industrial centers in China.[40] To achieve its goals, the Minister of Railroads for China, Liu Zhijun, embraced a "technology transfer for market access" strategy that gave foreign companies access to China contingent on them forming joint ventures with Chinese firms and agreeing to share their technology with Chinese producers.[41] The minister then invited leading foreign rail equipment companies including Siemens, Bombardier, Kawasaki Heavy Industries, and Alstom to assist in creating a family of rail technologies.

Over time, restrictions on these foreign companies increased as China's local manufacturers moved up the learning curve and value stack, from freight trains to light rail and then passenger trains. As discussed more fully in Chapter 3, the state also orchestrated the merger of two rail SOEs to create CRRC, which served as the centerpiece of the state's push into rail and effectively had monopolistic control of the domestic market. Once in place, CRRC then forced global rail equipment giant Bombardier to form a joint venture. In 2007, the country introduced its first high-speed rail line based on "borrowed" Western technologies including those sourced from Bombardier, Hitachi, and Kawasaki Heavy Industries (the two principal manufacturers of Japan's Shinkansen trains).

Phase two of China's high-speed rail development plan began in 2010, when the country launched its first high-speed train based on Chinese technologies. Estimates were that about 90% of the "Chinese" technology came from foreign companies.[42] To support its ambitions, in 2016 the state committed a whopping $549 billion to upgrade and expand the country rail network, with most of the investment targeting high-speed trains.[43] In addition to providing strategic direction through funding, China's National Development and Reform Commission (NDRC) was established to provide planning, issue operating licenses, and set standards. The NDRC also provided informal "guidance" for foreign firms, never in writing to avoid WTO conflicts. They then moved to effectively shut foreign firms out of key Chinese markets and segments, including the country's more recent movement into autonomous rail equipment and rail technologies that are connected to the Internet of Things. By 2019, the country had nearly 25,000 kilometers of high-speed rail lines, the most of any country in the world. In fact China has far more than the total high-speed lines operating in the rest of the world combined.[44]

China's domestic rail acumen has created significant international growth opportunities for the country. Phase three of the country's high-speed rail development plan involved globalizing Chinese rail technology and equipment. One report concludes that CRRC's ability to access state funding enabled the company to underbid foreign competitors by 20% to 30% on equipment sales opportunities in the United States and Europe.[45] A 2017 report estimates that the cumulative value of 18 different Chinese overseas rail projects was a staggering $143 billion, slightly more than the amount of the post-World War 2 Marshall Plan.[46] Much of this involved exports of Chinese manufactured products. In 2019, China exported $37.3 billion in rail equipment[47]—greater than the total sales of *any* of its global competitors.

Rail projects are typically extremely expensive. For the developing world, export financing is essential. Not surprisingly, rail has played a central role in the BRI initiative. A case in point is the gigantic China-Pakistan Economic Corridor, valued at $87 billion in 2020. The project has been called the crown jewel of the BRI and includes not only rail lines but also roads, bridges, tunnels, and port facilities. It is a "package deal," again playing to Enterprise China's strengths in linking domestic ecosystems. But the objectives of the China-Pakistan Economic Corridor went far beyond selling China's rail equipment and engineering services. Its full vision was to provide a land bridge connecting Chinese factories with Pakistan and beyond to the Arabian Sea. A side benefit was greater isolation of China's strategic and military adversary, India.[48]

It should not come as a surprise that China's ambition for industry hegemony would play out so well in the rail industry. Afterall, it is an industry that requires massive long-term investments. These have been provided by the state. Because the "buyers" are usually other state entities, China's growing political influence provides additional leverage. While many of CRRC's competitors win business through open tenders, over two thirds of China's overseas rail infrastructure projects from 2009 to 2019 were secured through government-to-government agreements.[49] The rail industry also needs substantial coordination between equipment providers and the state in terms of providing right-of-way access, locating and building platforms and stations, electrification, and so on. Again, the close alignment between Enterprise China and the state have proven pivotal. Finally, rail is an industry ripe with opportunity for smart track, freight and passenger monitoring, and the interconnectivity of machinery and software. Controlling standards, targeting related industries through MIC 2025, and utilizing the layers of network opportunities central to the structure of Enterprise China have produced a significant competitive advantage to the Chinese.

GOAL: FLIP THE DEPENDENCY RELATIONSHIP

In Chapter 2, we discussed the battles fought by Enterprise China to liberate itself from dependency on foreign firms and technologies. Enterprise China's broader ambition is to flip the direction of dependency with the West. It isn't enough that Chinese firms are free of Western dominance; rather, the ultimate ambition is to have Western firms depend on China.

Evidence of China's success with its third strategic pillar will be measured in large part by the degree to which it has reversed its dependency on foreign firms at three levels: (a) industry level, (b) business level, and (c) sales level. Each captures an important element of the dependency equation.

Dependencies at the Industry Level

Just as Enterprise China has targeted strategic industries in which it wants to reduce its external dependency, it would like to see that dependency reversed, or flipped. China seeks to have foreign firms dependent on it in strategic industries for the same reason it wants to unwind its dependency on foreign industries: asymmetric power and leverage. The greater the dependency, the lower the power and leverage of the dependent entity over profits, growth opportunities, and essentially all other decisions.

Growing International Dependencies on China

Putting the strategic role of an industry to the side for a moment, a 2020 study found that the United States was dependent on China for 414 categories of products. In this case, dependency on China was defined as importing "more than 50% of its supplies from China, and China control[ling] more than 30% of the global market of that particular good."[50] Examples of US dependency on China included:

- **Vitamins:** vitamin B2 (62%), vitamin C (74%), vitamin D (76%), vitamin B1 (85%).
- **Antibiotics:** penicillin (52%), tetracyclines (90%), chloramphenicol (93%).
- **Industrial products:** steel-toed boots (64%), welded-link chain (53%), vehicle jacks (83%), gantry chains (65%), shipping containers (66%), safety glass (73%), and metal castors (56%).
- **Metals:** tungsten (55%) and manganese (66%).
- **High-tech products:** laptop computers (93%), mobile phones (73%), projectors (52%), video games consoles (88%), microphones (58%), and lithium-ion batteries (51%).[51]

High dependency on China is not just a US problem. Australia was even more strategically dependent on China with 595 categories of products affected; in Canada, the number was 367; in the United Kingdom, it was 229. And globally, it seems that China's dominance has become increasingly clear in key industries. For example, by 2018, China was producing 70% of the world's solar cells.[52]

Example: Rare Earth Metals

Rare earth metals is an example of how China can achieve a position where foreign firms and countries are dependent on it and how it can use that position as leverage for other state objectives. Rare earths consist of 17 different natural elements, all of which are lower down on the periodic table. Examples include lanthanum, cerium, and praseodymium. They are essential in the functioning of a wide range of advanced products including hybrid cars, computers, wind turbines, lasers, fiber optics, and superconductors. They also act as catalysts for various chemical processes. Rare earths are found in many locations around the world but typically exist only in tiny concentrations. Consequently, they are costly to extract because significant volumes of earth must be removed to recover small quantities of rare earth metals. Given the environmental degradation and pollution that results from processing the basic elements, most of the world has stepped back from mining rare earths. In contrast, China has ramped up its production. China produced approximately of 85% of the world's output of rare earth minerals in 2019.[53] About 80% of US rare earth imports have come from China.[54] Japan was almost entirely dependent on China.

The imbalance in rare earth production gives China leverage in many contexts. In 2010, for example, China and Japan faced off in a diplomatic conflict involving a boat collision in disputed waters in the East China Sea. To press its position, China cut off its supply of rare earth metals to Japan. In response, Japan worked to recycle rare earths, moved its supply chains to other nations, and discovered rich supplies of rare earths in deep sea mud within Japan's exclusive economic zone. Despite these moves, it took Japan nearly a decade to unwind its dependency on China for rare earths.

Dependencies at the Business Level

As we note in Chapter 1, although China leveraged its abundant, cheap labor to establish itself as the world's factory, it recognized the risk of staying at the lower end of the value stack. Consequently, over the past two decades, it has invested more in physical infrastructure than the United States and Europe combined. This allowed it to build up a manufacturing ecosystem along many if not most points of the supply, manufacturing, and assembly chain. This ecosystem creates high switching costs for foreign firms that have become deeply embedded in it. For example, in 2019 retail giant Walmart relied on China for 26% of its supplies, and Target's supply exposure to China was 34%.[55] However, the dependency was actually higher than the numbers suggest because both retailers relied not just on the products themselves but second- and third-tier suppliers that were critical components of the final products Walmart and Target purchased. In addition, retailers not just in the United States but worldwide were dependent on the efficiency and reliability of the transportation and ultra-modern port facilities that could ensure that they received not just the right product at the right price but at the desired time.

Sometimes companies can be dependent on China because the end product has literally hundreds or thousands of components that are spread across China's production landscape. The breadth and spread of this interconnected set of suppliers create dependencies that are hard to undo. For example, US-based Medtronic's ventilators contain more than 1,400 parts. With pressure on the company to ramp up its production of ventilators during the early days of the coronavirus outbreak, Medtronic conducted a thorough review of its supply chain and concluded that almost 80% of its parts (more than 1,100) were actually produced in China. It was only after conducting this painstaking review that Medtronic realized how dependent it was on China for parts and components that went into its ventilators. The streamlined supply chains and just-in-time delivery systems perfected over the past decade have saved immeasurable amounts of time and money. However, that structure now means that even a small part sourced only in China at a tier below which a foreign firm has visibility can create a level of dependency for the company far beyond the value of the particular part. Unfortunately, much of this remains completely opaque to Western decision makers.

Dependencies at the Sales Level

Enterprise China is not limited to promoting supply dependencies. It is all too happy to ensure that foreign companies depend on China for the bulk of their revenue, providing those sales are only a small slice of the Chinese domestic market so that indigenous firms can still dominate at home. After all, when foreign firms are dependent on Chinese customers for the lion's share of their revenue, they are more likely to bend to China's approach and standards.

Over time, various companies have become heavily reliant on China for a high portion of their revenue. Exhibit 4.7 provides examples of American companies with some of the highest revenue exposures to China.[56] Even companies with lower overall revenue from China can nonetheless be more sensitive to that revenue (and its potential decline) when it represents a high portion of the firm's overall growth. Companies such as Apple, Intel, Tesla, SAP, and ASML would suffer major hits to their stock prices should sales in China dip compared to companies such as Mondelez, Nike, or McDonald's, whose proportion of sales in China are similar but those sales do not dominate revenue growth.

Company	Revenue exposure to China (%)
Wynn Resorts	75.2*
Qualcomm	66.6*
Micron Technology	57.1*
Broadcom	54**
Qorvo	52**
Texas Instruments	44.3*
IPG Photonics	43.1*

Exhibit 4.7 Examples of US Company Exposure to China Revenue
Source: Company documents (* 2019 data; ** 2018 data).

CONCLUSION

As we highlight, China is determined to be in as much control of its prosperity and destiny as possible. It is also acutely aware of the risk of becoming cut off and falling behind the West in a repeat of the Great Isolation. Equally, China abhors the possibility of the military, economic, and political subjugation that it endured a century ago. As a consequence, the first strategic pillar focuses on eliminating overdependency in key sectors. This was the focus of the MLP and amplified by MIC 2025. While achieving domestic content objectives would reduce China's external dependency, dominating domestically ensures it. However, in a connected world, competing globally, which means being able to set standards, is the final insurance that China can remain free from external dependence and increase its strength as a nation and ability to influence the world around it.

With the details now laid out of how China plans to achieve dual circulation, the key questions for foreign executives are as follows:

- What does this mean for me and my company?
- What should we do about it?

The answers to these questions are the focus of the remainder of the book. In Chapter 5, we address these questions for foreign firms competing *inside* China. In Chapter 6, we look at the answers for foreign firms competing *outside* China.

Chapter 5

HOW TO COMPETE
IN CHINA: STRATEGIC
OPTIONS AND ACTIONS

So far, we have examined how Enterprise China is more than a collection of Chinese enterprises; it is the combination of the state and commercial business in ways and to a degree never witnessed in modern history. We examined in some depth Enterprise China's three-part competitive strategy: eliminating dependence, dominating domestically, and competing globally. We also illustrated the progress Enterprise China has made on each pillar. Of the three strategic pillars, competing globally is the newest and consequently has the furthest to go before reaching its objectives.

Although it was discussed in Chapter 1, the level of control and influence that the state has on the Chinese economy is worth repeating here. Through 150,000 SOEs in China, the state directly controls 30% to 40% of the economy. The state dictates who runs these companies and how they run them relative to the strategic goals of the state. However, to think that the state's influence starts and stops with SOEs is a mistake. The state exercises significant influence over POEs and their leaders. The state choreographed the cancellation of ANT Financial's IPO as well as the humiliation of Jack Ma. It orchestrated the delisting from the NYSE of Didi. Both high profile events served as powerful lessons and reminders to the CEOs of Chinese POEs that the state's nod of approval is required for *all* significant strategic and financial decisions. Today, no Chinese POE would be foolish enough to fight against the state. As in ancient Rome, tribute must be paid, and political submission acknowledged. As we have said previously, Enterprise China is far more than just the domestic enterprises in China.

Although we have laid out Enterprise China's competitive goals and strategy, as well as the related tactics, many foreign executives have dismissed or discounted the threat. So have many diplomats, academics, and social sector leaders. Skeptics from all backgrounds have misinterpreted China's maneuvering as just another attempt at self-serving industrial policy, reasoning that the world has seen other such attempts come and go.

Other observers dismissed what we label Enterprise China because they expected that the increased commercialization of China eventually would undermine the centralization at the heart of Enterprise China. They believed that master planning and state control would cause the model to collapse under its own weight and inefficiency, as happened with the former Soviet Union. Others predicted that a wave of democracy and liberalization would usurp the Enterprise China model. However, after nearly two decades of counterevidence, these expectations have been beaten into full retreat if not complete defeat. In fact, the Enterprise China model is now more dominant and powerful than it was 20 years ago. To the surprise and disappointment of many in the West, Enterprise China can no longer be dismissed or discounted. As it moves forward, it has the potential to influence and disrupt a wide variety of foreign firms. This migration of power is captured in a recent McKinsey Global Institute report, which concludes: "Today, China is becoming less exposed in economic terms to the rest of the world [but] . . . the rest of the world is becoming more exposed to China."[1]

Given what we know about Enterprise China's path ahead and its past successes, foreign executives whose firms have operations in China naturally ask, "What can our company do to better compete in China?" In this chapter, we squarely take up this question and examine the strategic options and actions that foreign firms with operations in China might consider. Because other foreign firms do not have operations in China but nonetheless will be impacted by Enterprise China, we will examine their strategic options and actions in Chapter 6.

STRATEGIES FOR FOUR TYPES OF PLAYERS

Although more than one million foreign firms operate in China, there are not a million different reasons for being in the country. We can classify foreign firms into four categories by examining them in a grid along two axes (see Exhibit 5.1). The first is the extent to which they are in China to focus on upstream activities, such as raw materials, components, and production. The second is the extent to which they are there to focus on downstream activities, such as China-based distribution, marketing, and sales. In our model, firms can have a high or low emphasis on each dimension, yielding a simple but comprehensive two-by-two categorization scheme, which allows us to understand better the challenges that different firms will face while competing in China and how best to respond.

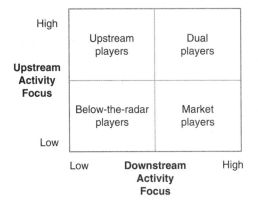

Exhibit 5.1   Foreign Players in China

Below the Radar Players

These companies have a low-low focus on both upstream and downstream activities in China. A surprisingly large number of US firms fall into the below-the-
radar category. A 2018 Goldman Sachs study found that the average revenue
from China for all S&P 500 firm was a mere 1% of their total revenue. Many
of these firms had quite limited upstream activities as well. Some are in this category because they are at an early, experimental stage of engaging with China.
Other firms seem to be in China with a low-low focus because so many other
companies are there and they don't want to be left out. In these firms, the executives we interviewed had a hard time articulating clear and compelling reasons for their small presence in China. Finally, a few firms operating below the
radar had had a bigger presence in China earlier in their histories, but over time
they experienced significant difficulties. Subsequently, they nearly eliminated
their upstream and/or downstream presence in the country. For example, on
the downstream side, even though International Paper generates more than one
quarter of its revenue outside the United States, in 2020 less than 2% of the total
came from China. In addition, although at one point International Paper had
had a reasonably sized upstream operation in China, by 2020 the company had
sold off most of those assets.

Regardless of the exact reason for foreign firms having a low-low presence in
China, the question remains: what are the implications of Enterprise China for
them now and what are their strategic options and action? The answers depend
somewhat on whether the foreign firms fall within or outside the targeted industrial sectors relative to MIC 2025 or Standards 2035.

For below-the-radar players in MIC 2025 or Standards 2035 targeted industries, the odds of survival in China are not good. The reasons are best illustrated
with an example. Fresenius Medical Care, based in Germany, is a top 10 medical

device maker globally. It does not have much in the way of downstream operations in China, and the country accounts for a low, single-digit share of its global sales. Fresenius also has relatively small operations upstream. However, its products sit in the crosshairs of the MIC 2025's medical devices target. Consequently, it could easily fall victim to China's national champion Mindray.

Mindray is more than twice as large as its closest domestic competitor, and it is growing faster in China than any of its major foreign rivals, including Fresenius. This growth is helped largely by national and provincial government officials directing Chinese hospitals to increase their purchases of domestically sourced medical devices to 70%, which is completely in line with the strategic objective of reducing external dependency and aligned with the local content and import substitution targets of MIC 2025. Consequently, Fresenius and other below-the-radar players in the targeted MIC 2025 segments would be wise to hedge their growth plans in China by laying down significant alternative bets in other markets. To survive in China at a small scale when national champions such as Mindray are looking to dominate domestically will require extraordinary superiority of product, likely discounted pricing, plus superior distribution. Without a value proposition that customers simply cannot ignore no matter how much pressure the state puts on them, the forces behind both reducing external dependency and domestic domination by national champions make the success prospects of these firms look dim. Fundamentally, below-the-radar firms that sit in targeted areas will need value propositions that national champions such as Mindray simply cannot come close to matching.

For those whose businesses sit outside targeted sectors, the immediate implications of Enterprise China are much milder. Assuming these foreign players continue to remain small-scale sellers and producers in China, the strength of their value propositions and business models in China, not Enterprise China's policies, will largely determine their fate in the medium term. Of course, longer-term moves by the Chinese government to promote import substitution and bolster indigenous Chinese firms' domestic position are likely to ripple across even untargeted sectors, putting pressure on foreign firms in this subcategory as well.

Let's look at a simple example to illustrate these points. Black Crow, based in France, is a renowned maker of freestyle skis. Black Crow sells some but not many skis in China, and it has minimal upstream activities there as well. Given that skis are not a targeted segment, as long as Black Crow skis are superior to Chinese rivals, it may be left alone to grow.

However, companies like Black Crow have no guarantees. Although Enterprise China is focused on targeted segments, it does not ignore everything else. Consequently, in 2019 a Chinese consortium led by Anta Sports acquired Amer Sports (maker of Armada, Atomic, and Solomon skis). Black Crow skis are great, but they share the freestyle space with a wide number of brands and makers and do not dominate their segment. What sort of distribution, sales support, and so on can Black Crow expect to capture in China compared to Armada, Atomic, or Solomon skis now that they are owned by a Chinese enterprise? It is safe to say that the executives at Black Crow ought to be concerned about this acquisition and its impact on Black Crow's future prospects in China—and beyond. The point here is that below-the-radar firms that lie outside targeted segments must nonetheless remain extremely vigilant or they could end up surprised and squeezed out as local Chinese competitors buy the technology and brands needed to dominate at home—and abroad.

If this were not enough, staying competitive in China may be difficult for below-the-radar players for one additional reason. Besides being small in China, their operations in China are almost always small within the global scope of their parent company. This means that China unit heads have a hard time capturing the time and attention of executives at the corporate level and getting the resources needed to stay ahead of their local competitors. For example, over the last decade Carrefour's revenue in China never exceeded 5% of global sales. So Carrefour sold 80% of its China business to local retailer Suning in 2019. Similarly, a number of other big foreign firms never reached a critical threshold in China and subsequently closed or sold off their Chinese operations, ceding control of the market to indigenous firms. We described Uber's struggles in Chapter 3. Other examples include Etam, Tesco, Amazon, and Forever 21. Local firms have benefited as a result. In just two years, according to one survey firm, local brands took their share of the top 50 brands in China from 18 to 30.[2]

Upstream Players

Florida-based toymaker Basic Fun is a classic example in the upstream player category. The company sources most of its raw materials (e.g., cloth, plastic, wood) and components (e.g., batteries, small electric motors) in China and concentrates nearly 90% of all its global production there as well. It then exports nearly all its products to more than 60 other countries. China accounts for just 2% of total revenue. For Basic Fun, any material price increases, supply disruptions, or labor problems in China ripple across the firm's entire global revenue stream. Disruptions in the company's China supply chain could mean that it cannot get its toys to market on time for buying seasons such as Christmas. Consequently, upstream problems in China can immediately and materially affect Basic Fun's margins and profits.

Even if firms such as Basic Fun do not encounter any problems relative to their upstream operations in China, they could be at risk downstream in other countries if tariffs target their exports from China. This risk was highlighted in the US-China trade war between 2018 and 2020. If foreign firms in China send an important portion of their China-based production to other countries, such as the United States, that have tariffs targeting Chinese exports, the global revenue impact for upstream players could be severe.

One of the strategic options for upstream players is sometimes described as "China Plus One." Within this strategic option, foreign firms typically establish "sister" upstream capabilities in an alternative country. For example, Japan-based

F-TECH is a key supplier of Honda components. F-TECH had a major brake pedal factory in Wuhan that supplied Honda's final assembly operations in both China and Japan. In keeping with a China Plus One strategic action, it also had a sister plant in the Philippines that primarily supplied Honda production facilities in Canada and the United States. When COVID-19 hit Wuhan and F-TECH had to shut down its factory there, its China Plus One strategy allowed it to increase its output in the Philippines to partially supply Honda's demand in Japan until the Wuhan factory could get up and running again.

As conceptually appealing as the China Plus One strategy is, it is sometimes more easily proposed than implemented. As noted, China has become the world's factory not just because it has abundant labor but because that labor possesses skills that are increasingly cutting-edge. In addition, the labor ecosystem in the key manufacturing centers in China enable over 200 million people to move flexibly across producers as demand fluctuates. This is all facilitated by a thoroughly modern physical infrastructure. As Jay Foreman, CEO of Basic Fun, puts it:

> China offers sort of a suite of benefits . . . a highly trained labor force, a well-financed infrastructure, a great safety and quality control regimen, excellent transportation and communication points....[Moving operations] would be really difficult. For example, if we went to Vietnam . . . it's only 10% of the size of China. So, if you just moved 5% or 10% of Chinese production into Vietnam, you're going to max out the capacity....You can go to India . . . but India's infrastructure is really not set up for this.[3]

Firms that are heavily dependent on China for their upstream activities can face difficulties independent of supply chain risks or tariffs. For example, leading Japanese air conditioner maker Daikin recognized that to grow, it had to expand its sales outside Japan. But to do that, it needed to make affordable air conditioning (AC) units. Given the high costs of labor, electricity, land, and other factors, producing the additional units in Japan at an attractive export price was just not possible. Consequently, its executives decided to move production to China in 2009. In the process, it gave Chinese rival Gree access to its advanced inverter technology in exchange for tapping into Gree's low-cost, mass-market production capabilities. Gree was a publicly listed company, but its largest shareholder was Gree Group, which was owned by Zhuhai Municipal People's Government (the local government of Zhuhai, the city in which Gree is headquartered).

Over the next few years, Daikin succeed in producing price-competitive AC units in China and exporting them to the rest of the world. In fact, it grew international sales to the point where they accounted for 80% of Daikin's total revenue by 2020. Daikin's upstream move into China (as well as that by other foreign firms such Lennox, Electrolux, Carrier, and Trane) helped reduce the country's external dependency and facilitated the target import substitution.

However, as we have emphasized, reducing external dependency through foreign firms' onshoring production is just the first of China's three strategic pillars. In alignment with Enterprise China's second strategic pillar, Gree leveraged the IP it extracted from Daikin to become the No. 1 domestic player in China. In less than a decade, Gree and other indigenous Chinese companies (notably MEDIA and AUX) grew to the point that they dominated over 70% of the domestic AC market, while foreign firms, such as Daikin, Lennox, Electrolux, Carrier, and Trane, saw their share of the market tumble despite their onshoring efforts.

However, the implications for upstream players such as Daikin do not stop there. In line with Enterprise China's third strategic pillar, Gree began leveraging its strength at home into global competitiveness abroad. In 2020 it generated $3 billion in international revenue (about 10% of its total). Its domestic and international sales increases gave it a growth rate double that of Daikin from 2014 to 2020. Its strengths at home enabled it to expand much more rapidly abroad.

Therefore, whether upstream players utilize a China Plus One strategy or not, they should take great care in protecting their IP, even when using China as simply a manufacturing base for sales primarily outside China. This means taking great care in selecting any JV partners and not underestimating local Chinese competitors' ability to extract technical insight and leverage it into increased competitive position—first at home in China and then abroad.

Market Players

Market players primarily have substantial downstream operations and investments in China and relatively little upstream. Consequently, they primarily import finished products to sell in China's huge and increasingly wealthy markets. Just as a picture is worth a thousand words, a concrete example is worth pages of theoretical description.

In the business-to-business space, Danieli has been a market player. This Italian company is the second largest supplier of steelmaking equipment in the world. To understand its position in China, we need to briefly provide some context relative to China and steel production more generally. In 1990 China produced just 8.1% of the world's steel. By 2000 this had doubled to 16%, and by 2013 China was producing more steel than the rest of the world combined. These were increases that no other country had ever made in such a short period. Importantly, virtually all the steel produced in China was made by indigenous Chinese companies. To capture such a large percentage of global steel production, Chinese steelmakers needed world-class steelmaking equipment.

Danieli saw the opportunity and set out to win as much of this business as it could. In 2003 when steel production in China took off, Danieli's global revenue stood at just €730 million. As steel production in China accelerated and it increasingly needed equipment to produce steel, Danieli's revenue soared. By 2010 its revenue had more than quadrupled to around €3.1 billion, mostly from the sale and installation of products made in Italy and exported to Chinese steel plants almost entirely owned by large SOEs.

Similar examples are abundant in the B2C rather than B2B space, and most firms can attribute their increased sales in China to the country's soaring per capita income. In 2008 China had approximately 450,000 millionaires, and by 2019 that number had more than tripled to 1.5 million. Swiss watchmaker Rolex was determined to capture a share of these affluent consumers' watch purchases. Like Danieli's, its strategy in China did not involve any local manufacturing; it imported 100% of its watches (nearly all from Switzerland) for sale to authorized dealers, who in turn sold them to consumers. To attract demand, Rolex focused its downstream activities in China on distribution via high-end retailers, celebrity endorsements (such as Chinese musician Lang Lang and Yujia Wan), and event sponsorships (for example, the Rolex Shanghai Masters tennis tournament). By 2019 China was Rolex's second largest market, and over a decade, sales there had more than quadrupled. By 2021, China had become the world's largest market for Swiss watches across all manufacturers.[4]

The implications of Enterprise China's competitive strategy for market players vary depending on whether the firms are focused on the B2B or B2C segment and whether their focus falls within sectors targeted by MIC 2025 sectors or their home country's export controls.

B2C firms whose products do not fall within MIC 2025 or Standards 2035 targeted sectors, such as Rolex, are unlikely to run afoul of import substitution efforts by China or any export controls imposed by their home country in the near term. This is not to say that Chinese luxury watch firms might not emerge or that some consortium might not buy a luxury brand to compete with Rolex in China and abroad as Anta Sports did with the acquisition of Amer Sports.

Nonetheless, for B2C market players, their challenge in China is not just the brand power, features, or pricing of their products; it also includes tapping into the marketing and distribution ecosystems in China, especially on the digital side of the equation. Throughout the world, including in China, digital marketing via social media and online sales platforms are increasingly important in the consumer space. This digital consumer space is quite large and sophisticated in China. As mentioned in Chapter 1, China is the biggest e-commerce market in the world. Alibaba, for example, does over $100 billion of revenue each year; about 88% of its total revenues are generated through its e-commerce platforms.[5] In addition to China being a large market with significant domestic players, it is also a tight and interconnected market. For example, Tencent's WeChat has over 1 billion users. It is hard to have a social media marketing impact in China without going through Tencent. In addition, Tencent's WeChat and Alibaba's Alipay control over 92% of all digital payments in China. In 2021 there were approximately 625 million people who owned smartphones in China and nearly 80% of these consumers utilized mobile payments dominated by WeChat and Alipay. This compares to less than one third of the total number of US smartphone owners who used mobile payments via their smartphones.[6] Unfortunately, many foreign firms in the B2C space are not well tied into the dominant Chinese digital ecosystems. To succeed in China, they will have to integrate with these platforms and the related ecosystems to gain better access and delivery to consumers. At the same time, as local Chinese brands gain credibility, some market players will also need to adapt their value propositions to evolving local tastes and buying patterns.

B2B market players in sectors targeted by Enterprise China will be most challenged going forward. Not only will China's import substitution policies drive them to invest in onshore production but also the strength of local competitors will be bolstered by China's efforts to build, buy, and "borrow" foreign-owned capabilities as outlined in the MLP and MIC 2025. One of the potential strategic responses to this situation is doubling down and adopting an "In China, For China" strategy, in which they make in China what they plan to sell in China and do both in ways that are customized to suit China's needs and political realities.

After the explosive growth of the steel industry in China subsided over the past decade, Danieli switched to an "In China, For China" approach. Downstream it set the goal of tripling its revenue in China to €1 billion. In pursuit of that goal, it tripled its employees in China to 1,200, of whom only about 30 (2.5%) were international expatriates. Its Chinese employees were deployed across both downstream and upstream activities. Upstream, Danieli substantially increased its investments in local R&D, design, and production capabilities. It felt it was making these moves ahead of its two biggest perennial global competitors — German SMS and Japanese Primetals. The moves also helped prepare Danieli for increasing encounters in China with indigenous firms, such as state-owned China Metallurgic Group (MCC) and 2 of its 13 specialized subsidiaries, CERI and CISDI. These firms target the same Chinese steel producers that had been Danieli's customers for years. Despite taking a proactive approach, holding onto old customers in China or acquiring new ones proved difficult for Danieli because CERI and CISDI had the benefit of state-ownership, subsidized debt, and state influence on both SOE and POE purchases of steelmaking equipment, plant construction, and modernization contracts. To succeed, an "In China, For China" move by one-time market players requires faith that future revenue will more than offset the new upstream investments.

This may not always be the case. Some market players in targeted sectors may determine that bolstering their upstream capabilities in China simply costs too much relative to anticipated returns. In this case, foreign firms have two fundamental options. The first we term the "Fight Fire with Fire" option, and the second we label "The Long Stall."

In the "Fight Fire with Fire" option, market players do not invest upstream but rather double down on their existing downstream strategy. This makes the most sense when the firm's value proposition is quite compelling, hard for indigenous firms to copy, and the foreign firm believes that it can continually increase

ENTERPRISE CHINA

the attractiveness of its value proposition. Through this they may be able to keep a compelling lead on indigenous firms, despite those firms having advantages, such as privileged access to SOE customers, subsidized funding, and helpful administrative guidance to SOE customers to buy from indigenous firms.

The second major alternative for market players that believe that heavy investments in upstream activities won't make attractive returns is what we term "The Long Stall." Unlike the "Fight Fire with Fire" option, in this case firms do not double down on their downstream operations or capabilities in China but rather limit their investments downstream and simply try to extract as much value (primarily revenue) from the existing operations for as long as possible. Essentially, firms pursuing this option determine that while their value proposition to Chinese customers may be superior, they estimate that indigenous rivals' privileged access to SOE customers, subsidized funding, helpful administrative guidance to SOE customers to buy from indigenous firms, and so on, will allow those indigenous firms to eat away at the foreign firm's value proposition over time. Consequently, these foreign firms determine that the best course of action is simply to invest some time, money, and effort to fortify their downstream operations and thereby delay their eventual exit as long as possible—collecting profitable revenue along the way.

This highlights the third general strategic option for market players, which is to exit the market. Some market players may determine that not only are investments upstream unjustified but that continued support of even their existing downstream operations are also unjustified. For example, Microsoft announced in fall 2021 that that it was withdrawing its LinkedIn business from China. Microsoft launched LinkedIn in China in 2014. By 2020 it had 54 million users. However, the gains came at a cost. "We're also facing a significantly more challenging operating environment and greater compliance requirements in China," LinkedIn executive Mohak Shroff wrote in a 2021 blog post. "Given this, we've made the decision to sunset the current localized version of LinkedIn later this year."[7]

Ultimately, those market players that stay to one degree or another are likely to survive, let alone thrive, only to the extent that their value propositions are so superior to indigenous firms that customers in China (industrial or consumer) simply can't resist them despite any advantages that might be bestowed on indigenous rivals. However, to have a chance for medium- and long-term growth, they will also need to keep far ahead of their Chinese competitors in terms of customer value propositions. In many cases, this will mean leveraging global R&D efforts for technological advantage by aggregating the power of their global talent to benefit their Chinese operations. It may also require a commitment to lowering key costs through the amortization of technologies, brands, and so forth, across a global revenue base. This may be more doable in the early days of competing with Enterprise China because this is a time when local Chinese players are relegated to tapping only domestic scientific talent and unable to access global scientific diversity, while at the same time amortizing their innovation costs across only domestic revenue streams, resulting in higher R&D costs per unit. The longer-term prospects, however, are not as bright.

Dual Players

The dual players category includes a wide variety of companies, such as Apple, Coca-Cola, Nike, Honeywell, Airbus, and Yum Brands. All have significant downstream operations, generate substantial sales in China, and have significant upstream operations as well. Dual players differ from upstream players in that they see significant revenue opportunities in China. To them, China is not just a good production platform. In many cases, they differ from market players in that they feel that a strong upstream position in China can support a downstream platform, and vice versa. Dual players believe that China requires a comprehensive strategic positioning.

As a consequence of their significant upstream and downstream investments in China, most dual players have some form of an "In China, For China" strategy. However, the upstream operations of some dual players, such as Apple and Nike, are not just for China but also for the rest of the world. Other dual players' upstream operations in China are much more constrained to China. As we have noted all along in this chapter, the implications and strategic options for these players also vary somewhat depending on whether or not they are in sectors targeted by MIC 2025 and Standards 2035. In the following sections we explore examples of foreign firms in these various subcategories.

In China, For China and the World in Un-targeted Sectors: Nike
Nike is a dual player that derives nearly 20% of its revenue from China. Consequently, it is in China for the roughly $8 billion in revenue that it generates there. It produces equipment, apparel, and shoes "In China, For China" but also for the rest of the world.

In terms of downstream opportunities, Nike sees significant "headroom" or growth both in the absolute size of the market and in terms of the share it can capture. This headroom is in part a function of the fact that Nike operates in non-targeted segments. This does not mean that it does not have indigenous Chinese rivals; it does. Nor does it mean that these local competitors are not capable; they are. Rivals such as Li-Ning and Anta are not to be underestimated. It just means that Enterprise China is not strategically targeting the sectors of sports equipment, apparel, and shoes and consequently does not devote significant time, money, and political clout to these industries. The other factor driving Nike's belief in significant future headroom is the fact that indigenous brands do not yet dominate domestically. Nike believes that as long as it remains flexible and tailors its products to local Chinese consumers, it can leverage its global brand power to sustain its strong position among the growing segment of fashion-conscious and sophisticated Chinese consumers.

On the upstream side, Nike recognizes a variety of challenges and risks associated with having too much of its sourcing and production based in China. Nike began reducing its dependency on China for products shipped to the rest of the world several years ago. For example, in 2012, roughly one third of Nike products for global sale were produced in China. By 2017 that figure had dropped to 12%.[8] Much of the diversification of upstream capabilities that left China migrated to Vietnam, where Nike made roughly half of its shoes for global sales in 2020.[9] However, getting the balance right in terms of upstream activities in China has been challenging. For example, customers outside China have put mounting pressure on Nike to ensure that it does not receive supplies (including raw materials such as cotton) from Xinjiang in northwest China. The autonomous territory, home to the Turkic Uyghurs and other ethnic minority groups, has come under scrutiny due to worries about forced labor and religious persecution. Nike has acknowledged the issue and expressed its commitment to limit supplies from the region. In response the Communist Party mouthpiece, the *People's Daily*, called for broad boycotts against Nike and other members of the Better Cotton Initiative (BCI). Dozens of Chinese celebrities subsequently terminated contracts or said they would cut ties with Nike—moves the state media praised.[10] Since the appeal to boycott Western brands was made, Anta Sports Products, China's largest domestic sportswear brand, has seen its market share climb at the expense of both Nike and Adidas.[11]

The fact that Dual Players like Nike operate in un-targeted sectors does not insulate them from being targeted—both inside and outside China. In fact, this is the inherent risk of pursuing an "In China, For China" strategy. Linkages in Nike's upstream and downstream value chains, including the use of its brand in and outside China, create both strengths and risks. Nike, like many dual players in similar situations, has tried to mitigate the risks by reducing its upstream dependency on China. As we mentioned earlier, Nike has done this by moving production out of China. Besides Vietnam, major investments have gone to Mexico and other countries. The risks on the downstream side, both inside and outside China, have been harder to contain because any moves away from the Nike brand inherently cause Nike to lose the leverage and power of its brand.

In China, For China and the World in Targeted Sectors: Apple

A variety of dual players have significant upstream investments in China, while garnering significant revenue downstream as well. But unlike Nike, these players operate in targeted segments. Apple is an example of such a firm.

For Apple, China has been an important source of revenue for more than a decade. In 2020 the consumer technology giant took in more than $40 billion in China. On the surface this appears to be a great number, but it is down from a peak that approached $60 billion in 2015. Apple's biggest driver of revenue in China has been its iconic iPhone. However, over time it has seen its smartphone market share in China decline. Some of this has been due to the increased functionality of local Chinese smartphones and their significantly lower prices, but some of the loss has been a function of larger ecosystem challenges. For example, as noted earlier, Chinese consumers prefer Alipay and WeChat Pay over Apple Pay by a massive 10-to-1 margin. Apple depends on various aspects of Chinese government approval for segments of its business, including its app store, and it has been stymied by the government at different times. For example, in 2019 Apple CFO Luca Maestri said, "The app store in China is a large business for us.... This issue around the approval of new-gain titles . . . is affecting our business right now."[12]

However, Apple's challenges as a dual player in China do not stop at maintaining or growing revenue within China's borders. Because Apple produces in China not just for China but for the rest of the world, challenges in China can ripple through its entire global value chain. For example, Apple assembles 100% of its over 250 million iPhones in China. Consequently, import tariffs by the United States (or any other country) of 10% to 25% on those phones can hurt sales and certainly profits outside China. During the height of the trade war between the United States and China from 2017 to 2019, Apple found a way around this for the moment by exporting its phones to Singapore and allowing them to "cure" before re-exporting them to the United States.

Although Nike reduced its dependency on China for its upstream activities that provided products for sale globally, Apple and other dual players like it face more challenges in diversifying upstream activities out of China. Given that many of Apple's products are targeted for import substitution and that Apple sells more than $40 billion worth of products and services in China, it must keep a lion's share of what it plans to sell in China produced in China. However, its challenges don't end there; this is only the beginning.

Apple utilizes an estimated 2 million to 3 million workers in China via strategic partners such as Foxconn, a scale hard to replicate anywhere else. At least as important as the size of the workforce is Apple's ability to flex this workforce up and down by hundreds of thousands of people according to seasonal demand shifts—something impossible to achieve in any other country including the United States. What's more, few other countries can match the quality of Chinese workers at a comparable cost. Apple CEO Tim Cook has noted:

China has moved into very advanced manufacturing, so you find in China the intersection of craftsman kind of skill, and sophisticated robotics and . . . computer science.... That intersection, which is very rare to find anywhere . . . is very important to our business because of the precision and quality level that we like. China has extraordinary skills . . . ICT manufacture[s], among other things, the AirPods for us. When you think about AirPods as a user, you might think it couldn't be that hard because it's really small. The AirPods have several hundred components in them, and the level of precision embedded into the audio quality—without getting into really nerdy engineering—it's really hard. And it requires a level of skill that's extremely high.... The number one reason why we like to be in China is the people. China has extraordinary skills.[13]

The integration of the ecosystem of suppliers that provide the various components for products such as iPhones, iPads, and AirPods; the quality of physical infrastructure that enables the smooth movement of parts, components, subassembly; and final assembly of these products within China, plus the transport to world-class airports and seaports for export out of China to scores of countries around the world is difficult to match in countries with lower labor costs. Consequently, the difficulty in replicating the ecosystem and physical infrastructure also keeps Apple and other dual players heavily invested in upstream activities in China and makes diversifying away from China challenging, costly, and slow—though Apple made some small migrations of iPhone assembly to India and iPad production to Vietnam in 2021.

If all that were not enough, dual players such as Apple that operate in targeted segments are vulnerable at both ends of their value chain. Enterprise China has and will continue to facilitate national champions such as Huawei as the state attacks dual players such as Apple all along their downstream links. As mentioned, Apple already has seen its market share and revenue decline significantly in China as a result. Embedding a firm deeply in China's downstream networks opens the door to nearly endless attacks by Enterprise China, making the acceleration of revenue growth in China extraordinarily challenging. However, as we'll read in the pages ahead about Honeywell, it is not impossible. At the same time, if a firm's upstream activities serve more than just China, the greater the depth and scope of those operations, the greater the risks for global supply chain disruptions, as well as reputational threats already examined for upstream players. While dual players may appropriately consider China Plus One and other diversification moves, as illustrated with Apple, these options may not be so easy to find and may take time to nurture before they can be realized.

In China, For China with Partners: Coca-Cola China

One way for dual players to limit their risk and investments is by working closely with Chinese partners. Coca-Cola has embraced this approach in China. Coca-Cola's business model in China includes three components: beverage concentrate production, which is carried out in a company-owned factory in Shanghai; bottling, which is managed through two joint ventures; and marketing and branding, in which Coke takes a dominant but not exclusive role.[14] Coca-Cola has specifically involved Chinese partners on the bottling side, especially SOEs, in an effort to protect itself and facilitate business relationships in China.

Coca-Cola's current structure was initiated largely by a restructuring of its bottling operations in late 2016. The new structure in China included a joint venture with COFCO (for the northern part of the country). COFCO is an SOE officially known as China Oil and Foodstuffs Corporation. It is also China's largest food processing company. The new JV of COFCO Coca-Cola is 65% owned by COFCO and 35% owned by Coca-Cola. For its operations in the south, Coca-Cola sold its minority ownership position in its bottling operations to Swire Pacific, its Hong Kong–based partner since the mid-1960s.[15] In 2020 John Swire & Sons of London owned 55% of Swire Pacific, listed on the HKG Exchange. Within southern China, Swire Coca-Cola partnered with nearly 20 local companies in setting up municipal bottling operations. Examples included Swire Guangdong Coca-Cola (62.96% owned by Swire Pacific) and Shanghai Shenmei Beverages and Food Company (53.6% owned by Swire Pacific). In almost every case, Chinese municipal governments held equity stakes in the Chinese partners and were instrumental in securing approval of the joint ventures.

The plethora of partnerships reflects Coca-Cola's strategy of increasing local responsiveness and removing operating encumbrances. The networks of municipal partnerships no doubt reflect lessons learned in 2009 when Coca-Cola proposed a $2.4 billion acquisition of Huiyuan Juice—China's largest juice company at the time. This high-profile acquisition was rejected by Chinese authorities.[16] At the time, it was the largest proposed foreign acquisition in China, and the proposed acquisition and subsequent rejection garnered significant global press. With the government in Beijing saying that the deal would be bad for competition, Coca-Cola recognized that its global size and status wouldn't necessarily translate into unimpeded upstream investments in China. For these investments, Coca-Cola determined that it would need to partner with local entities within Enterprise China, specifically municipal governments, to ensure that it had upstream capabilities in China that would satisfy its downstream opportunities.

In 2016, Muhtar Kent, then chairman and CEO of Coca-Cola, explained the importance of these local connections in China:[17]

> *We produce, distribute, sell and operate locally. Partners are part of the local culture in every market and community in which we operate. We create value for all our stakeholders through this franchise system.*[18]

Because Coca-Cola's upstream activities were "In China, For China" and not the rest of the world, or really any other country, the upstream risks (supply disruptions or reputational) to a large extent were confined to China. These confined upstream operations also lowered Coke's external public relations exposure by being embedded in JVs. Forming the bottling JVs largely with municipality-owned SOEs also helped mitigate supply risks because the government was incentivized to ensure that the plants operated at full capacity. However, the most valuable part of Coca-Cola and its greatest source of profits has always been its concentrate. The production of concentrate is confined to a factory that is fully owned and controlled by Coca-Cola. Dual players that have both their upstream and downstream activities largely restricted to China and operate in untargeted segments may find the partnership approach of Coca-Cola a smart and effective way to structure their China operations.

Deep In China, For China: Honeywell

Companies in targeted industries that cannot easily separate their key technologies and crown jewels from other links in the chain, as Coca-Cola did, may find insights in a more "solo" strategy as exemplified by Honeywell. Honeywell has been a dual player with an "In China, For China" strategy for nearly two decades. Shane Tedjarati was the architect of Honeywell's strategy in China beginning in 2004. Since then, the firm's revenue in China has grown from $360 million to more than $6 billion in 2020,[19] making China Honeywell's largest market outside the United States. From the outset, Tedjarati sought to embed both himself and Honeywell in China. For himself, Tedjarati learned Mandarin to the point that he often held meetings with Chinese officials without interpreters. For Honeywell, the company pursued opportunities and sales that often helped Chinese companies achieve strategic targets set by Beijing. By 2021 Honeywell China had facilities across more than 30 cities and employed more than 13,000 people.[20] After living in China for over 20 years, Tedjarati commented:

> China's macro trends, such as the digital economy, the Belt and Road Initiative (BRI), Beautiful China, smart manufacturing and so on, bring tremendous opportunities for Honeywell to play a bigger role in this dynamic market. Honeywell has more than 20 branches with more than 3,200 local employees in the countries along the "belt and road." Customers don't just want to buy our products, they want us to provide a range of solutions, from software to hardware, to help them meet the challenges and win the future.[21]

Honeywell's "In China, For China" strategy is now so deep that the company seeks not to be among the best foreign companies in China but to become *the* Chinese competitor and be benchmarked against influential local companies. As evidence of how far it has come in achieving that objective, in 2020 when Honeywell opened a new R&D center in Wuhan, Chinese Premier Li Keqiang spoke highly of Honeywell. "I shouldn't do any commercial promotion for any company," he said. "But I highly appreciate this move [by Honeywell]."[22]

Although Honeywell's deep "In China, For China" strategy hasn't eliminated all risks, it has helped mitigate many. For example, in 2019 the *People's Daily* named Honeywell for possible blacklisting because it was a supplier involved in US arms sales to Taiwan. Specifically, Honeywell supplied engines for tanks sold to Taiwan. However, Honeywell argued that it delivered its equipment "directly to the US government and had no control over the Taiwan deal."[23] Tedjarati commented, "I have a very, very close relationship with Chinese officials. We have intimate discussions."[24] Those deep relations helped Honeywell escape the subsequent list of sanctioned US defense companies.

Most dual players try to operate at the higher end of the value curve. They try to stay ahead of emerging Chinese competitors by increasing the technical capabilities and functionality of their products. Honeywell has largely taken this approach, but when pressed, it added a "turn and attack" strategy to its repertoire. For example, a Honeywell unit, Garrett Motion, produced turbochargers for vehicles. These were some of the best turbochargers on the market and they commanded a price premium. Tedjarati commented that soon after the introduction of its superior products, 100 Garrett look-alikes appeared on the market. "We had Carrett, Farrett, Parrett, Tarrett—you name it," Tedjarati said. "All at 40% of our cost and 50% of our capability. And they sold well." To ensure that Honeywell was deeply embedded in China, it did not just try to move away from these competitors by migrating to the even higher-end of the performance (and price) curve, but it turned and attacked the imitators head-on. Garrett soon produced a "no-frills version of its turbocharger" that was price-competitive with the knockoffs. The move worked brilliantly. "Of those 100 local players, only three survived, and they became our suppliers," Tedjarati said.[25]

However, Honeywell's deep, solo approach to operating "In China, For China" is not for the faint of heart or for fair-weather friends of China. As noted, Honeywell has pursued this deep, solo strategy over decades. It has been led by an executive who demonstrated deep, personal commitment over that entire time. It required Honeywell headquarters to allow Honeywell China to pursue its own course, including actions that might be somewhat controversial, such as helping Enterprise China move up the value chain and reduce its external dependency in targeted areas such as aerospace and help SOEs with Belt and Road Initiative efforts. As illustrated by Honeywell's top executive in China, this deep solo strategic option also requires consistent efforts at the subsidiary's highest executive level to personally mirror the strategy of the unit. Without this, a deep, solo "In China, For China" strategy will likely fall short of intended objectives.

Not Just In China, For China But Becoming Chinese: Yum China

In the most extreme cases, some dual players may take their "In China, For China" strategy to the point that they decouple their upstream and downstream value chains in China from those they have outside China. Three conditions are common for firms that pursue this option. First, they have significant potential for revenue growth in China. Second, they have a high portion of their critical upstream supplies that are based in China. Third, they judged the risks (operational and reputational) of having their value chains outside China linked to their value chains in China as substantial.

Yum China is an example of this option. Yum traces its history in China back to the late 1980s with the formation of KFC in Beijing. In November 1987 KFC opened its largest restaurant in the world adjacent to Tiananmen Square in the heart of Beijing, making it the first Western fast food company to set up shop in China.

In 1997, PepsiCo grouped the KFC, Taco Bell, and Pizza Hut brands as a subsidiary under the name Tricon Global Restaurants. Within a few months, Tricon was spun off as a separate company, and in 2002 it was formally renamed Yum! Brands. When Yum became independent, KFC had about 800 restaurants in China, far surpassing its nearest Western competitor, McDonald's. By early 2021, KFC had a whopping 7,300 restaurants across China. Much of that growth was due to adapting KFC's menu to better meet Chinese tastes and price points. New and popular items included egg tarts, congee, curry pork chop rice, and the Dragon Twister, a wrap similar in preparation to Peking duck that includes fried chicken, cucumbers, scallions, and duck sauce.

Yum also grew its Pizza Hut brand in China but at a slower rate. Yum opened its first Pizza Hut restaurant in China in 1990 and by 2020, it had over 2,300 restaurants there. As with KFC, it modified Pizza Hut's menu items to reflect Chinese tastes. New menu items included toppings such as shrimp and salmon and bases such as mayonnaise instead of tomato and cheese. Yum also redesigned Pizza Hut to be a decidedly more upscale experience for its customers compared to its sister restaurants in the United States.

Yum did not open its first Taco Bell in China until 2016, and by 2020 it had only 11 restaurants in the country, almost all in Shanghai. In China, Taco Bell was also positioned as more of an upscale establishment, selling crayfish tacos and Japanese beer rather than downscale refried beans and cheese burritos familiar to US consumers.[26]

In 2005 Yum began to explore non-US brands and dining concepts that more directly targeted Chinese tastes. That year it launched a new food brand called East Dawning, based initially on merging KFC's approach to fast food with Chinese cuisine. The concept evolved over time and eventually focused on "serving gourmet Jiangnan cuisine to tourists and visitors in transit."[27] In 2011 Yum acquired Little Sheep, a hotpot restaurant chain founded in Inner Mongolia in 1999. Yum streamlined operations, closed underperforming stores, and developed a more consistent and up-market brand. By 2020 the company was operating nearly 300 Little Sheep restaurants in 130 cities around the world.

Yum China was larger than the rest of Yum Brands businesses around the world by 2015. But sales and profits were languishing due to rising local competition and supply chain issues in China. It was "In China, For China," but it was still a foreign company. Subsequently, a decision was made to spin off Yum's China operations to allow the US company to focus on sharpening its brands in the United States, while providing the same benefits to its China operations. Yum Brands CEO Greg Creed commented on the objectives of the spin-off:

> *Following the separation, each stand-alone company will be able to intensify focus on its distinct commercial priorities, allocate its own resources to meet the needs of its business, and pursue distinct capital structures and capital allocation strategies . . . This will provide a clear investment thesis and visibility to attract a long-term investor base suited to each business.*[28]

Yum China became a wholly independent company based in Shanghai but listed on the NYSE on November 1, 2016. It immediately became a member of the US *Fortune 500*. It operated as a master franchisee of Yum's iconic KFC, Pizza Hut, and Taco Bell chains but had full and complete autonomy over its strategic future, paying only a royalty back to the original parent.

Since being split off, independent Yum China has doubled down on its efforts to become a more fully Chinese company. In 2018 Yum China launched COFFii & JOY coffee shops as a direct competitor to Starbucks in China. By the end of 2019, the company had 53 COFFii & JOY stores in China. In 2019, Yum China announced plans to partner with SOEs China Petrochemical Corporation (Sinopec) and China National Petroleum Corporation (CNPC) to start a franchise business for its brands embedded in the two companies' combined 80,000 gas stations.[29] By 2020, Yum China had become the largest restaurant company in China.

To make itself even more Chinese and embed itself even further in China, about five years ago, Yum China began to build a digital ecosystem for sales. In China, unlike the United States, fast food sales are heavily influenced by consumers' use of smart devices. Consequently, Yum China created a digital membership program including the launch of a new YUMC Pay app that spanned all of the company's brands and restaurants. By the end of 2019, Yum China had over 240 million members. The company also launched KFC Pocket Store, a mobile game app that "invited customers to personalize and cultivate their own KFC stores [including the ability] to unlock new products and design the customers' storefront to further augment guest experience."[30] The company also partnered with Alipay to create "Smile to Pay," a system that enables customers to use facial recognition to pay for their orders.

Yum China's efforts to embed itself in China as a Chinese company were rewarded in 2020 when it was named the Official Food Services Sponsor of the Olympic and Paralympic Winter Games in Beijing 2022. This prestigious designation allowed the company to use the "imagery of the Beijing 2022 Olympic Winter Games as well as marks of the Chinese Olympic Committee"[31] in its advertising and promotional activities. At the time of the announcement, Yum

China had more than 9,200 restaurants in over 1,400 cities in China. It had a staggering 577 restaurants just in Shanghai and 535 more in Beijing. After more than 20 years in China, Yum was no longer just "In China, For China," but it was a Chinese company.

CONCLUSION

The strategic options and actions for foreign firms with operations in China in large part depend on the configuration of those operations. Firms with few operations upstream or downstream (below-the-radar players) have very different challenges and options relative to competing in China with Enterprise China compared to firms that have significant operations and investment in China both upstream and downstream (dual players). In addition, whether the foreign firm lies in a sector targeted by MIC 2025 or Standards 2035 also has a significant impact on strategic options and actions.

The one common element is that being in China means that the relevance of China's first two strategic pillars (i.e., reducing external dependence and dominating domestically) is high. Though we did not elaborate much in this chapter, the third pillar of competing globally is also relevant. To the extent that Enterprise China is able to successfully reduce its external dependence and dominate domestically, it will leverage both of these achievements to come after foreign firms on their home turf, as well as in other countries around the world in which these foreign firms have important operations and aspirations. As a consequence, all foreign firms with any business in China, regardless of size, may want to consider the value of engaging Enterprise China in China today in order to delay or reduce Enterprise China's ability to compete with them outside China tomorrow.

While various firms that had operations in China have made the decision to exit the country, to think that an exit does not have implications for future competition with Enterprise China outside China is to ignore or discount Enterprise China's third strategic pillar. We see no evidence that ignoring or discounting this strategic pillar is a wise move. Exiting China today may only allow the unrestricted growth of profit sanctuaries to fund global expansion tomorrow. While it may make sense to exit China, those firms may be wise to use the time right now to strengthen their global and domestic positions to better defend against an almost certain global attack by Enterprise China down the road.

In our next chapter, we will discuss the strategic options for firms that do not have any operations in China. Numerically, these foreign firms vastly outnumber those that do have operations in the country. Some executives might think that with no operations in China, they are immune from competitive conflicts with Enterprise China. However, our research, experience, and forecasts suggest that is merely wishful thinking. Consequently, in Chapter 6, we review the strategic options for these firms.

Chapter 6

HOW TO COMPETE
WITH CHINA: STRATEGIC
OPTIONS AND ACTIONS

In Chapters 1 through 4, we discussed at length the competitive strategy of Enterprise China. We first focused on its efforts to reverse its external dependency. We next discussed its intent to dominate domestically. We subsequently examined how Enterprise China plans to leverage its dominance at home into leadership abroad. In Chapter 5, we explored the strategic options and actions that foreign firms with operations in China might consider. In this chapter, we zero in on the strategic options and actions for firms that have essentially no operations in China but nonetheless may find themselves in competitive battles with Enterprise China.

Although roughly 1 million foreign companies have operations in China, the vast majority of firms have no operations there at all. By one estimate, 115 million businesses exist worldwide. Another estimate pegs the number at 295 million.[1] Although the precise number is impossible to know, we safely can say that today more than 99% of the firms around the world do not have operations in China.

TWO COMMON REACTIONS

In our interviews with scores of executives whose firms fall in this category, we encountered two common reactions to the rise of Enterprise China. The first group we label "content but curious." The second we describe as "nervous but nonplussed."

117

Content but Curious

The first category of executives whose firms have no operations in China recognize that China is an important country economically. They acknowledge that China has grown and today is the second largest market in the world. They are not blind to the fact that China is the largest exporter in the world and that its exports now reach virtually every corner on the planet. They admit that Chinese firms are increasingly expanding overseas and setting up shop in both developing and developed markets. While they acknowledge all this, they still feel that China is quite removed from their day-to-day realities. Consequently, spending lots of time trying to understand China is hard for them to justify. One American CEO in this group commented:

> To be honest, I don't spend a lot of time thinking about China. To me it is like a news story in a faraway city in the US. Did I hear about a mudslide or a forest fire in some location across the country? Sure. And it might even be an interesting story. But it doesn't impact me, and I quickly forget about the headlines and move on.

Typically, these executives run firms that have strong positions in their home markets. Many are leading companies that offer services that they believe are immune to Chinese competition. For example, in the United States, we interviewed the CEO of a company that owned a large portfolio of car washes across several states. He was a capable business executive, and his portfolio of car washes was worth many millions of dollars. However, while he was curious about China, he was mostly content with his knowledge that China wasn't knocking on his door. He wasn't worried because he believed that no Chinese firm could come in and understand the mentality of US car owners relative to washing their cars. He was content that it would take a Chinese company years to understand the local real estate dynamics of site selection for car washes. He was convinced that it would be nearly impossible for a Chinese company to understand the ins and outs of local, state, and federal politics and regulations for getting building approvals—not to mention the dynamics of local construction once the approvals were in hand. Still, given the increasing car sales in China, he was curious as to how often and where Chinese drivers washed their cars. Perhaps he could learn something from the Chinese. But maybe not. Ultimately, he was curious about China but principally content that no Chinese firm would ever be able to set up shop and succeed in his backyard.

Other executives who were curious but content lead firms that make products rather than offer services. Quite often these executives felt that their firm's products were at little risk of being undercut on prices by cheaper Chinese-made goods. For example, we interviewed the CEO of a firm that manufactures mobile homes. He was convinced that mobile homes could not be made in China to

American specifications and shipped in a cost competitively way across the Pacific. Furthermore, because the manufacturing of mobile homes is a rather labor-intensive business, the executive felt that it was just not possible for a Chinese construction firm to set up shop in the United States and manufacture locally in a way that would be successful. In particular, he doubted that any Chinese firm could come in and understand how to recruit and supervise skilled and semi-skilled labor in a way that ensured both the quality and speed necessary to succeed in this business. He also noted that it would take years and years for a Chinese firm to understand the US input supply chain and the distribution and sales channels associated with his industry. He was curious about how Chinese construction firms could build massive apartments in China, but he was content that they would never be able to come to the United States and challenge his mobile home manufacturing business.

Most of the content but curious executives ran businesses that were primarily domestic in their scope and focus, but not all. Those that did have international operations tended to focus on countries that were not quite so puzzling as China. These international markets were often proximate geographically, culturally, linguistically, or all three. Those content but curious executives whose firms had international operations but not in China were for the most part not in China because they simply had better and less challenging expansion opportunities elsewhere.

Nervous but Nonplussed

The second category of executives were quite nervous about Chinese exports, as well as Chinese firms' international expansion, but they were nonplussed or bewildered as to what to do about it. Often that bewilderment was accompanied by feelings of resignation. As one executive put it, "I know that Chinese companies could challenge me either through exports or setting up shop here, but what can I do about it? How can I or my firm push back China if they [sic] decide to invade?"

We interviewed the CEO of a medium-sized US cosmetics company who acknowledged that Chinese firms had their eyes on the United States and Europe, where most of his firm's sales were. However, he felt that his firm's focus on natural ingredients made it difficult for Chinese exports to steal market share from him and thought that the all-natural niche was perhaps too small to be of interest to a large Chinese cosmetics company. At the same time, he was nervous because he had seen Perfect Diary (PD), a large and growing Chinese cosmetics company, rise since its founding in 2016 into a major "direct-to-consumer" powerhouse in China. He was nervous in particular because his firm had also grown by avoiding traditional brick and mortar retail channels and had instead focused on an e-commerce approached stoked by the clever use of social media. He wanted to believe that PD, or some other Chinese firm, never would be interested in expanding outside China into the United States or Europe, but he had no idea what to do if it did. Surely his company's competitive advantage would be enough to dissuade the Chinese from becoming a direct competitor. But if not, he acknowledged being nonplussed at the thought of going up against what was presently a non-competitor.

REASONS FOR <u>NOT</u> BEING IN CHINA

While these two categories of executives differed in their views of risks and potential for Chinese exports and expansion to wreak havoc on their home turf, they shared a commitment not to expand into China in the foreseeable future. While the vast majority had never had operations in China, a few had once had business there but had subsequently withdrawn. They were doing their best to keep China at arm's length.

In the interviews with both categories of executives, we uncovered a long list of reasons for avoiding China that didn't differ much whether the executive was "content but curious" or "nervous but nonplussed." What follows are the top five reasons that these executives gave for not having operations in China:

1. "We're Too Small"

One of the most common reasons we heard was size—"we're just too small to be in or bother with China." Here are a few quotes from our interviews:

- We only have four employees. Why should my company care about China?
- My company has 12 employees. What am I supposed to do in China?
- Our company has revenues of about $6 million per year. We don't have the bandwidth to take on China right now. To do this properly, we would need new skills that we can't afford. And even if we had the money, I wouldn't invest it in a market that I don't understand that is 6,000 miles away.

Most of these firms were also not in other international markets. It is hard to argue with the point that a firm needs to be a certain size before it makes sense to expand internationally, including into China. However, most companies that had this as their top reason also felt that their small size meant that Enterprise China would not have much interest in them or their markets. This may not necessarily be the case because in some situations these small firms operated within large industries that Enterprise China has targeted.

2. "China Isn't a Strategic Priority for Me Personally"

Many executives we spoke to had never warmed to China and remained determined to keep their companies disengaged from China because of personal preferences. In our interviews, some readily admitted that being in China *might* actually be good for their business, but they still were determined to steer clear. Either they simply disliked China, or they preferred to focus their energies on other countries instead. One Canadian CEO told us:

> *In my early 30s, I lived in France for four years. I love France and Europe more generally. Now that I am back at our corporate headquarters in Calgary, I look forward to going back to Europe as often as possible. I like its restaurants and hotels. I like the cobblestone streets and town squares. And I like keeping my French up. It shouldn't surprise those who know me that I have pushed our company's expansion there—in Europe. To be honest, I have never been to China. I wouldn't even know where to start. Maybe the Chinese market would be great for us. It's just not for me.*

Top executives' preferences can always exert an influence on firm direction. But the smaller the company is, and more particularly if it is privately owned, the more top executives' personal preferences can dictate the company's strategy and actions. Consequently, it is easy to see how a lack of personal experience in or with China, limited personal bandwidth, or just a personal lack of interest in China could cause leaders to stick with the familiar and the comfortable.

3. "We Have Better Opportunities Elsewhere"

Beyond the personal preferences of leaders, executives often noted that their firms had international expansion opportunities elsewhere that were not as politically, culturally, or economically complicated as China. They didn't necessarily view China as a negative opportunity, but they simply had better prospects elsewhere. For them, China represented an opportunity, but so did Brazil, the United Kingdom, or California, for that matter.

Even executives in firms of substantial size noted that they had to look carefully at their international expansion opportunities and prioritize them. This applied not just to setting up operations in China but also to decisions about including China more broadly in their upstream supply chains. Some commented that they *could* buy components or products from China but that the associated complications made other options more attractive, at least for now.

Companies that have made this determination include a who's who of the largest and most powerful companies in the world: Allstate, Munich Re, National Grid, CVS, Charles Schwab, Lloyds Banking, Netflix, AT&T, Adobe, and Marathon Oil, among many more. These are companies that have decided that China will not figure prominently in their strategic plans. They have only so many resources and limited bandwidth, and they choose to spend them elsewhere.

4. "Our Industry Isn't China-Centric"

No doubt some industries are naturally more prone to competition or disruption from China than others. Some industries have low levels of international trade, are not technology-intensive, or are so domestic in nature that China and Chinese firms are simply not in the picture. Executives in such industries were not shy about dismissing any need to be in China or worried about competition from China. One CEO of a New York–based water treatment company told us:

> We are a water treatment company. We work with factories and farmers to ensure that their water emissions are clean for the environment. It's all about local service and relationships with some technology thrown in for good measure. How would I break into China? It takes years to form relationships. For the same reason, how are they going to break in here?

We encountered similar responses from executives in the custom printing, fast food, dry cleaning, health care management, and construction industries, among many others.

5. "We Tried It, Didn't Like It, and Went Back Home"

The idea that the rising tide of China lifts all boats sounds good, but actually isn't true. Some boats rise, but others spring a leak and sink. Many foreign companies are not competing in China now for a simple reason: they tried it, didn't like it, packed their bags, and went home. Their absence is a testament of their disappointing results or frustrations that many companies have had working in China.

It isn't just US companies that feel this way, but companies from Europe, Canada, Japan, and beyond. In one 2019 study, nearly a quarter of German companies operating in China reported that they were planning to relocate all or part of their business out of China.[2] In another study carried out by the British Chamber of Commerce in China, 71% of executives believed that doing business in China in 2020 was more difficult than the previous year.[3] Life in China is getting harder, not easier. Some high-profile firms that pulled up stakes in China include these:

- **Amazon:** In 2019 Amazon announced that it was shutting down its China marketplace business.[4] The company had entered China 15 years earlier through the acquisition of a domestic online retailer, Joyo. That company was rebranded Amazon China in 2011. After several years of growth, the company hit a brick wall and saw its market share dwindle to less than 1%. Its biggest barrier was competition with Chinese tech giants Alibaba and JD. Both had powerful local ecosystems that allowed them to lower costs and speed products to customers much faster than Amazon. And both had the full support of the state.

- **The Home Depot:** US do-it-yourself retailer The Home Depot set up operations in China in 2006. It quickly opened a dozen stores with great hopes for the future. It took the company several years to realize that the Chinese do not really like working on home renovation projects. There, DYI projects are most often viewed as a sign of poverty. Chinese customers also have problems moving heavy tools, lumber, and accessories in crowded urban centers. By 2012 The Home Depot pulled the plug on China, closing its stores and writing off $160 million in after-tax losses.
- **Fashion companies:** French fashion company Etam was once a major player in China. In the late 1990s, the company had over 700 stores and sales of $134 million in the country. By 2014 the company had nearly 3,100 stores in China representing about three quarters of its total stores worldwide. The key to its success: its trendy and affordable Western brands, which struck a chord with Chinese women. However, the combination of a decline in the ready-to-wear business, rising local competition, and Etam's inability to adjust led to rapidly declining sales. In May 2018 Etam sold much of its Chinese business to an investor group in Hong Kong.[5] Other fashion and apparel companies to leave China include New Look, a UK-based retailer with 130 stores in China. It decided to walk away from China in 2018. Another was US-based Forever 21, which announced in May 2019 that it would shutter its 11 stores in China. Another example was Old Navy, which pulled the plug on its China operations in 2020.[6]
- **Uber:** As we noted earlier, after two years of heavy investment, Uber sold its China operations to its largest rival in the country, Didi, in the summer of 2016.

Given the increasing sophistication of Chinese competitors, bewildering and opaque regulations, and the Chinese state's eagerness to put its thumb on the scale in favor of domestic companies, it's not surprising that many foreign firms that had operations in China subsequently threw up their hands in despair and left.[7]

WHY IT'S HARD TO HIDE FROM ENTERPRISE CHINA

With all this in mind, it's easy to wonder if it is right for most firms to even have operations in China. The answer is clearly no. We have no doubt that most firms without operations in China today are fully justified and that the quotes cited previously make sense given the idiosyncratic circumstances ascribed. Additionally, not every firm should be worried about competition with Enterprise China, via exports or directly. Executives who feel that their industry and business are just too local for Chinese firms to ever pose a direct threat could easily be correct. Nonetheless, given Enterprise China's successes and ambitions, taking an "only the paranoid survive" or "forewarned is forearmed" attitude may be wise.

Growing Exports from China

As we discussed in Chapter 4, over the last 20 years China has increased its exports more than 12-fold. In the process, it has become the largest exporter in the world. That being said, limits exist to exports from China (and any country). Furthermore, Chinese exports may not grow as fast in the next 20 years as they have over the past 20 years.

This may be the case for at least a couple of reasons. First, as we will discuss in greater depth in Chapter 7, an important part of why China was able to capture the benefits of its low-cost labor was the massive internal migration of labor from rural farms to urban factories. That migration is largely over, and China's labor costs are increasing. As its costs increase, China's ability to penetrate foreign markets via low-cost exports may diminish. Second, exports are most profitable when they are standardized with few modifications added. However, industrial customers and retail consumers do not have identical needs and preferences around the world. Many want products and services tailored to their specific needs, tastes, and preferences. These two factors put some natural limits on all exports, including those from China.

However, to think that Enterprise China will gracefully bow out and let other lower-cost countries take China's current share of global exports is wishful thinking. China is not going to sit idly by while Vietnam, Indonesia, and India try to push it out of the way. Enterprise China needs the foreign currency, profits, and employment that comes from its exports. Therefore, what we have seen in auto parts and cars may be a preview of what we are likely to see in other segments. Auto part exports from China soared from 2000 to 2014 from near zero to $4 billion. However, over the next four years, they stagnated and were basically flat. Rather than simply accept the stagnating results, Enterprise China moved up the value chain to full passenger vehicles, and those exports soared from 428,000 vehicles in 2015 to 760,000 in 2020. Thus, executives whose firms do not produce commoditized products and therefore feel that their products are less vulnerable to cheap Chinese exports may want to take an extra look at Enterprise China in terms of its ability to move up the value chain when it comes to exports. How China's exports are positioned in the value chain today is unlikely to be totally predictive of where they will be tomorrow.

Additionally, Chinese exports often have an intangible source of cost advantage that leads foreign executives to underestimate the potential of Enterprise China to further lower its export prices to penetrate the home turf of these foreign executives. In one company we worked with, a Chinese municipality promised a battery materials company that it would assist it in building a 1.2 million square foot factory and finance all the equipment, which would then be paid back through taxes collected on global sales as well as a small percentage of ownership in the venture. This support would have given the company tremendous cost advantages over foreign rivals. These kinds of subsidies allow Chinese companies to undercut foreign firms outside China on price. As efficient as a foreign firm might be in its home market, it may lose out to cheaper Chinese competitors that have cost advantages that are nearly impossible for foreign firms to replicate.

Some executives we interviewed were less worried about Chinese exports posing competitive problems because they believed their home government would step in to block or curtail the Chinese. And in some case these hopes have borne fruit—at least initially. For example, in November 2011, two US companies filed suit claiming that Chinese firms were selling solar panels in the United States at below production costs. In 2012 the US Department of Commerce determined that Chinese-made solar panels were "being sold, or likely to be sold, at less than fair value."[8] In 2015 the International Trade Commission imposed company-specific tariffs that ranged from a low of 11.45% to a high of 165%. Not surprisingly, solar panel imports from China subsequently dropped from a high of $2.8 billion to a low of $392 million in 2020. Problem solved, right? Well, not exactly.

As solar panel imports from China declined, solar panel imports from Vietnam rose to $1.6 billion. US imports from Malaysia also rose to $2.3 billion and from Thailand to $1.4 billion. In 2020, imports from these three countries accounted for 80% of all solar panel imports into the United States.[9] How did these three countries suddenly soar into the solar panel production and export stratosphere? It turns out that it was Enterprise China. In 2020 Chinese firms accounted for 75% of all solar panel production globally, including production that it had moved from China to Vietnam, Thailand, and Malaysia.[10] However, some experts contended that the volume of exports coming out of these countries to the United States was greater than the production capacity in those countries, which suggested that Chinese firms were merely trans-shipping production done in China through subsidiaries in these countries to the United States.[11]

Therefore, foreign executives who feel their operations are insulated from Chinese exports because they are far up the value chain or are protected by politically imposed barriers might benefit from a healthy dose of paranoia about Enterprise China's determination and ability to move up the value chain or maneuver around political barriers. Exports are strategically important to Enterprise China, and this fact isn't going to change. They drive profits at home and stoke the fires of its profit sanctuaries today that drive overseas expansion tomorrow. Exports also provide an initial beachhead and learning opportunity that can accelerate and facilitate later global expansion into those foreign markets. Finally, exports make important contributions to China's foreign exchange reserves, which are vital to international expansion via overseas JVs, acquisitions, and greenfield projects. Therefore, while there are forces working against increased exports from China, Enterprise China is unlikely to give up its exports without a major fight.

Enterprise China's International Expansion

As we noted in Chapter 4, exports are not the only way that Enterprise China seeks to expand globally and is therefore not the only means by which foreign firms with no operations in China might nonetheless find themselves in competition with Enterprise China. Enterprise China seeks to acquire foreign firms both to reduce its external dependency and to expand its global footprint and competitive position. Even with the continued scrutiny of Chinese acquisitions by US and European regulators, the odds that Chinese foreign acquisitions will be completely blocked seems remote. In addition, Enterprise China has dramatically ramped up its foreign direct investments through greenfield projects where no acquisitions are necessary. As we mentioned in Chapter 4, China's outward FDI has soared 14,417%, and its foreign assets have swelled from 2.3% of GDP to 15% over the past 20 years.

Regarding all this, foreign competitors should keep in mind an important irony. In our interviews, many of the executives who were least worried about Chinese firms invading their shores tended to be in industries that were (a) local and (b) outside traditional strategic sectors targeted by either MIC 2025 or Standards 2035. However, Chinese acquisitions or greenfield projects that are least likely to engender tough foreign government scrutiny will be in exactly those sectors.

We are not predicting that Enterprise China will forsake its focus on reducing external dependency in key sectors or abandon its strategy of acquiring foreign firms in these key sectors. What we are suggesting is that foreign executives should not be surprised if Enterprise China increases its global activities in sectors likely to receive less rather than more foreign government scrutiny and have less rather than more import protection. For example, Wanda's investment in movie theaters did not fall within any of the targeted sectors in the MLP, MIC 2025, or Standards 2035. Nor did it run amuck of US national security interests. Consequently, the acquisition happened largely unimpeded. In summary, although Enterprise China has and will maintain a focus on key industries and sectors, its third strategic pillar of winning globally in order to influence globally is not confined to strategic industries and sectors.

In addition, executives in industries that feel they are relatively immune to or insulated from the onslaught of centrally controlled SOEs should keep in mind that Enterprise China is not just limited to SOEs. Enterprise China includes many of the most nimble and entrepreneurial private Chinese companies or publicly traded enterprises. Furthermore, as Enterprise China, embodied by these or other firms, expands globally, it does not need to target you or your competitors directly in order to have a competitive impact on you. Their moves up or down your value chain can have a profound impact on you and your company. You may find Enterprise China encroaching upstream. It may not be buying your competitors, but it may be buying up or pushing out your old suppliers or suppliers to your suppliers. Conversely, you may find Enterprise China encroaching downstream. It may not be buying your competitors, but it may be buying up or pushing out your customers or the customers of your customers.

Many people are surprised to discover how much progress Enterprise China has made in expanding its FDI. Why? In part because we naively assume that because we don't see Chinese named companies in the grocery stores or auto malls, they aren't there. In many cases, they are out of sight and therefore out of mind. Few foreigner consumers know that brands as far ranging as Volvo, Pirelli, Suunto, Brookstone, Sunseeker, Atomic, Smithfield, Fila, Wilson, Harvey Nichols, Hoover, GE Appliances, Lenovo, and Club Med are now Chinese owned. Other Chinese-owned companies with less-well-known brands but with a substantial presence in their industries include Anker (consumer electronics), Cirrus Wind Energy (energy), Complete Genomics (health care), Nexteer Automotive (automotive), Riot Games (entertainment), Addax Petroleum (energy), Teledyne Continental Motors and Mattituck Services (aerospace), Terex Corp. (machinery), Triple H Coal (mining), and Zonare Medical Systems (health care).[12]

A 2019 report by the European Commission found that fully one third of European Union assets were foreign owned. Of this total, nearly 10% were owned by companies based in China, Hong Kong, or Macau. This is up from just 2.5% in 2007. By comparison, the shares of European Union companies owned by US and Canadian firms dropped from 42% to 29% during the same time period.[13] In the United States, Chinese FDI soared from just $1.6 billion in 2009 to nearly $38 billion in 2019.[14] Enterprise China owned an estimated 2,400 "American" companies in 2019, as well as 191,000 acres of land.[15]

Beyond controlling ownership positions, a significant chunk of the equity in many companies—often national icons in their respective home countries—are held by Chinese entities. In 2021 it was estimated that Chinese investors owned some £143 billion of assets of major UK companies, including Lotus Cars, Manchester City football club, Royal Albert Dock in Liverpool, as well as shares in Thames Water and even London's Heathrow Airport.[16] Other prominent global companies with major Chinese equity stakes include Snapchat, Hilton Hotels, Spotify, Norwegian Air, Reddit, Universal Music Group, Warner Music, Airbnb, Sharp, and Lexmark. And the list keeps growing.

While it is tempting to ignore China, it is impossible to remain fully insulated. Enterprise China is on the move. To quote John Lennon, "Life is what happens while you are busy making other plans." Putting your head in the sand comes with big risks. Why? Because like it or not, what is happening *in* China is affecting what is happening *outside* China. And the dominos are falling in the most unexpected places. For example, in the summer of 2019, China announced that it would curtail purchases of US agricultural products and threatened additional tariffs on farming goods coming from the United States.[17] This led to a plunge in agricultural commodity prices, and with it, big drops in orders from US farmers for US-made John Deere tractors. In some locations, tractor and planting equipment orders dropped as much as 50%. In other words, John Deere's US business got whacked because of policies undertaken by the Chinese state directed at another industry a world away.

COMPETING WITH ENTERPRISE CHINA OUTSIDE OF CHINA: STRATEGIC OPTIONS

It seems that whether you never competed in China or tried it and left, the effects of Enterprise China are never far away. So where does this leave foreign firms without operations in China? What are the strategic options for them? We divide this discussion into three sections. The first section examines the option of waiting for China to change. The second section explores upstream strategic options and actions. The third section dives into downstream options and actions.

Wait for China to Come Around

Given the high levels of volatility and uncertainty, perhaps a wise strategy for foreign firms outside China is to wait it out. The rationale for this strategy goes as follows:

> With so much exposure to Western values and with so much of its economy at stake, it is inevitable that China will change its confrontational ways. It has to, if it is to survive. After all, China—no matter how large its economy grows— will always be a small player compared to the overall global economy. How long it will take for China to appreciate the futility of its grand ambitions is uncertain, but change it will. So, in the interim, it's better to wait on the sidelines as the Chinese tide eventually recedes.

Few would argue with the wisdom in seeking clarity before acting. Strategy is a commitment to a certain future, and unless you know what the future holds, perhaps it is better to avoid making big commitments. We readily acknowledge that the future posture of Enterprise China is uncertain. As Yogi Berra once quipped, "It's tough to make predictions, especially about the future." Certainly, China may yet alter its course and reverse the initiatives it has embraced for the past 20 years. We might all be surprised as China transitions to a period of greater accommodation and cooperation with the West. The internal politics in China may change and past commitments to MIC 2025 and beyond may be dismantled or abandoned. The trajectories that seem set today may be altered tomorrow.

Yet, if we are correct that trajectories can and sometimes do change, an even more confrontational and ambitious Enterprise China is also possible. Instead of lightening up, China could double down on its present plans. It could pump more money into foreign investments while hampering foreign enterprises operating in and around China. And the state could act even more forcefully to promote Chinese SOEs and POEs at home and abroad.

While we can't know the future, ominous clouds on the horizon dim hopes that China will become more democratic, pro-Western, or conciliatory in its engagements with the rest of the world. In our interviews with state officials in

China and participation in forums involving high-level state officials, we have not seen any hints of backpedaling on the country's three-part competitive strategy. If anything, China seems to be taking a firmer stance against the West as opposed to following a more accommodative path. Its successes are fueling its confidence, and its confidence is fanning its ambitions. One indication of this is its increasingly aggressive stance against foreign firms that rub it the wrong way. For example, when clothing retailer H&M decided to stop sourcing from the Xinjiang region of China over human rights concerns, the company's apps were blocked on key platforms throughout China.[18] You couldn't even order a car to pick you up at an H&M store, nor would H&M stores in China appear on Baidu Maps. No doubt state officials knew there would be blowback and negative reporting of what happened. They didn't seem to care.

Some hoped that the Biden administration would usher in a new era of accommodations by China. This does not appear to be happening. To welcome in the new Biden administration in January 2021, China announced a new set of rules that applied to both Chinese companies operating overseas and foreign firms operating in China. The rules banned Chinese companies and Chinese citizens from complying with "unjustified" laws and sanctions imposed by foreign states. Chinese firms were also permitted to sue foreign firms in Chinese courts when they complied with yet-to-be-defined "unjustified" foreign laws. The new rules allowed the Chinese government to order Chinese companies to simply ignore what it viewed as inappropriate foreign laws.[19] Then in August 2021, China proposed a new set of rules targeting data-intensive companies that used complex corporate structures to circumvent restrictions on foreign listings.[20] The message was clear: China would place state control and internal politics over the commercial interests of its companies. Those who continue to believe that China will come around and let Western-style capitalism prevail may be waiting a long time. China's commitment to Enterprise China seems as firm—if not firmer—than ever.

What people in the West often miss in predicting relations with China is the preeminence of ideology in the thinking of Chinese leaders. It may be most accurate to think of China's conflict with the West as an ideological one that is manifest through commercial competition. Matt Pottinger, former deputy White House national security advisor in the Trump administration, put it this way:

American businessmen, wishing for simple, lucrative commercial ties, have long resisted viewing U.S.-China relations as an ideological struggle. But strategic guidance issued by the leaders of both countries make clear the matter is settled: The ideological dimension of the competition is inescapable, even central.[21]

Ideology is built on core values and worldviews and does not change quickly or easily. Perspectives tend to drift, but essentially no overnight shifts in ideology have occurred in the history of the world.[22] And because China's dominant ideology is closely linked to its national identity and pride, we can expect Enterprise China to press its case all the way to the backyards of completely domestic firms based in scores of countries around the world. Consequently, we have a high degree of confidence that tensions and disruptions will continue for the foreseeable future, *even for domestic firms* in the United States (and elsewhere), which casts a shadow on the merits of the "wait and see" strategy.

Upstream Strategic Options

Foreign firms without operations in China may nonetheless be using parts and components several steps up their supply chain that originate in China. Sometimes, these inputs are hidden from a company's view, as was the case for Medtronic that we highlighted in Chapter 4. Mitigating China-based supply chain disruptions or other risks invariably means diversifying away from Chinese suppliers. This is relatively easy when the supply input is not critical to the company's overall business model or when the Enterprise China–controlled supply inputs pretty much run on autopilot or are relatively easily substituted. This tends to be the case for low technology, commodity inputs.

Determining your company's supply chain risk profile is a prerequisite to understanding the range of available strategic options. We can best capture these options by examining them in the context of two variables:

- The level of management engagement dedicated to working with the company's Chinese suppliers. Here, management engagement is a proxy for the importance of Chinese supplies to the company's overall business model.
- The degree to which the industry is at risk of being disrupted. Other than shutting down or choosing to compete in a different industry, companies have little-to-no influence on their risk of being disrupted.

The strategic options for foreign firms with Chinese supply chain exposure are shown in Exhibit 6.1.

Status Quo

Given our discussion of the risks of Chinese supply chain disruption, foreign leaders may be tempted to think that *all* companies should be racing to diversify their supplier bases away from China. This would be a mistake. Staying the course may be the smart thing to do, particularly if the imported products are of low profile or are commodity products. If this is your company, you are in luck! It doesn't mean that you don't have to periodically reassess your suppliers' costs and performance levels. But you would need to do this anyway. The good news is that taking a status quo approach doesn't require much additional management

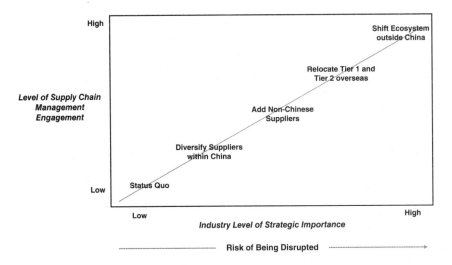

Exhibit 6.1   Strategic Options for Foreign Firms Outside China

bandwidth. This means that foreign leaders can stay focused on other issues, including what's happening at home.

Diversifying Suppliers within China

As product complexity increases and as the importance of the imported product goes up, diversifying one's suppliers may be a smart move. In many cases, the firm will find multiple suppliers within China that it can add to diversify its base. Adding suppliers reduces the disruption risks when sourcing from a single vendor. At the same time, adding one or two more Chinese vendors necessitates a commensurate increase in the engagement levels of home country leaders.

Let's consider the US houseware products industry—an industry that highly depends on Chinese manufacturing. In 2020 the average size of houseware products companies in the United States was just $19.4 million. Of this group, 61% of companies produced all of their products outside the United States, mostly in China. Typical of these companies is Skorr Products, a New Jersey–based importer of chafing dishes and stands used in the restaurant industry. In 2010 the company made all its chafing dishes in the United States in its own in-house factory. Ten years later, it outsourced all its production to three manufacturers, all located in Jiangmen, Guangdong Province, China. Skorr's product mix did not require highly specialized equipment nor did the company emphasize highly customized product designs or customer solutions. Standardized designs and lack of proprietary technical skills made the outsourcing of manufacturing an attractive option for Skorr. However, to lower its supply risk, it diversified its suppliers within China. This also reduced the bargaining power of a single vendor.

Adding non-Chinese Suppliers

As products grow in complexity and as technology intensity increases, the number of specialized vendors and sub-vendors usually goes up and value chains typically become more complex, commanding an increasing amount of head office management attention. At the same time, the embedded technology starts to capture more of the attention of the Chinese state, and with this, the risk of disruption grows. In this situation, a foreign firm would typically consider some geographic diversification by adding a non-Chinese supplier. A good example would be Google-owned Nest thermostats. In 2021 the company moved aggressively to expand its supplier base away from China to Taiwan and Malaysia.

Replacing Chinese Suppliers

GoPro, the sports-camera company, is an example of a manufacturer that replaced its China-based suppliers. Traditionally, GoPro sourced it compact cameras from GoPro Hong Kong. It in turn sourced products from Woodman Labs. Woodman Labs received key components from Moduslink Electronic Technology, based in Shenzhen, China.[23] In 2019 the company's CFO, Brian McGee, announced that GoPro would shift production of US-bound cameras out of China to Guadalajara, Mexico. Of the move, he said:

> We expect most of our US-bound cameras will be in production in Mexico in the second half of 2019. As stated previously, our decision to move most of our US-bound production to Mexico supports our goal to insulate us against possible tariffs as well as recognize some cost savings and efficiencies.[24]

Shifting Entire Supply Chain Ecosystems

In rare cases, foreign importers may want to shift to an entirely new ecosystem outside China. This move may be warranted under two extreme scenarios. In the first case, a dominant company (for example, Tencent or the merged Sinochem Group and ChemChina holding company) may seek to block direct exports of finished products or inputs and components to foreign customers. Sometimes this decision is made with the support or direction of the Chinese state. This could leave a foreign importer dangerously exposed. While possible, we view this scenario as highly unlikely, especially when the products or components reverse China's external dependency and in fact create a dependency on China for foreign firms.

Under the second scenario, foreign firms may be blocked from engaging with Chinese vendors because of events transpiring in their home country, such as trade restrictions or reputational risks to the company. An example of the latter would be diversifying away from Xinjiang-based suppliers because of reputational risks—whether real or perceived—that the imported goods were produced via slave labor or by religiously oppressed workers.

For companies with no operations in China, setting up an entirely new supply chain may be their only option. However, transforming to an organization that is entirely independent of China upstream inputs is a heavy lift, especially for firms that are less experienced internationally. It may be worthwhile only under the most extreme circumstances.

Additional Upstream Actions

Beyond taking efforts to advance their supply chain diversification, foreign companies with no operations in China can do a few other things to shore up their supplier bases. These include:

- **Building inventory reserves:** Although this goes against the conventional wisdom and financial benefits of just-in-time and lean manufacturing, when revenue capture is more valuable than carrying costs, this may be an option worth considering.
- **Allocating older products and components to upstream connections in China:** Although Enterprise China wants to be involved on the cutting-edge products, sourcing second-generation components to China may dull or even blunt the wound of a related supply disruption.
- **Blocking "end-runs":** Ensuring that Enterprise China suppliers cannot go around you directly to your customers by boosting your integration capabilities may also be a wise move.

Gauging Dependency on China

The fundamental issue for companies with no operations in China but which have upstream exposure to China is the extent of their dependency on China. The greater the dependency, the closer should be the examination of the nature of their upstream connections to China and consideration of their strategic options. The further upstream a firm's connection to China and the smoother those connections have been over time, the easier it is for companies to get lulled into the belief that all is well and that any risks are minor or can be easily addressed in the future. Often an unexpected event or crisis is necessary to expose submerged dependencies. As we noted in Chapter 4, this was the case for Medtronic. The company came to understand the level and extent of its upstream dependency on China only after the COVID-19 pandemic. Unfortunately, trying to reconfigure or dramatically change one's upstream connections to China in the middle of a crisis is not ideal. Thus, forewarned is forearmed.

Therefore, and as counterintuitive as it may seem, when the waters are calm is the best time to dive below the surface and inspect whether the hull of the ship has drag-inducing barnacles attached. Unfortunately, mapping out supplier relation-ships is a painstaking process. A product like a personal computer, for example, may have 200 components. A typical chainsaw has 26 major components plus dozens of sub-components and individual parts. A single-lens reflex (SLR) camera includes a battery, pentaprism, focusing screen, digital sensor, display, and view-finder. Each of these components has its own supply chain, and many are hid-den from the final assembler and the end buyer.[25] Determining the ownership of these suppliers, especially determining the full extent of their affiliations with the Chinese state, can be difficult, time consuming, and error prone. Deconstructing the broader ecosystem of interdependent suppliers while deciphering their level of exposure to state ownership and influence can be mindbogglingly difficult. Trying to map all this out in the middle of a storm is exactly the wrong timing.

Even when fully or reasonably understood, changing links in the upstream chain can be difficult because of interoperability challenges. Components in complex products are designed to work seamlessly together through hardware and software integration. Given these interconnections, every supplier is dependent on the next, leaving the foreign owners highly susceptible to *any* disruptions that might emerge from rewiring the system. Adding a new supplier in, say, Malaysia adds risks to the entire system. While invariably product compatibility problems *can* be overcome, they may take months to sort out and result in great costs to the company and its other suppliers. Take Japanese television maker Sharp as an ex-ample. It produces ultra-thin panel cells in Japan. It then exports these to China, where additional components are added, including backlights.[26] Shifting some of these back-end operations to a new supplier outside China would introduce huge risks to Sharp's entire production system and ultimately to its ability to bring its televisions to the global market in a timely manner.

At the end of the day, given that one third of the world's value-added manu-facturing happens in China, the odds that something in your upstream chain is located in China are considerable. Therefore, there is no better move to make *to-day* than to fully examine and understand the extent of that exposure. From that informed base, determining which upstream strategic options are best becomes a much easier task.

Downstream Strategic Options

Although assessing your upstream exposure to Enterprise China may be hard to de-termine, measuring direct downstream exposure is much easier. Executives know who their customers are and if any of their key customers are Chinese entities and whether those purchasing entities are inside or outside China. In most cases, executives also know who the customers of their customers are, and therefore can reasonably assess their direct downstream exposure. That exposure becomes most problematic when those components, products, or technology fall within the tar-geted segments for reduced external dependency by Enterprise China.

If a foreign firm sells components, products, or technology directly or indirectly to Chinese enterprises, having a bit of paranoia may be a good idea. Enterprise China may not be able to achieve its targeted levels of higher import substitution and lower external dependency in every segment, but its determination to do so should not be underestimated. It may be that a foreign firm's component, product, or technology is so unique, so far advanced, so hard to copy or substitute that it is at low risk of having its revenue from Enterprise China interrupted. But as we have illustrated earlier, Japanese, German, French, and US firms in the high-speed rail sector to one degree or another all thought they too were in solid positions. A decade later, not only were they not selling as much to Enterprise China, but Enterprise China was taking market share away from them across the world. And this pattern is not unique to rail equipment.

We have examined at length Enterprise China's success and continued determination to capture downstream opportunities via both exports and direct international sales through global expansion. Compared to countries such as Germany, Enterprise China has a lot more room to grow in terms of not just absolute export sales but export sales relative to its growing GDP. For example, if China's exports relative to GDP were similar to those of Germany, China could add nearly $5 *trillion* in exports, which is more than the total annual GDP of Germany. Compared to virtually all developed countries, Enterprise China has room to more than triple its international expansion relative to its GDP. In terms of foreign investments, if China's foreign asset levels relative to its GDP were in line with the United States, Germany, or Japan (leaving the extreme case of Switzerland out of the equation), it would amount to an additional $3 *trillion* in Chinese FDI. This increase in foreign assets alone would be more than the annual GDP of all countries except the United States, Japan, Germany, and of course, China's own GDP.

Going forward, will Enterprise China take an additional $8 trillion in international revenue opportunities via increased export sales and direct international sales? Even if they do, it won't happen overnight. But it would be a mistake to underestimate Enterprise China's determination to push forward. As China advances overseas, the main implication for firms with no downstream operations in China is that you won't need to look far for a competitive encounter with Enterprise China. Enterprise China is bringing the fight to you.

In the process, firms with no downstream operations in China that thought they might thereby be insulated will discover that they are not. Even if Enterprise China does not target them or even their industry, these firms are likely to at least feel the ripple effects through greater market volatility. This greater volatility likely will happen due to a variety of factors, including:

- **Misunderstood motives:** Enterprise China's motives and moves are neither wholly commercial nor completely political. Viewing Enterprise China's competitive moves through only one lens or the other leads to misunderstandings, miscalculations, subsequent adjustments, and consequently greater volatility.

- **Mistakes and missteps:** Chinese leaders of overseas companies often are inexperienced in foreign markets. Inexperienced Chinese leaders as a consequence could lack cultural awareness, have limited languages skills, and be more prone to misread cultural and political cues that are intuitive to local managers. The resulting mistakes and missteps could also amplify volatility.
- **Masked ownership:** The equity and non-equity ties of Chinese companies to home networks of other companies and government entities are often opaque. This can cause foreign executives to make their own mistakes relative to Enterprise China in their backyard, which in turn could amplify volatility.
- **Mispricing:** As Enterprise China expands internationally it may spend too much on acquisitions or misprice products. The resulting ripple effects on asset prices and sales prices could increase volatility.

The effects of these challenges involve not only the amplitude of the wave via increased volatility but also the dispersion or reach of the wave. Let's consider smartphones as an example of how smaller local firms may be disrupted by Enterprise China. Beyond Samsung and Apple, the top global producers of smartphones in 2020 were Chinese (Huawei, OPPO, Vivo, and Xiaomi). In addition to these experienced players, there are newcomers, such as Shenzhen-based realme, which shipped 100 million smartphones in just 37 months, seven months faster than Apple.[27] Still, no matter where you are in the world, success in the smartphone business requires both effective integration of hardware and software with a supporting ecosystem of apps and large corporate size to capture economies of scale, including those relative to purchasing various inputs and components.

How will this affect non-Chinese suppliers for the smartphone industry? Huawei may provide a preview. Nikkei, in partnership with Tokyo-based research specialist Fomalhaut Techno Solutions, deconstructed Huawei's Mate 40E and found that roughly 60% of the total value of components were made in China, which was twice as much as the Mate 30, the previous model.[28] As this example illustrates, non-Chinese suppliers, often smaller component manufactures from the developed and developing worlds, could increasingly be exposed and forced to bend to Enterprise China's rules if they want to stay in business or find their business shifted to indigenous Chinese suppliers. In these situations, two main responses are possible. Foreign firms can "Fortify and Defend" or "Advance and Attack."

Fortify and Defend

When facing an imminent attack, a tried-and-true strategic option is to fortify and defend your castle. This works best when the castle is strong in the first place and in an advantageous and defendable position in the second place. In terms of fortifying and defending the downstream portion of a firm's business, the process starts and ends with customers. Any local firm's advantage over Enterprise China has to include its understanding of and relationship with its customers. Knowing what matters to customers and what drives winning value propositions constitutes a defensive moat that can be dug deeper and wider.

For example, if your primary customers are highly price sensitive, thinking that these customers won't switch to Chinese options for lower prices is folly. Enterprise China may have lower cost structures or may enjoy lower costs of capital. Some Chinese competitors may even benefit from direct or indirect subsidies embedded in the Enterprise China system. In any case, the only defense is to lower your costs so that you can be price competitive while not obliterating your margins. This may mean diving into and improving the input and manufacturing costs. But it may also involve lowering your customer transaction costs. And as a domestic company with a strong understanding of your customers, you have an advantage of knowing your customers' hot button buying concerns. For example, we worked with one company that provided equipment financing to its customers. Although this customer could not beat Chinese competitors directly on the price of the equipment, it reduced the time for financing approval from one week to four hours. While the key terms of the financing (specifically interest rates) were not profoundly better than the competition, the reduced transaction cost widened the moat around their business.

In providing this example, we are not implying that all customers are primarily price sensitive. They are not. Customers can also place high value on tangible aspects of the product they buy (e.g., quality, reliability, and durability) as well as intangible aspects (e.g., brand, reputation, and convenience). To the extent that customers value intangible aspects of the value proposition, Enterprise China is at a disadvantage. Culturally and linguistically those elements are often harder and take longer to understand. To the extent that these aspects of the value proposition are relevant, they are a wise place to dig a deeper and wider moat.

Fortifying and defending may be particularly important relative to intellectual property. This often means establishing rock-solid firewalls from cyberattacks. It also means reviewing restrictions relative to existing strategic partners who have *any* access to or understanding of your IP. It also means ensuring that employees don't unintentionally leave clues, cues, and breadcrumbs on social media or through other channels that the Chinese can pick up.

Although product and service technical IP is important to protect, so too is unpatented but important insight and knowledge regarding customers, markets, suppliers, regulators, and regulations. This "IP" tends to reside in people's brains, and therefore, it is important to review, refine, refresh, and bolster your human capital systems. The following are key questions to ask and answer well:

1. Do you know who your key talents are that Enterprise China most likely would try to poach?

2. Do you know how satisfied and engaged these high performers are, and therefore how much of a flight risk they are?
3. Do you have in place financial retention incentives for key employees?
4. Do you have in place nonfinancial incentives, such as career and succession planning, development programs, and recognition and reward schemes?
5. Do you have an identified and strong bench to replace key talent in case the unintended loss happens?

Advance and Attack

The opposite strategic option of "Fortify and Defend" is to "Advance and Attack." Rather than waiting for Enterprise China to secure a beachhead and then launch an inland assault on your well-fortified and defended position, determine where Enterprise China is the most vulnerable and advance and attack preemptively. For example, if a Chinese firm were in the process of opening a greenfield operation, it would be preoccupied with constructing and setting up that operation. While this is happening, consider locking in any local suppliers that it might later seek out. Also, spend extra time with customers that the Chinese firm might want to win, and lobby regulators who supervise or approve aspects of its business. Hiring more key talent and preempting the loss of existing talent through retention contracts might also be wise. Finally, the timing could be ideal to double your marketing efforts or promotion activities.

Because a key objective of Enterprise China's international expansion moves is to capture revenue opportunities, a critical area of focus for the "Advance and Attack" strategic option is customers. Local companies know the customers, speak the same language, and have an insider's knowledge of the marketplace. Rather than wait to be forced to improve or innovate after Enterprise China is up and running, a wiser option is to focus on improving customer service, customizing touch-points, and creating bespoke solutions *now*. These moves often indirectly strengthen the firm's brand. Additional efforts to reinforce brand names and logos can also help amplify the disadvantage that entering Chinese companies may have when their brands are less well known, when their product or brand names can't be easily or effectively translated, or when the traditional and especially social media channels are not well understood by the new arrivals.

A portion of an "Advance and Attack" strategy might also involve intelligence reconnaissance on the new arrivals. Seek to gather information about *their* customers and suppliers. Carefully review their applications for patents. Pour over their regulatory and other public filings. Take a public tour of their new plant. Explore LinkedIn and map out personal relationships among their key executives. Track what job openings they post, the qualifications they are looking for, and how much they pay. This is a two-way street, and failure to seek out information that is legally accessible represents a significant missed opportunity.

CONCLUSION

As we noted at the beginning of this chapter, 99% of all businesses do not have operations in China. However, this can leave executives in these firms underestimating their upstream exposure to and their eventual downstream confrontations or competition with Enterprise China.

In terms of upstream exposure, the common problem is that the risk of exposure to China is typically many steps upstream in the value chain. Consequently, the risk and exposure remain out of sight and out of mind until some sort of event lowers the tide and reveals the rocks below the surface. Trying to react at that point typically presents fewer degrees of freedom than when a proactive assessment is done and when strategic options are identified and debated in advance. The strategic options we have offered are not the only ones, but they provide a reasonable framework and continuum for consideration.

In terms of downstream risks, our research and experience indicate that unless Chinese exports or FDI already have had an impact on Western firms, most foreign executives significantly underestimate the potential conflicts with the Chinese in the future. Although we will examine in the next chapter factors that could derail Enterprise China's ambitions and strategy, the magnitude of both additional exports and direct international expansion ($8 trillion) that would simply put China on a relative par at a country level with the likes of Germany or the United States is staggering. To think that because Enterprise China's exports or direct investments have not resulted in a competitive confrontation with you yet is not a safe prediction of what is likely to happen in the future. As with upstream risks, doing an assessment and identifying strategic options and actions when the waters are calm is much easier than in the middle of a raging storm.

These anticipatory assessments may require putting impressions or stereotypes of China to the side, especially if they were formed years ago. China has changed in terms of its economic power and ambitions. This, in combination with a competitive strategy that has been relatively consistent and cohesive over the last nearly 20 years, only focuses that power, like a magnifying glass does to the sun's rays. Gaining a more informed and accurate assessment of Enterprise China likely requires some direct experience. Few things can substitute for actual travel to and time in China. When you go, and we encourage many visits, you might want to stay in a Chinese versus Western hotel and avoid tourist guides to help you see the "sites." You are likely to get more of a real picture of the place if you venture out into the offices and factories and even Chinese homes.

Putting travel restrictions that curtailed visits to China during the COVID-19 crisis aside, as valuable as direct experience can be, it is not always possible to the desired degree. Therefore, it is important to read broadly on what is happening politically, culturally, socially, and economically. Gather information relevant to your industry's upstream and downstream value chains in China. And look at multiple sources of data, not just the channels that reinforce your stereotypes or confirm your worldview.

The rationale for executives whose firms don't have operations in China doing so much advanced learning and planning is found in every corporate safe harbor declaration: Lack of past disruptions, interruptions, conflicts, and competition with Enterprise China may not be indicative of lack of future disruptions, interruptions, conflicts, and competition with Enterprise China.

Chapter 7

CAN ENTERPRISE CHINA BE DERAILED?

Across the previous six chapters of this book, we have had three major objectives. First, we sought to highlight that taking a traditional competitive analysis approach to China that focuses on Chinese enterprises and not Enterprise China can cause executives to miscalculate the risks and opportunities relative to competing in and with China. Second, we tried to bring to greater light and provide a deeper understanding of Enterprise China's three-part competitive strategy. And third, we endeavored to examine the strategic options and actions that foreign companies can pursue in responding to Enterprise China, both in China and abroad. Through all of this we have argued that foreign executives should take Enterprise China's strategic objectives and plans as seriously as the Chinese do.

However, just because Enterprise China has strategic objectives and plans and just because those plans have enjoyed notable success to this point does not guarantee that Enterprise China is predestined to succeed in the future. Therefore, in this chapter, we have two objectives. The first is to highlight the key factors that could derail Enterprise China's strategy. The second is to provide an empirically based assessment of the extent to which those risk factors push Enterprise China's competitive strategy toward derailment. Achieving both of these objectives enables business executives to know what to closely or casually monitor and helps them to better judge the implications, strategic options, and appropriate actions as conditions change over time.

We have organized the factors that could derail Enterprise China into four major clusters. The first section examines how competing forces in China have the potential to destabilize the foundation on which Enterprise China's competitive strategy is built. Next, we lower the microscope and examine each of the three pillars of Enterprise China's competitive strategy and the factors that could derail them.

CROSSCURRENT DERAILERS

Thus far, China's success in providing a unified and aligned approach to its competitive strategy has been impressive. Many in the West have been surprised by the ability of the state to plan and coordinate investment strategies and complex regulations over an extended period—now approaching two decades. However, in Chapter 1 we emphasized that equating Enterprise China with just the central government or with just central SOEs is a mistakenly narrow view. As a point of reemphasis, "the state" of course includes the central government, but in the context of Enterprise China also includes provincial and municipal governments. As testament of why this is the case, it is worth pointing out again that 99.9% of all SOEs are owned by provincial and municipal government entities, not the central government.

Ownership Isn't Everything

Even though we have stressed it previously, it bears repeating. Viewing Enterprise China as consisting of only SOEs is also a mistakenly narrow view. Clearly SOEs of all types and sizes are important, and collectively they constitute at least 30% of the country's total GDP. However, as our several examples illustrated in previous chapters, the government has been willing to, and is capable of, exerting substantial influence on POEs to ensure that the actions of nongovernment-owned commercial enterprises align with state objectives. Thus, the total portfolio of enterprises in Enterprise China includes both SOEs and SIEs.

Even with this more complete view of what constitutes Enterprise China, looking only at the surface of its past successes risks not seeing the full and more complex picture. Digging deeper into the important relationships helps bring to light powerful and often competing crosscurrents that lie below the surface. In this section we examine those crosscurrents and their implications for the stability and future success of Enterprise China's competitive strategy. However, this examination requires a short primer on "Vertical China" and "Horizontal China"[1] because these two fundamental forces are driving the various crosscurrents.

Vertical and Horizontal China

Vertical China refers to a system in which all key decisions are made at the top and pushed down through the provinces and cities. The old China dominated by Mao captured the essence of Vertical China. In those days, a Chinese company's general manager would take orders and receive direction from above concerning key aspects of the business such as production targets and had little ability to deviate from the orders of central command. This was the predominant system in China up until the early 1980s.

Then began a decade or more of what could be called the "workaround years." Ambitious Chinese entrepreneurs eager to get rich started making their own deals. Laws were routinely bent or broken through creative workarounds. This was a time when local government-owned companies making cement were signing deals with Western fast-food chains merely because they owned the land where a restaurant would be built. Little by little, both municipal and provincial governments, as well as many companies, stopped following top-down rules and directives and started coming up with their own.

As China's economy began to move beyond central planning and as Deng's economic freedoms began to take hold, China slowly but surely shifted to a new model of decision-making called "Horizontal China." The move represented a shift from ideology to pragmatism. It was Deng Xiaoping who opened the door to this by putting pragmatism ahead of ideology. In this vein, perhaps Deng's most famous quote was, "I don't care what color the cat is so long as it catches mice."

In Horizontal China, decisions are made within and by the members of the network. Horizontal China is facilitated by urbanization and China's increasingly world-class infrastructure, which allows for speedy communication and the efficient transfer of goods. Horizontal decision-making is also encouraged by the increasingly prosperous and educated middle-class in China who have no patience for central planning or the inferior goods that result.

Horizontal China has another set of friends: mayors and governors. Rather than simply obeying directives from Beijing under Vertical China, mayors and governors in Horizontal China can heavily factor into their decisions their own local interests regarding economic development, jobs, and the reinforcement of their political power. Put simply, Horizontal China is an affront to the power and authority of Beijing.

The irony for Beijing is that it promoted Horizontal China in part because many floundering non-central SOEs needed to find their own way to survive; the central government could not be the financial backstop for them all. Yet, in encouraging these SOEs and their lower government owners to find their own way, the central government unwittingly undermined its own authority and control. The ascendancy of President Xi Jinping came as the Communist Party was fearing that it was becoming economically irrelevant. Xi's policies are a blend of an ambition to shift power back to Beijing, while at the same time holding onto Deng's commitment to pragmatism.

Risks of Blending Horizontal and Vertical Models

Xi's attempt to include both horizontal and vertical aspects of China is fraught with risks. Politically, an undertaking to move the central state back to becoming the center of all things risks conflicts with increasingly powerful mayors and governors, tech tycoons, and an affluent middle class. Yet, a lack of such a centralizing or consolidating effort could allow provinces and cities that are as large as many countries to go in different directions from each other and from the central government.

While we do not predict that the networked, state-centric Enterprise China model will disappear, we simply want to highlight that the current efforts to consolidate power in Beijing are not universally supported and therefore are not destined to succeed with no chance of failure. Much of Enterprise China's competitive success thus far has come from the central government formulating a unified strategy and provincial and municipal governments supporting and largely following the plan. Should the current balance buckle and proponents of Horizontal China push back with force against Vertical China, much of the last 15-plus years of stability relative to competitive strategy could be put in flux.

This fundamental derailer notwithstanding, Enterprise China faces additional potential derailers. These are linked to each of the three strategic pillars in Enterprise China's competitive strategy. In the next three sections, we examine the potential derailers for each pillar.

DERAILERS OF REVERSING DEPENDENCY

Thus far, China has come a long way in reversing its dependency on foreign products and technologies. Nonetheless, looking forward, one must wonder if this pillar could be derailed, and if so, by what forces? The answer hinges on a key challenge at the heart of Enterprise China: reducing its dependency.

At its core, if China is to continue to shake off its external dependency, it needs technologies that are competitive with, or superior to, those being developed elsewhere. As we discussed earlier, China is not blind to the limits of borrowing or buying technology from others and recognizes that over the long term it must be able to generate innovations and new technologies on its own. However, just because a company or a country decides that it wants to move from foreign-acquired to homegrown innovation does not mean that results automatically will come. While China's targeting of technology-intensive industries and its efforts to control global standards are important steps forward, the country must out-innovate foreign firms to reduce and reverse its external dependency.

History demonstrates that successful innovation does not happen by edict or simply by opening a money spigot. A key driver of innovation within a company is a more open and free culture and entrepreneurial leadership, which empowers and encourages people to experiment.[2] SOEs typically favor the opposite: a more top-down and autocratic approach. Considering this clash, one must question how compatible the dominant leadership style in SOEs is with the general tenets of successful innovation. It is no wonder that most of China's innovative progress has come through the country's POEs.[3]

Irrespective of whether a company is set up as an SOE or POE, Chinese enterprises are also burdened with vigorous government oversight of their business activities. One uniquely Chinese hurdle is that all companies with more than 50 employees must have a Communist Party representative on site. This oversight does little to foster experimentation, the lifeblood of innovation. The fact that most of Huawei's impressive advances in 5G have come from its tech centers *outside* China underscores the challenge of innovating inside China. The bottom line is that extensive state oversight risks muddying decision making, skewering rewards, and suppressing innovation overall.

This raises doubt about the ability of Chinese firms to move from expropriating technology to inventing it—from borrowing or buying to building. The cases of several high-profile tech titans don't bode well for China's innovative future. For example, facing heightened government scrutiny, Jack Ma of Alibaba essentially disappeared from public view for much of 2021. That same year Colin Huang, chairman of e-commerce company Pinduoduo, and Zhang Yiming, founder of TikTok, both announced that they would be stepping down to "try new things." If innovative leaders are suppressed or pushed out, will Enterprise China be successful at producing the homegrown innovations needed to reduce external dependency?[4]

Two decades of research has well documented that the organizational culture changes and the new leadership capabilities required to successfully transform a company or a country from imitation and expropriation to creation and innovation are staggering. To be clear, the question goes not to the intelligence of Chinese or their innate ability to innovate. This is not in doubt. The question goes to the culture and systems needed to bring out, foster, and support the transfer of that intelligence and creativity into market-ready innovations. This is the same fundamental challenge for organizations in any country. Unfortunately, the majority of companies from *all* countries fail in such transformational attempts. To think that Chinese companies will disproportionately succeed where others have failed simply defies the odds, particularly in an environment of strong state oversight.

If Enterprise China's strategy of developing its own technologies and products stutters or stumbles, the slow growth in innovation could actually become a drag on productivity for the next 10 years or more. For a simple analogy of why we predict this, imagine a baseball team that had a solid history of scoring runs by hitting singles. It decides to transform itself into one that scores primarily by hitting homeruns. Is it reasonable to think that lifelong singles hitters can instantly or easily transform into homerun hitters? No, it will take some time as singles hitters swing harder in order to hit homeruns. However, as these single hitters swing hard for the fences, it is likely that they will strike-out or pop-out more often. Any baseball buff will know that famous homerun hitters, such as Babe Ruth, were also the leaders in strikeouts. A key question then is: Will the system tolerate, let alone encourage, more strikeouts during the transition to hitting homeruns, especially because not just the hitters will do worse but the team overall will likely score fewer runs during the transition as the hitters strike out or pop out more often?

The alternative is to simply replace the singles hitters with homerun hitters now. However, even then, the system will have to tolerate more strikeouts under the new model for success. It's just one of the consequences of swinging for the fences, just as failure is a natural consequence of trying to build rather than buy or borrow innovations.

To reiterate, the problem is not that Chinese workers or managers are not creative or innovative. They are as clever and creative as anyone else on the planet. As other research has shown,[5] in Enterprise China, the problem is that the structural, governance, corporate cultural, and leadership changes required just don't seem to be in the cards.

To the extent that Enterprise China cannot as easily extract technology from others as it has in the past or cannot acquire the technology by buying the external firms that own the technology and products on which it is overly dependent, it will increasingly need to innovate and invent its own technology and products to replace those on which it has determined it is overly dependent. Numerous leadership, cultural, and systemic barriers appear to stand in the way of this third and critical tactic relative to this first strategic pillar. Consequently, in the short to medium term, many firms actually could hurt their growth as they swing for the fences of homegrown world-class innovation and invention and strike out.

DERAILERS OF DOMINATING DOMESTICALLY

Of the three pillars of China's competitive strategy, ensuring that Chinese firms dominate domestically is arguably the easiest to ensure and therefore the least likely to be derailed. After all, by edict China *could* send every foreign firm in the country packing. That it chooses not to do so is evidence of the many competing forces that shape China's position at home and abroad.

While China's trajectory for domestic domination seems unassailable, foreign firms and products continue to play important roles in China. For example, although FDI around the world dropped 35% due to the impact of COVID-19, FDI inflows to China actually increased 6% in 2020. They went up again in 2021 to a record $174 billion, including in the targeted areas of high tech. Enterprise China's high debt burden and lower profits compared to its external rivals put some limits on indigenous firms' ability to fund further domestic growth. Ironically, all other things being equal, Enterprise China's first strategic pillar of reduced external dependency and its focus on import substitution and higher levels of local content creates an incentive for foreign firms to invest more in China and grow their operations there rather than trying to export their goods to China. Thus, in pushing strategic pillar No. 1 and encouraging import substitution, China may make it temporarily hard for indigenous firms to dominate at home. However, executives should take care not to interpret invitations or pressures to invest in rather than export to China as a sign that Enterprise China is backpedaling on strategic pillar No. 2.

Another factor that could create a speedbump in China's march to domestic domination is the country's shift to services. As China's population becomes wealthier and more mobile, the demand for services has and will continue to grow. In 2020 services accounted for 54.5% of China's GDP, followed by the manufacturing sector at 37.8%, and agricultural at 7.7%.[6] It was projected that between 2022 and 2023, services would represent 7 of the top 10 fastest growing industries in China.[7] This shift to services favors Western firms, which transitioned to services decades earlier and for which many have significant competitive advantages. Marketing, branding, advisory, audit, and database management are examples of services where Western companies have strong leads and commanding market shares.

Even in manufacturing, Enterprise China is facing headwinds, in part because the country's external dependencies and its stymied domestic domination are intertwined. Nowhere is this more evident than in the semiconductor industry. As we have already documented, despite Enterprise China's ambition and goal of producing 70% of its semiconductors onshore by 2025, it wasn't even one third of the way there in 2021. Notwithstanding significant efforts and massive investments of money, China still imports the vast majority of its needed semiconductors, primarily from Taiwan, the United States, Japan, and South Korea.

Another potential derailer of Enterprise China's strategic pillar of domestic domination is a tougher and more assertive World Trade Organization (WTO), of which China became a full member in December 2001. Joining the WTO meant that China—at least in theory—was required to revise its commercial laws, lower barriers to trade, guarantee intellectual property rights, and allow foreign investment in its service sector, which includes banking, telecommunications, insurance, and retail.[8] Thus far, few outside China would dispute that China has failed to live up to many of these commitments. The 2021 US Trade Representative's Report to Congress on China's WTO compliance concludes:

China's record of compliance with the terms of its WTO membership has been poor. China has continued to embrace a state-led, non-market and mercantilist approach to the economy and trade, despite WTO members' expectations—and China's own representations—that China would transform its economy and pursue the open, market-oriented policies endorsed by the WTO. At the same time, China's non-market approach has imposed, and continues to impose, substantial costs on WTO members.[9]

In response, the United States has tended to take a more unilateral approach and has thus far not exerted maximum pressure on the WTO — or China — to address examples of Chinese noncompliance. A CATO Institute study concludes as follows:

> *If the [United States] really does want the Chinese economy to be more market-oriented, it should make better use of WTO rules by filing more complaints against China. While it is often accused of flouting the rules, China does a reasonably good job of complying with WTO complaints brought against it.*[10]

If the United States and other nations unilaterally or multilaterally ramp up pressure on China to reduce its domestic firm bias and to provide equal treatment to foreign firms, Enterprise China's domestic domination ambitions may come up short.

DERAILERS OF WINNING GLOBALLY

The leaders in China have little doubt in Enterprise China's ability to compete globally. In a speech commemorating the 70th anniversary of the Chinese Communist Party's rule in 2019, Xi asserted, "There is no force that can shake the foundation of this great nation. No force can stop the Chinese people and the Chinese nation forging ahead." In our interviews with Chinese officials, many pointed to the dramatic rise of Chinese firms on the *Fortune* Global 500 as evidence of China's unstoppable nature. Many beamed with pride when in 2020 China passed the United States (124 firms versus 121) and took over the No. 1 spot on the list, and in the multiyear process passed 19 countries including global stalwarts such as Switzerland, the United Kingdom, France, Germany, and Japan. They sustained and increased their lead in 2021 (see Exhibit 7.1).

So spectacular has been the rise of the number of Chinese firms on the Global 500 list that some have argued that the country has or soon will achieve "escape velocity," allowing it to remain No. 1 in the global orbit of the top 500 companies for decades to come. These observers believe that, unlike the case with Japan, which declined significantly from its zenith, no gravitational pull is strong enough to ever bring China back down to earth and cause its numbers to fall. However, we offer several reasons and point to empirical data that put this unstoppable global ascent into question.

In fact, we think that the same gravitational force that caused Japanese firms to fall from their lofty global heights are at work and are likely to have a similar impact on China. That gravitational force in a word is people. Like Japan, China soon will (a) not have enough workers at the bottom, (b) not generate enough productivity to offset the negative effects of its shrinking workforce, and (c) not have the right business leaders at the top to solve these two

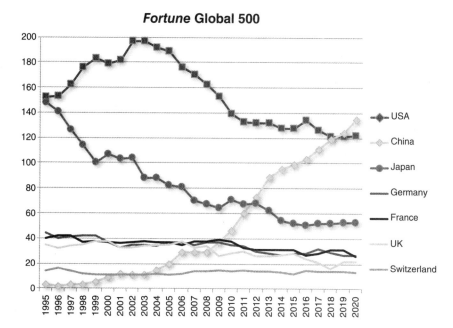

Exhibit 7.1   Number of *Fortune* Global 500 Firms by Country
Source: Fortune Global 500 List 1995–2021.

fundamental challenges. Together, these forces threaten China's third strategic pillar of winning globally.

Declining Number of Workers

In terms of workers at the bottom of the pyramid, China is about to experience what Japan has been struggling with for the last two decades—a declining working age population (ages 15 to 64). Although separated by a generation, Exhibit 7.2 graphically illustrates the rise and fall of the working population for both China and Japan.

But what is behind these declines? In China's case, many scholars have pointed to its "one-child policy" implemented in 1979, one year after Deng Xiaoping began the economic reform of the country. No doubt this policy had an impact, but China's birth rate and subsequently its live births began their precipitous fall a decade *before* the implementation of the policy, following a nearly universal pattern of declining birth rates associated with rising standards of living. How much of China's decline was due to the one-child policy and how much would have happened anyway as GDP per capita more than tripled is hard to say. Whatever the relative effect of either, the outcome is the same—significantly fewer people are being born in China, leading to worrisome declines in the workforce in the future.

The Rise and Fall of Working Age Population (WAP)

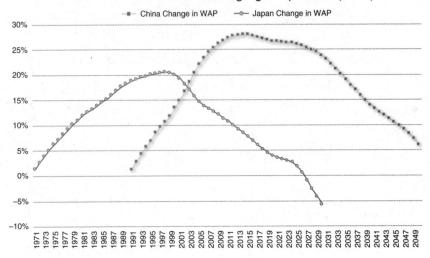

Exhibit 7.2   The Rise and Fall of Working Population in Japan and China

Source: UN Population Project.

Based on our analysis of United Nation's data, over a 25-year period from China's peak in 2015, its working population will decline 13.1% by 2035. However, as Exhibit 7.2 illustrates, China's working age population decline is predicted to continue far beyond 2035, out to 2050. By then, its working population will have declined by 200 million people from its peak. To put this into perspective, that equates to more people than the total current working populations of Germany, France, the United Kingdom, Italy, Belgium, the Netherlands, and Switzerland combined!

Steep Decline in Young Workers

A closer examination of China's working population decline provides additional insights. Even though China's initial decline looks somewhat gentler than Japan's, this is not true for those aged 15 to 24. The decline slope for this particular group is as steep as Japan's overall decline curve. Our analysis shows that the decline for these younger workers in China started in 2007 and was an impressive 33.7%, or 80 million people, over that 15-year period (see Exhibit 7.3). We highlight the early and steep fall of this group because many Chinese firms have relied heavily on younger workers for their current success, in part because of the flexibility of these workers and also because of the lower wages they are paid. Fortunately for China, the decline in this group of workers is projected to slow, declining by only 30 million between 2020 and 2050.

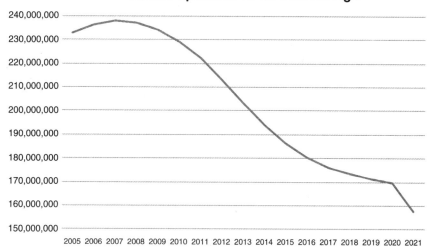

Exhibit 7.3 The Fall of Young Workers in China
Source: OCED, UN Population Projections.

Reliability of Demographic Predictions
But how confident can we be in these projections of working population out 10 or 20, let alone 30 years? Such extrapolations must be the stuff of fortune-tellers and crystal balls, right? Not so. The reason is simple. If someone was not born in 2015, that person cannot be in the workforce in 2035. The only way to make up directly for a missing person not born in a given country is by bringing in someone else born in another country. However, foreign workers have never been a major source of labor for China. In 2015 less than 1/10 of 1% of those living in China were foreigners. By comparison, the city-state of Singapore had more than 1.6 times as many foreigners living there as in the entire country of China. Other contrasts are similarly stark. In 2020 the number of registered foreigners in Switzerland was 29% of the population; for both the United States and Germany, the number was 15%. No evidence suggests that China will revise its long-standing aversion to immigrants, highly trained or otherwise.

Inability to Maintain High Productivity Improvements

A declining population is a serious issue, but it is not necessarily the kiss of death if productivity improvements exceed workforce declines. Unfortunately, in Japan's case, rising productivity did not make up for its falling population. For 20 years leading up to 1997, the peak of Japan's working population, the country averaged 13% per year in productivity gains. But in the two decades that followed, it averaged less than 1% per year. In essence, not enough people worked smarter or more efficiently enough to compensate for fewer people working in Japan.

The same pattern is evident for China. In the 20-year run-up to China's working population peak, China's annual productivity gains averaged an impressive 13.8% (slightly higher than Japan's 13.0%). However, a more granular examination reveals that in the last four years, China's productivity growth averaged just 5.7%. In other words, its productivity growth rate was decelerating just as it needed to accelerate or at least stay in place (see Exhibit 7.4 with GDP measure in current local currency).

The key question is, Can China make up in productivity gains what it will lose in working population? To address this question intelligently, we must examine the key factors that have been responsible for China's impressive productivity growth thus far and then analyze whether these factors are likely to improve, stay the same, or decline going forward. This analysis is made easier because most economists at the macro level and most business strategists at the company level point to the same three key drivers of China's past productivity: small numbers, internal migration, and technology expropriation.

Small Numbers

The first factor that worked in China's favor in the past was small numbers. In 1994 when China's GDP was just $564 billion and its GDP per capita was only

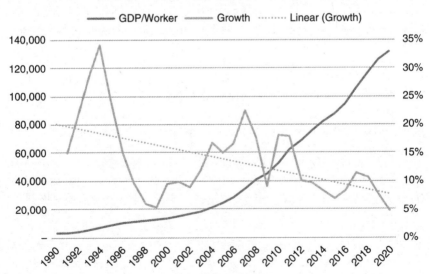

GDP per Worker and Productivity Growth

Exhibit 7.4   China's Slowing Productivity
Source: World Bank.

$473, major increases in productivity were much easier to achieve than in 2014, when GDP hit $10.48 trillion. Working off a small base helped China's productivity gains average 15.5% from 1995 through 2013. Thereafter, working off a much larger base has limited annual gains to a much lower number (5.7%). In summary, whether productivity is measured in GDP per capita or GDP per labor hour, as GDP gets larger and larger, it becomes harder and harder to maintain the same rate of productivity growth. When you also have a falling number of workers, the constriction only compounds the challenge because to sustain the same level of domestic growth you must squeeze even greater productivity out of fewer workers. For example, if your workforce falls by 10%, in order to maintain a 6% growth rate, productivity from that smaller workforce must increase from an annual rate of 6% to 17.8%. The challenge of achieving this over long periods is obvious.

Internal Migration
Another factor that elevated China's economic growth in the past was internal migration. While economists do not agree on the exact magnitude of its impact, most believe that China gained great improvements in productivity by people migrating from rural areas devoid of modern machinery and technology to urban areas in which factories were loaded with both. The magnitude of this leap in productivity was multiplied by the staggering numbers involved. In a special report issued in 2016, China's National Bureau of Statistics notes that there were 282 million internal migrant workers in China. According to the report, 53.9% of the migrant workers were young, between the ages of 15 and 40. Thus, in the two decades leading up to the peak in working population, China captured significant improvements from people, especially young people, moving from less productive rural jobs to more productive urban jobs. However, because the number of young workers peaked in 2008 and is projected to decline sharply through 2025, China simply has fewer and fewer young workers left for further migration. Consequently, the productivity bump that this internal migration provided in the past is now mostly over.

Moving Past the Lewis Turning Point
Worth noting is that productivity gains via the migration of people from rural to urban areas is not new or unique to China. The United States saw the benefits of this a century ago and Japan experienced the benefits after World War II. However, the time always comes at which a country exhausts its supply of excess rural labor and as a consequence loses that source of productivity gains. That point is termed the Lewis Turning Point (LTP). Two key indicators show when a country has reached the LTP: a dramatic slowing of migration and an increase in wages, specifically for those who have migrated. This is exactly what has happened recently in China. Over the past 10 years, the rate of urban worker migration has dropped precipitously and turned negative in 2020 (see Exhibit 7.5).

Migrant Workers Numbers in China

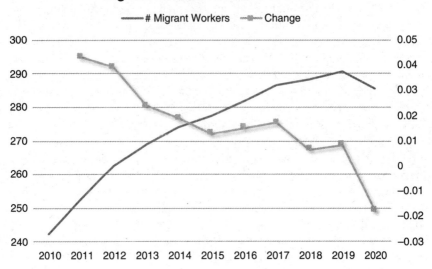

Exhibit 7.5 Number of Migrant Workers in China
Source: China Bureau of Statistics.

Wage Increases and Slowing Internal Migration

A key sign that internal migration is slowing is the rising wages of those who already have migrated, which is exactly what has happened (see Exhibit 7.6). The increase in 2011, 2012, and 2013 averaged 15.6%. Wages continued to increase from 2014 to 2019 and averaged 7.2% per year. Wages increased again in 2020, though at a much lower rate of just 2.8%. No doubt, some of this low increase can be attributed to the impact of COVID-19 in China that year.

Determining the exact moment that China reached the LTP is not as important as the general consensus among scholars that China reached that point before 2018.[11] To the extent that China has passed the LTP, future gains in productivity via massive internal migration of workers from low productive rural jobs to more productive urban jobs is diminished.

Ghost Cities and Additional Migration

Beyond the math related to determining when China moved past the LTP, scholars point to the additional evidence provided by the large number of "ghost cities" built over the last decade that remain largely unoccupied. The logical conclusion is that most of those who wanted to move to the cities from rural areas already have done so. Some reports estimate that in 2021 over 65 million Chinese homes are unoccupied, almost all located in urban areas.[12] This is enough to house the entire population of France! If China has already reached the LTP,

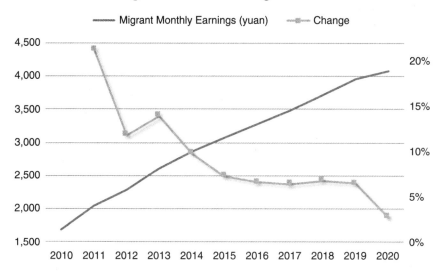

Exhibit 7.6 Earning Increases of Migrant Workers in China
Source: China Bureau of Statistics.

China's recent announcement that it plans to move another 250 million people from rural to urban areas by 2025[13] may be wishful thinking. Only time will tell how large or small the next wave of internal migration will be, but any productivity gains from it will certainly be far less than before. Lower productivity because of limited internal migration will only amplify the downward gravitational pull of China's declining workforce.

Limits to Expropriating Technology
Expropriating technology from foreign companies has been a third factor and a major driver of China's past productivity. At the macro level, signs suggest that foreign firms are increasingly resistant to Chinese demands to accept this technology-for-market-access trade-off. Importantly, at a macro level, inward FDI is slowing. According to United Nations Conference on Trade and Development data, FDI inflows into China from 1990 to 2005 increased an average of 28.8% per year. However, from 2006 to 2010 the rate slowed to 10.8% per year. From 2011 to 15 it dropped again to 3.5% per year. From 2016 to 2020, it averaged just 2% per year. As we mentioned earlier, this is still impressive compared to other countries. It nevertheless portends to a dramatically lower inflow of foreign investment that could bring with it new technologies. To the contrary, we see a growing list of tech companies that have been shut out of China (Uber, Facebook, and Amazon are but a few examples) or others including Seagate, Panasonic, Epic

Games, LinkedIn, Yahoo, and Sony that have recently closed shop completely or radically reduced investments in China because the technology-access trade-off was not worth it to them.[14]

Other Workforce Challenges

In addition to a drop in young people available for factory jobs, those who are available increasingly don't want to work in factories.[15] Furthermore, young workers in China are notorious for their propensity to move from job to job to increase take-home pay, saddling Chinese firms with high and expensive turnover rates. The cost of this high turnover only increases as workers perform more skilled jobs. Consequently, as Chinese firms pay more to recruit and retain needed workers, overall costs go up, which puts upward pressure on prices or downward pressure on margins. If Chinese enterprises push prices up to protect margins, their goods and services risk becoming less price competitive versus other locations in the world.

Productivity Challenge Summary

In summary, China must make up for the loss of working population with greater productivity, but the odds don't look great for three main reasons:

- The law of large numbers will work against China.
- Chinese industries will have fewer opportunities to benefit from less productive rural labor moving to more highly productive urban jobs.
- Chinese companies will have fewer opportunities to boost productivity through the expropriation of technology.

If the odds of outsized productivity gains that would offset losses in the workforce look bleak, then the prospects that the domestic economy will continue to soar also look dim. Given how dependent Chinese firms on the Global 500 list have been on the domestic economy for their ascent thus far, any domestic slowing makes the prospects of improved global competitiveness and staying on the list look quite grim. The same would be true for new firms trying to make their debut.

Leadership Shortfalls

Even if China's domestic economy slows or stagnates, can't Chinese executives throttle up their export and international sales engines to compensate and still achieve the country's global competitiveness objectives? In theory they could. For example, despite Switzerland's small domestic economy, Swiss firms have maintained an outsized presence on the Global 500 list over the years, precisely by doing that. Why can't Chinese executives avoid the fate of Japan by being more like the Swiss—in essence, by becoming more global? While possible, we don't think they will for the same reasons the Japanese executives did not.

The Pull of Gravity

The inability of Enterprise China to offset declining domestic opportunities with exports and international sales is based on three primary factors. First, if you have a main domestic engine delivering 85% of your total revenue thrust and it sputters, two auxiliary engines that combined deliver 15% of thrust just won't cut it; even if you could throttle them up, if the main engine sputters, the rocket will decelerate. Second, trying to make those small auxiliary engines bigger while rocketing into space is no easy task. This is true in part because export and international sales engines require different "engineers." Put more plainly, driving revenue through those engines requires different business leaders with distinct experiences and capabilities. Specifically, a leader who has succeeded domestically is not at all assured of succeeding internationally.[16] In fact, the required leadership capabilities are quite different.[17] If these needed global leaders weren't part of the crew during liftoff, getting them up to the rocket in flight is challenging, even if the rocket is decelerating. Third, if you have neglected developing these global leaders internally and if external leaders are hesitant to join your mission, you are in double trouble. In this case, the odds are that even if you scramble to develop the leaders you need, you will run out of time to throttle up your export and international sales engines and your total revenue thrust will not let you reach escape velocity. In short, gravity will pull you into a ballistic descent, just as we saw with Japanese firms.

Learning from Japan

To illustrate in more detail the dynamics that could hamper Enterprise China's global competitiveness, let's dive a bit deeper into the case of Japan. In 1995, auxiliary export and international sales engines contributed about 10% and 5%, respectively, to the total sales of Japanese firms. Growing these auxiliary engines on the fly was extraordinarily challenging. To complicate matters, Japanese executives did not give up on the main engine (domestic sales) when it first sputtered. On average, they waited seven years before trying to throttle up their export engines. The surge when they finally hit the switch added about 10% to total company revenue—helpful, but not nearly sufficient to offset the loss of thrust from the main domestic revenue engines. Perhaps their export engines would have continued to gain momentum, but unfortunately, they hit an unexpected and major air pocket in 2008 with the Global Financial Crisis and Great Recession. Japanese exports dropped 25.4% during the crisis.

This slowing of momentum was compounded by the fact that Japanese firms did not have the right leaders to throttle up their international revenue engines. Put simply, the leaders who can make and sell at home are not necessarily the same leaders who can successfully produce and sell abroad. The leadership capabilities are quite different, and it takes some time to develop these international leaders.[18] Japanese firms needed a combination of Japanese leaders who had lived and worked in different parts of the world and also non-Japanese leaders with strong international experience. Unfortunately, both were in short supply.

For example, our research and consulting with Japanese firms found that from 2005 to 2010 a full 98% of the top executives and members of the boards of directors of Global 500 Japanese firms were Japanese nationals, most of whom had little overseas experience.[19] Experienced foreign global executives, young and old, could easily see this. Consequently, often the best and brightest foreign leaders were hesitant to join Japanese firms. As they looked up, they saw few if any top leaders who looked like them. In addition, without superior Japanese language skills, they simply did not believe they could rise to the top. As a consequence, foreign leaders viewed Japanese firms as having a "bamboo ceiling"(a term Black coined in the late-1990s), meaning that non-Japanese leaders could go so far but no further up the hierarchy. Faced with diminished career prospects, often the best and brightest foreigners didn't join Japanese firms, or if they did, they didn't stay. This left Japanese firms without the diversity of leadership at corporate headquarters and in overseas affiliates around the world necessary to successfully drive international sales.

As a consequence of not having the right Japanese leaders with international experience or the best and brightest foreign executives, Japanese firms' global competitiveness inched up exactly when it needed to soar. For example, exports ticked up five points to 17.8% of GDP. Japanese firms started from a low base and increased their overseas investments until foreign assets constituted 31% of GDP. With this increase, international sales moved up as well. By 2020 nearly 50% of Japanese revenue thrust was coming from exports and international sales. If this was the case, why did the number of Japanese firms on the Global 500 list fall? Simplified, domestic sales for these companies stagnated with the stalled Japanese economy, and the increased thrust from exports and international sales were not enough to offset the fall in domestic sales. Finally, because the Global 500 list is just that "global," Japanese firms' ability to stay on or fall of the list is a function of their relative total revenue growth. Consequently, while domestic sales combined with increasing export and international revenues pushed overall revenues up, the increase relative to their global rivals was not enough to keep them from falling off the list. Consequently, Japanese firms lost 65% of their peak share of the Global 500 list within less than a generation.

Most unfortunately, we predict that even though the decline of Japanese firms on the Global 500 list has stopped, the country will not see a recovery and resurgence. This is in large part because the profile of executives and board members has not changed much in the last 20 years. Specifically, we took a random sample of 20 of the 52 Japanese companies on the 2018 Global 500 list and found that nearly 97% of all executives and more than 98% of all board members were still Japanese nationals.[20]

Chinese Similarities in Trade and Investment   Everything we just described that contributed to the decline of Japanese firms' global competitiveness is also evident today among Chinese firms. As with the Japanese, the size of Chinese firm's auxiliary export and international sales engines is small. In 1995 Chinese export engines accounted for about 18% of thrust relative to GDP. In 2019 it was essentially unchanged at 17.8%. In 1995, international sales (proxied by outward FDI stock) accounted for about 2.4%. In 2019 it had moved up significantly to 14.6% but still lagged far behind its German, French, British, and US competitors. With its exports and international sales constituting roughly one third of its total revenue thrust, in 2020 Enterprise China was only slightly better positioned for global competitiveness than Japan Inc. in 1997.

Here it is important to reemphasize that global competitiveness is a relative race. Consequently, we need to compare Enterprise China's balance and progress against global rivals (see Exhibit 7.7). In terms of exports, China has fallen

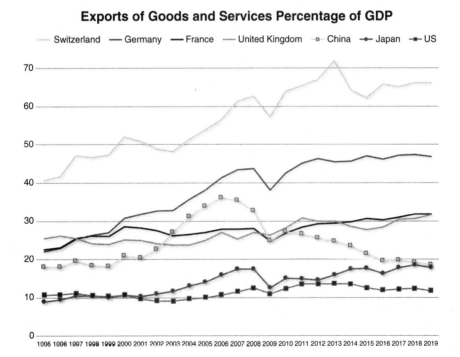

Exhibit 7.7 China's Relative Exports
Source: World Bank.

further behind key rivals in Europe, especially the Swiss, and lost ground to Japanese and US rivals as well.

What about international expansion? On this dimension, even though Enterprise China has increased its overseas presence, it lags every other major country, including Japan, and the gap seems to be widening, not narrowing (see Exhibit 7.8).

Leadership Parallels with Japan   What about the issue of leadership? Don't Chinese leaders have the benefit of all this history and analysis? Can't they see and avoid the mistakes of the Japanese executives? Theoretically they can, but so far, we see little to no evidence that they are paying much attention. Take the most obvious issue of diversity. As with the Japanese firms, we took a random sample of 20 Chinese firms on the Global 500 list and reviewed the diversity of their executives and board members (see Appendix 1). Using 2018 data, we found that diversity levels among the senior ranks of Chinese companies was nearly identical to those of Japan: just under 97% of all executives and just over 97% of all board members were Chinese nationals, most without significant

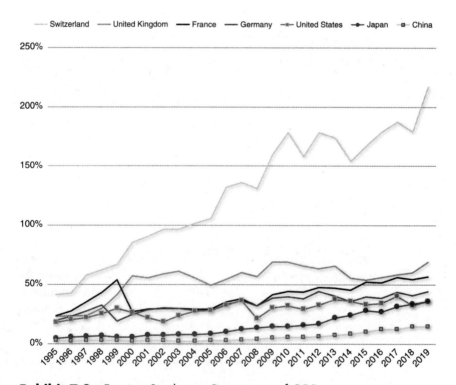

Exhibit 7.8   Foreign Stock as a Percentage of GDP
Source: Adapted from UNCTAD World Investment Report 2020.

international experience. These levels would have been even higher except for a few exceptional firms in our random sample that were beginning to diversify their leadership. If you remove these three firms, the other 17 had only Chinese managers in *every* executive leadership position.

Like the Japanese, Chinese companies have a hard time attracting and integrating foreign leaders. Language is a barrier. But unlike Japanese, which is really only spoken in Japan, Chinese companies could hire ethnic but internationally experienced Chinese from Singapore, Taiwan, and other locations for talent. But our interviews indicate that wide cultural differences between these locations and China represent a major barrier to full integration. The few Chinese firms that have managed to attract and retain globally experienced foreign executives have done so by making English an official company language, such as Lenovo.

While we know of no established threshold, research has demonstrated,[21] and our experience confirms, that when the international composition of leaders is misaligned with international revenue, growth slows and profit lags. The reason is simple. The world in terms of cultures, languages, politics, regulations, supply chains, customer preferences, and technologies is just too big and diverse for executives of one nationality from the center of their home country to put their arms around it all. It does not matter if executives are from Switzerland or the "Middle Kingdom." To be globally competitive, all companies need to be able to attract and retain the best and brightest leaders irrespective of nationality. They need their ideas, their experiences, and their ability to empathize with different cultures and connect personally with different markets. And they need to integrate this diverse group of talent into aligned and engaged teams within the firm.

Impact of Productivity Drag on Global Expansion and Competitiveness

In Chapter 4, we made the case that domestic domination created profit sanctuaries that were needed to fund expensive global expansion and competitiveness. To the extent that a shrinking workforce and declining productivity drag on the domestic economy, Chinese firms have less profit to be put into their global war chests. This is true even if Chinese firms dominate domestically. While this point may be obvious, it is worth emphasizing. Part of the problem for Japanese firms trying to remain globally competitive was that the domestic economy stalled for nearly 15 years. GDP in 2008 was $5.01 trillion. GDP in 2020 was $5.05 trillion, with a high of $6.2 trillion in 2012 and a low of $4.3 trillion in 2015. If Enterprise China's leaders are not able to take sufficient compensatory action and the Chinese domestic economy continues to slow and eventually stagnates, its firms will be left with less capital than expected for global expansion and competitiveness. This risk is amplified by the fact that China's level of debt relative to GDP, especially for SOEs, is such that it cannot in perpetuity compensate for the lack of profit by dolling out more borrowed money. The collapse of the Evergrande

Real Estate Group in the fall of 2021 was widely scrutinized as a harbinger of the interest of the state in propping up highly indebted and poorly run Chinese enterprises. Consequently, if, like their Japanese counterparts, Chinese firms are unable to internally develop or externally recruit capable global leaders, the negative effect of this loss of funding will likely be amplified.

CONCLUSION

Our analysis highlights an important dichotomy. On the one hand, the potential power of Enterprise China's three strategic pillars should not be underestimated nor should its commitment to them be trivialized. Implemented effectively and completely, Enterprise China's competitive strategy has the potential to negatively affect foreign firms in a substantial way. On the other hand, the actualization of this potential is not predestined or assured.

As we have outlined, several factors could derail Enterprise China's competitive strategy. Political crosscurrents could diminish the government's iron-fisted control over SOEs and POEs. Lack of innovation could lead to continued external dependency. Continued external dependency and multilateral and unilateral moves by foreign countries could reduce domestic domination. And a shrinking workforce and lower productivity could stall China's domestic economy and place a gravitation pull on China's ambition for global competitiveness. In our final chapter, we look further out and broaden our field of vision. We start by clarifying four major misconceptions about Enterprise China. We then provide additional recommendations that focus on creating the vibrant organizations that will be ready to confront the general challenges of an assertive Enterprise China going forward.

Chapter 8

PREPARING FOR THE TURBULENT WATERS AHEAD

O ver the past 40 years, we have witnessed and participated in a great awaken-ing of the Chinese giant. Chinese customers have generated trillions of dollars in revenues for millions of companies. Chinese factories have produced trillions of dollars' worth of products and lowered costs and expanded choices for billions of consumers around the world. While some have had qualms about doing business with China, others believed that engagement would over time result in the diminishment of China's authoritarian bent and commitment to Communist rule. In the end, the liberalization of China many had hoped for did not materialize.

That notwithstanding, the rise of China has been impressive. In 2020 for the first time ever, China outspent the United States on R&D. That same year, China housed 77% of the world's installed production capacity of lithium batter-ies; the United States controlled just 10% of global capacity, and the European Union controlled only 4%. In 2020 China spent 4% of its GDP on biotech R&D; the United States spent just 2%. By 2020 China had also taken the lead in a range of technologies central to artificial intelligence, as well as 5G wireless, facial rec-ognition, and factory automation. For every electric vehicle sold in the United States, four are sold in China.[1] While China still lags and is trying to catch up in many areas, it is moving quickly and has a trajectory that suggests that it may yet achieve the objectives of its three strategic pillars over the next decade or so.

Enterprise China is the key operating unit in the process. It is a vertically and horizontally networked model that places the state at the center of decision-making, strategy formulation, funding, and partnership formation. To those in the

West, the Enterprise China model is a paradox. It encompasses what most Westerners view as irreconcilable tensions between the state and free markets. And yet somehow the model has worked and has not collapsed, defying the predictions of many. If anything, Enterprise China seems to be moving steadily ahead, though as we discussed in the previous chapter, its ultimate success is not foreordained.

Enterprise China goes far beyond past attempts by other countries at industrial policy. It is driven by commercial strategies and tactics with strong state ownership, guidance, support, and influence. Even though the competitive strategies of Enterprise China have been hiding in plain sight for nearly two decades, often they have not been well understood by foreign executives. One reason is because the strategies bend the norms of business-government engagement.

In Chapters 5 and 6 we explored strategic options for foreign firms competing in and with Enterprise China. For foreign firms with operations in China, the relevant strategic options varied depending on the configuration of their operations and whether those operations were segments targeted by Enterprise China or not. For foreign firms without operations in China, the most relevant strategic options also varied depending on whether their operations were within or outside the targeted segments. We also pointed to several examples in which foreign firms that thought they were safe from conflicts or competition with Enterprise China ended up in the competitive crosshairs.

In Chapter 7, we pointed out that notwithstanding the huge progress that has been made, Enterprise China's competitive strategy has a variety of weaknesses, and we examined at some length the factors that could derail it all. Specifically, we pointed out that the political crosscurrents within China had the potential to shake the foundations of the Enterprise China model. Other forces had the potential to derail individual components of Enterprise China's competitive strategy.

No matter the dents that Western business and government actions may make pushing back against the Enterprise China model, it would be naive and imprudent to assume that a quick and sure derailment of the model is imminent. It seems reasonable to start from the assumption that China's economy will not implode or that Enterprise China will not self-destruct soon or quickly. Rather, foreign executives would be better off to start from the premise that Enterprise China will be sticking around, that it will continue to pursue its three-part strategy with continued commitment and skill, despite wishful thinking to the contrary.

ARE WE ON THE ROAD TO DECOUPLING?

Looking to the future, fully predicting how the Enterprise China model may evolve is difficult. However, we anticipate that it will continue to use the model to play offense rather than defense. This is consistent with the Chinese state's approach to other initiatives, including geopolitical challenges involving the South China Sea, Hong Kong, the rising power of technology-based POEs, and potentially Taiwan. It is worth highlighting again the words of President Xi in a speech given during the 100th anniversary of the CCP in July 2021, when he lashed out at the West—and more particularly the United States—saying that China would not tolerate "sanctimonious preaching" from other nations. "We will never allow anyone to bully, oppress or subjugate China.... Anyone who dares try to do that will have their heads bashed bloody against the Great Wall of Steel forged by over 1.4 billion Chinese people."[2] Considering this rhetoric, thinking that China will reverse course anytime soon would be a mistake.

Since coming to power, the tone of Xi's speeches has grown more assertive and the country's actions more aggressive, not the reverse. This, combined with the country's track record of success, has led some to conclude that China has already taken a step toward some form of decoupling from the West. Fundamentally, decoupling between China and the West is about the two economic systems moving away from each other, not closer; loosening the connections, not tightening them; and lowering the level of integration, not raising it. At the same time, rising nationalism and growing protectionism in the West suggest that the road to decoupling runs in both directions.

Some worry that the endgame may be the complete decoupling of China's economy from the West. This has been referred to as hard decoupling, and some have speculated that this could happen by design, while others have argued that it could result from unintended consequences. In either case, it would end in the creation of two essentially independent economic systems, two different regulatory approaches, two separate markets, two competing technology platforms, and so on. The nature of hard decoupling was captured by K. Johnson and R. Gramer, writing in *Foreign Policy:*

> *Decoupling refers to the deliberate dismantling—and eventual re-creation elsewhere—of some of the sprawling cross-border supply chains that have defined globalization and especially the U.S.-China relationship in recent decades . . . . [It represents] a potentially historic break, an interruption perhaps only comparable to the sudden sundering of the first huge wave of globalization in 1914, when deeply intertwined economies such as Britain and Germany, and later the United States, threw themselves into a barrage of self-destruction and economic nationalism that didn't stop for 30 years.*[3]

Such an outcome would cost both China and the rest of the world dearly. In 2019 McKinsey pegged the economic value that could be lost due to hard decoupling at between $22 and $37 trillion or between 15% and 26% of global GDP by 2040.[4] These estimates are staggering. While not quite the same as the mutually assured destruction in a nuclear war, hard decoupling is an outcome that few rationally minded people would want. Economically speaking, it is a lose-lose scenario for both China and the West.

While politicians and political analysts joust about the notion of hard decoupling, as business strategists we believe that Enterprise China's competitive strategy neither calls nor allows for hard decoupling. Achieving the objectives of its third strategic pillar and winning globally is simply not possible via a hard decoupling. China cannot win the Standards 2035 race if hard decoupling is the endpoint. The reality is that the world is too big for Enterprise China to simply impose its will on others. At the same time, China cannot achieve its vision of being among the strongest nations in the world as a self-contained and isolated island. It trod this path once, and it did not work out well. And it would work even less well in today's interconnected world. We see no indication that China intends to go down this dead-end path again. Nonetheless, China is big enough that it can leverage its domestic scale into international influence and global competitiveness. Importantly, the logic and ambition to do so is explicit in public documents and statements.

Consequently, even as Enterprise China seeks to reduce its external dependence and seems to be moving in the direction of decoupling, it will still import key technologies and products from foreign firms. It cannot do otherwise until it has viable import substitutions. Otherwise, it risks shooting itself in its economic foot (or worse) depending on the criticality of the imports it wishes to substitute and on which imports it wants to reduce or even eliminate.

Likewise, even as Enterprise China seeks to dominate domestically, it will still allow foreign firms to operate in China. In fact, in some areas, foreign firms will continue to dominate in China unless and until indigenous firms have the technologies, products, services, and prices to offer at least somewhat close to competitive alternatives. China cannot do otherwise, or again it risks shooting itself in its economic foot, especially if the products and services those foreign firms produce and provide *in* China are critical.

If Enterprise China did not have its third strategic pillar of influencing and winning globally, hard decoupling could be a plausible endpoint. But as long as China maintains its third strategic pillar, it must pursue its first and second strategic pillars in the context of this three-dimensional chess game. For example, if China insists on reducing its dependency on external semiconductors before reasonable import substitutes are available, it risks losing billions of dollars in exports in two key ways. First, if it insisted on using primarily its own semiconductors and did not have adequate supply, it would lose billions because it would simply not have the finished products for export. Second, if it created sufficient supply but its semiconductors embedded in export products lacked quality or functionality, customers could, and in many cases would, simply refuse to buy the products. China could not force external customers to purchase products made with inferior components.

As another example of these dynamics, consider the commercial aircraft industry. What would happen if Enterprise China insisted on dominating airplane manufacturing domestically through indigenous companies before it had reasonably comparable offerings? Chinese planes could start falling from the sky or at a minimum face perpetual repairs. What would the Chinese public do? They would do what the flying public anywhere would do. They would stop flying—at least on Chinese-made planes. Despite its strength, the Chinese state could not force the public to get on planes they viewed as dangerous. Whether planes or semiconductors, China cannot achieve the aims of its third strategic pillar without a reasonable approach to its first two.

This all being said, we are not suggesting that Enterprise China will not play hardball and use every tactic we have described and discussed to its full advantage. It will. At the same time, we are not predicting that Enterprise China's economic ambitions will necessarily supersede the state's geopolitical interests in Taiwan or elsewhere in the region. We are only saying that if you take a hard look at China's competitive strategies and tactics and at the general consistency of their implementation over nearly two decades, some of the political speculation and debates that occupy print and digital space are of limited practical utility to business executives.

CLARIFYING MISPERCEPTIONS

Before we shift the discussion to the broader implications of Enterprise China on the "rest of us," we want to pause and provide some additional clarifying points. We begin by reviewing frequent misperceptions about China more generally and Enterprise China more specifically.

Misperception 1: China Wants to Drive All Foreign Companies Out

As we briefly mentioned, we sometimes hear politicians and even business executives claim that "China wants to drive foreign companies out of China." Certainly, examples abound of foreign companies leaving China. Many of these firms claim that they were "forced" out by unfair practices, regulations, and policies by commercial rivals, as well as the state. No doubt this has been the case for certain foreign companies. Some of the highest-profile examples are digital media giants, such as Google, Facebook, Reddit, Dropbox, and Wikipedia. Others have been legacy media giants, such as the *New York Times, Wall Street Journal, Washington Post, Bloomberg*, and the *South China Morning Post*. However, it is important to note that in most cases in which a foreign firm was pushed out or blocked, China had a reasonable, indigenous alternative in place to fill the void.

Despite these high-profile examples, the vast majority of foreign companies that have entered China have remained. Foreign firms operating in China run the spectrum of industries, including semiconductors, apparel, fast food, retail, factory automation, pharmaceutical, and many more. Companies as varied as Walmart, Coca-Cola, Siemens, Rockwell, Honeywell, Tesla, General Motors, Panasonic, and

Bayer have become fully entrenched in China and enjoy stable operations. They are not at risk of being shut down or otherwise blocked by the state anytime soon.

However, this is not to say that the nature of competition and regulation these companies face *within* China are not different or even unique; they are. It is not even to say that the playing field is level between foreign firms in China and their domestic rivals. Enterprise China is a different type of competitive beast than found anywhere else in the world. Its objective is not to eliminate all foreign competitors but to first ensure reduced dependency and second to dominate domestically. If your firm is in the way of these first two objectives *in* China, expect a rough ride. If not, you are likely to experience China as a competitive market, but no more so than other tough and competitive markets such as Japan, Germany, the UK, or the United States.

Misperception 2: Foreign Companies Barely Make Money in China

Growing trade and political tensions between China and the West have led many to believe that foreign companies are in desperate straits in China, but this is by no means the universal case. China is a hugely profitable country for many Western companies. This is true for companies that import from China, those that import into China, and those that follow an "In China, For China" strategy. Case in point: Wynn Resorts now generates more than 75% of its revenue and 77% of its profit from its operations in Macau. Another example: General Motors has numerous joint ventures in China, but because it owns less than 50% of these ventures, it doesn't report the resulting revenue. However, it does report equity income, which for China amounted to $1 billion in 2019.[5] To put this in context, GM's total net income in 2019 was $6.6 billion. Likewise, it would be safe to say that other companies such as Qualcomm, which counts on China for two thirds of its global revenue, and Micron with 57% of its revenue coming from China[6] are capturing the bulk of their profits from China. This is consistent with annual surveys from the US-China Business Council (USCBC) that have found that for the 2015 to 2020 period, between 91% and 97% of member companies reported that their Chinese operations were profitable.[7] No doubt the stock prices of numerous foreign companies worldwide would go into free fall if their China businesses suddenly disappeared.

The myth that foreign companies are *all* losing out in China is perpetuated by a dearth of public data on firm performance. Many companies do not break out country-specific profit but only report revenue and profit by larger geographies. In our interviews, not a single executive would go on the record to discuss profit in China. But privately, many assured us that they were "most pleased" with their results. One executive described his firm's financial performance in China as "the best kept secret in the company." Another executive told us, "Amongst our global operations, we are doing particularly well in China."

Even if China-specific profit and revenue data were reported, the numbers would almost never tell the full story. Why? Because many Western companies take advantage of accounting rules to shift profit from one country to another. This can be done to lower overall taxes or as a means of moving profit out of China for strategic purposes or simply for the optics. Wholly owned foreign enterprises can also shift money out of China by making payments for "services rendered" to sister subsidiaries or the foreign parent company. These payments can also include royalties from their China operations as another means of shifting profit. Look carefully and you will find representative offices in small countries such as Singapore or Switzerland with revenue and profit that far outweigh the miniscule size of the local office. Of course, none of this shows up directly in any financial statement. The creative accounting is all perfectly legal but has led many to accept at face value that China is a money-losing proposition. Again, this may be the case for some companies but not for those that have mastered the market and made peace with Enterprise China.

Misperception 3: Enterprise China Is Merely a Tool of the CCP

Another comment we frequently heard in our interviews was "Enterprise China is just a tool of the CCP." We agree that Enterprise China is a powerful instrument that extends the reach of the state. As we have highlighted, many of the initiatives associated with MLP, MIC 2025, and China Standards 2035 are designed to increase the relevance and legitimacy of the CCP. After all, power increases when exercised. But the state is much more than the CCP with its strong ties to the central government in Beijing.

As we have stated previously, the central government is a powerful actor in the overall state, and Enterprise China helps strengthen Beijing's power within the country. However, to think of China as totally a top-down political system is both narrow and naive. Power in China is much more widely dispersed than most in the West appreciate. The country is simply too large and complex for the CCP to run everything from Beijing. China has organized itself on provinces, autonomous regions, and municipalities, each with its own power structure. Big city mayors are no longer going to Beijing with heads bowed and hands out. While mayors are not free to lead their cities in any direction they fancy and are constrained to follow dictates from Beijing, they have some latitude in how they interpret and implement guidance or even dictates. Since the mid-1980s, for example, municipal governments have been permitted to engage in major investment projects without the approval of Beijing. This has led to a broad and deep patchwork of investment and development initiatives with some cities strongly promoting high technology investments and others supporting more basic manufacturing that generates jobs for millions of rural migrant workers.[8]

Misperception 4: Foreign Governments Will Never Accept Enterprise China

Given perceptions that the state has put its thumb on the scale of competition in China in favor of its indigenous firms (especially the ones it owns), it would be understandable to expect that foreign governments will take a confrontational approach to Enterprise China, fighting the Chinese state at every opportunity. Such expectations are born out of public statements by the leaders of many countries in support of the rule of law and some form of free market capitalism. This may lead many to expect that foreign governments will collectively or independently but harmoniously rise up to block Enterprise China's aggressive tendencies. This has not yet transpired to the extent many predicted and may never reach that level.

While some foreign governments have taken a confrontational approach vis-à-vis Enterprise China and China, most have not. In fact, a number of countries are doing the exact opposite; they are emulating China. Given what they see as successes in China, some foreign governments are experimenting with Enterprise China–like models for economic development at home. Arguably this is most prominent among countries that have been on the receiving end of the Belt and Road investments that we discussed in Chapter 4. Consequently, certainly in countries such as Pakistan, Indonesia, and Vietnam, we expect to see more state-owned enterprises fashioned after the Enterprise China model to pop up.

Even among those countries that do not necessarily admire or seek to emulate China, many have taken a schizophrenic or passive-aggressive approach. The reason for this is that while many countries feel that their firms have been and are now unfairly disadvantaged by the Enterprise China model, these same countries are often dependent on China for a wide array of products. Consequently, they risk painful retaliation if they push too hard. Australian foreign minister Marise Payne acknowledged the power dynamic in July 2020 during meetings in Washington, DC. "The relationship that we have with China is very important," she said. "We have no intention of injuring it. But nor do we intend to do things that are contrary to our interests."[9] Likewise, Germany pushed the European Union to sign a large investment deal with China in December 2020 without waiting to consult the incoming Biden administration. The Germans also have distanced themselves from the United States in terms of opposition to Huawei and Chinese-based 5G technology.[10]

US dependency on China in key areas such as masks, ventilators, and pharmaceuticals was made abundantly clear when those products were in short supply in the early days of the COVID-19 pandemic. The US government subsequently utilized the Korean War–era Defense Production Act to encourage the domestic pharmaceutical industry to work with the US military to create a public-private consortium for essential medicine production. Although under President Trump the

United States took a more direct and confrontational approach to China via tariffs, the Biden administration has embraced a more indirect approach. For example, the United States launched a series of workshops and handbooks designed to inform policymakers in places such as Latin America and Central Europe on the perils of using Chinese technology for their next-generation 5G networks. In the summer of 2021, legislation was also working its way through the US Congress that authorized foreign aid funds for countries in Central and Eastern Europe to buy non-Chinese 5G telecom equipment.[11] In June 2021, the US Senate passed a bill that provided $52 billion in funding for the US semiconductor industry. The bill included a 30% boost in spending for the National Science Foundation.[12] The government also authorized US Department of Energy to issue loans to accelerate the development of advanced battery technologies.[13] The Biden administration also organized a task force "including the secretaries of commerce, transportation and agriculture to help reduce the exposure of US companies to Chinese supply chains."[14]

In the final analysis, it would be naive to think that all governments will push back on China or that those that do will act consistently. Even the strongest countries, such as the United States, have demonstrated that they will push back on some things but not all things and that as administrations change, targets and tactics can and will be significantly modified. For business leaders, this means that although it is likely wise for them to try to influence their government officials, they are unlikely to find consistent partners in their governments. The onus is on foreign businesses executives to dive deep into determining the competitive strategies, motivations, and tactics of Enterprise China and then formulate explicit strategic options and actions without relying on home governments for strong leadership or direction.

ADDITIONAL RECOMMENDATIONS FOR FOREIGN EXECUTIVES

With these clarifications in mind, we offer several additional general recommendations for foreign companies that are currently or will likely interact with Enterprise China in the coming years. These recommendations focus less on the specific strategy options reviewed in Chapters 5 and 6 and more on what Western companies can do to create the vibrant organizations that will be ready to confront the general challenges of an assertive Enterprise China. On the importance of being fully prepared for the challenges ahead, we are reminded of the oft-cited aphorism from Benjamin Franklin: "By failing to prepare, you are preparing to fail."

1. Manage Your Bets

Most companies' strategies for engaging Enterprise China are iterative processes that evolve over time. Yet, once formed they take on an air of permanence.

A Canadian executive we interviewed provided a military analogy when describing the process for his company's efforts in China:

> When we came to China we were like an army under constant attack. We first fought it out for a beach-head, and then took heavy casualties to reach high ground. Once there, we set up a camp and have been in build mode ever since. Over the past 15 years we have accomplished a lot. We established a joint venture partnership with a major Chinese corporation affiliated with the municipal government, established an office, and with our partner built a factory, and put together a complex supply chain. We have finally reached a point of stable success.

In setting up successful operations in China, virtually every executive we interviewed listed developing good relationships with Enterprise China among their top three success factors. Importantly, relationships with Enterprise China are both difficult to establish and difficult to change. They are difficult to establish because local ecosystems, with Enterprise China serving as the hub, are tough for outsiders to understand or navigate alone. Enterprise China has the power and relationships required to open doors, secure contracts, and facilitate transactions. Once established, these relationships are tough to alter because the dependency inherent in them is hard for foreign firms to escape. This makes foreign company strategies less flexible and fluid than they may be in a pure market setting.

This lack of strategic flexibility isn't necessarily a bad thing. Maintaining a strong relationship with Enterprise China can make sense if the world remains stable. But what if local conditions change or markets shift? What if a company needs to introduce a new business model and establish new partnerships in adjacent industries or in faraway locations in China? What if trade frictions arise or nationalism drives away customers? What if Enterprise China squeezes the foreign firm in order to secure its own domestic domination? At a moment in time when Chinese state media proudly run articles on Western—and particularly American—economic and political decline, it would be naive to count on Enterprise China leaping to the rescue of any foreign firm regardless of the strength of the relationship in the past.

As uncertainty and risks rise, foreign companies need real options in their interfaces with China. A real option is an economically valuable ability to make (or abandon) some choices, or in this case strategic decisions, at some point in the future. The "real" aspect of an option refers to tangible products or services as opposed to financial instruments where different types of options may be at play. With real options, executives structure investments, operations, and projects in ways that preserve rather than cut off choices down the road such as to expand, redirect, or downsize projects or investments depending on economic, technological, or market conditions in the future. In the context of Enterprise China, although we have examined its competitive strategies and tactics and outlined the potential implications, strategies, and actions for firms, circumstances and dynamics can and likely will change. Therefore, it makes sense for executives to consider potential key changes that could arise and how they can position things today to preserve those real options down the road.

For example, we reviewed the strategic option of China Plus One—having a sister plant outside China—for market players in Chapter 5. This diversification move may be easy to implement today or difficult depending on how locked into China a company's upstream operations are and how many viable locations there are to create a "Plus One" sister plant. However, the real option is to preserve the ability to expand and diversify production, as F-Tech did when COVID-19 hit its main plant in Wuhan. F-Tech deliberately managed issues of capacity, space, equipment, labor access, and so on to ensure that it could exercise the real option of moving production capacity from Wuhan to the Philippines.

From an economic perspective the cost of preserving an option has to be weighed against the value of being able to exercise the option. This, of course, involves complicated calculations but, more important, estimations. Because the actual value and costs of real options are not fully realized until some point in the future, completely accurate calculations of the value of a real option are not possible. Nonetheless, foreign companies (whichever of the four categories of configuration applies to them from Chapter 5) can estimate the value of a potential real option. For example, F-Tech could estimate the cost of keeping increased capacity and space in its Plus One plant in the Philippines. It could also estimate the lost revenue if its plant in Wuhan were shut down, as well as the revenue it could capture while its plant in China was idled and its sister plant ramped up to capture its lost output.

Committing to real options is like taking out an insurance policy. It creates costs (both current and future) and provides few immediate benefits, but if exercised, it delivers the promise of considerable value. Given some of the risks we have outlined, especially for foreign firms with significant upstream or downstream operations in China, examining and creating real options may be a prudent move.

2. Guard Your Company's Global Reputation

Companies doing business in and around China face significant reputational risks. What is said and done by a company's leaders in China may reverberate around the world. Likewise, a company's actions and communications outside China can be highly damaging to a company's reputation in the country. Generally, reputational risks come in two forms: those that are based on cross-cultural misunderstandings and those that result from the perception of being overly "cozy" with the Chinese state.

Avoid Cross-Cultural Mistakes
Most often, embarrassing missteps are based on a lack of cultural awareness and poor cross-cultural communication skills. In these situations, the foreign

company's intentions are typically good, making it all the more difficult to recognize when reputational damage may have been done. Case in point: Dolce & Gabbana. The Italian fashion house found itself in a public relations crisis in November 2018. The company had spent months preparing for a major fashion show in Shanghai. To help set the stage, it created a promotional video, titled "Eating with Chopsticks," which it placed on the company's social media accounts worldwide. The video featured an Asian woman, wearing fashionable clothing, fumbling to eat Italian dishes like spaghetti and pasta using chopsticks.[15] It seemed like an innocent way to humorously highlight the blend of East and West. Unfortunately, social media sites, starting in China, were set afire with claims that Dolce & Gabbana was racist and had stereotyped the Chinese in a most unflattering way.

What started in China could not be contained, and soon the story spilled over to the rest of the world. This then led others to dig up an old video of Stefano Gabbana (the company's co-founder) making unflattering comments about the Chinese. Gabbana claims his personal Instagram account had been hacked and that the comments had never actually been made. In response, celebrities demanded a boycott of the company, products were removed from shelves, the fashion show was canceled, and the company suffered a major *global* brand crisis.[16] As is typical in these matters, the company and its leaders soon apologized and claimed a deep love for China and asserted that this entire episode had unfairly cast the company in a negative light.

Cross-cultural missteps can be damaging to a company's reputation. And they can be difficult to control without constant monitoring. Many Western companies are adept at tracking social media sites for potential stories that are detrimental to their reputations. But too often their monitoring stops in their home country. Few Western companies actively track what is being said in China. Consequently, bad news stories may reach a fever pitch in China before they capture the attention of top executives back at headquarters.

Monitoring, as important as it might be, isn't preventative. Foreign firms also need to conduct more China-targeted employee training on core company values and standards to ensure that they are not violated in China. As an example of how a lack of strong training comes into play, McDonald's came under fire in 2020 after one of its branches in Guangdong Province displayed a sign saying that "black people are not allowed to enter."[17] A Twitter firestorm soon erupted, complete with pictures and videos. While the sign was quickly brought down, local employees failed to fully understand the importance of McDonald's global standards.

Beware of Perceptions of Getting Too Cozy
Western companies that are perceived to be too cozy with the Chinese state also risk damaging their global reputations. On these matters, Western companies face a nearly impossible task of appeasing the Chinese state—whose support

they need to function within the country—while at the same time remaining true to norms and values outside China and back home. For example, Coach and Givenchy were forced to apologize to China for producing T-shirts that apparently identified Hong Kong as an independent country. Other companies, including Marriott, Swarovski, Medtronic, Calvin Klein, McDonalds, Delta Airlines, and the NBA, have also publicly apologized to China for "inappropriately" siding with Taiwan or Hong Kong by referring to them as countries in their ads or in the maps they have produced. Other companies such as Mercedes-Benz have offered formal apologies for including a quote from the Dalai Lama in an Instagram post. Not only are apologies requested, but they must be public and show a sufficient level of contrition. However, the apologies of companies and their acts of contrition to China can be viewed negatively outside China and back in their home countries. For example, when Houston Rockets general manager Daryl Morey apologized to China for showing solidarity with pro-democracy protesters in Hong Kong, former 2020 US Democratic presidential candidates Robert "Beto" O'Rourke and Julián Castro, as well as US Sen. Ted Cruz, blasted the apology.[18] "The only thing the NBA should be apologizing for is their blatant prioritization of profits over human rights," Cruz said. Castro agreed, saying the United States should "not allow American citizens to be bullied by an authoritarian government."

In many cases, companies are damned if they do and damned if they don't. For example, Disney suffered a major blow to its global reputation with the release of its film *Mulan*. Some of the outdoor shots were filmed in Xinjing. No doubt in an attempt to curry favor, Disney publicly thanked the Chinese authorities for their support of the film. However, the province had become a hotbed for human rights complaints largely relating to the Uyghur ethnic minority group. While Disney had hoped that its support for Xinjing would position the company—and the film—in good standing in China, social media sites in the West fanned the flames of controversy. In the end the Chinese government shut down all coverage of the film in China, leaving *Mulan* to languish at the box office there. In a dual blow, Disney's reputation took a hit in both China and the United States.

Beyond appeasing the Chinese state with carefully chosen words and at-the-ready "heartfelt" apologies, Western companies face an even larger challenge: responding to rules and regulations that are inconsistent with their home country values. Many of these rules govern the collection and sharing of sensitive data with the Chinese state. As an example, many Western executives in China report being pressured to facilitate China's social credit system that uses data on such things as credit scores and parking tickets to determine social benefits and even employment opportunities for Chinese citizens. Western companies may also be required to share information with the state on employee use of video games, access to unauthorized websites, consumption of unhealthy food, or smoking habits. Others are either directly or indirectly involved in helping the Chinese state implement a massive facial recognition database tracking system.[19] Even when the company isn't forced to share this data, it knows that in China its global confidentiality norms are at risk. For example, in 2021 Apple opened a data storage center in Guiyang, China, to house the personal information of its Chinese customers. However, as part of Apple's grand bargain with the Chinese, the operations of the plant were largely turned over to a state-owned Chinese firm that was given access to the digital keys that controlled the encryption algorithms.[20] To many observers, it appeared that Apple had one set of rules for China and another for the rest of the world. Clearly, the optics were not good.

The perception that either by word or deed a Western company is helping to build an Orwellian state in China can have important public reputation consequences. But the pressures don't stop at China's doors. In many cases Western executives have even been strong-armed by the state to share proprietary databases containing sensitive information collected and stored *outside* China. Defying these requirements would at a minimum severely curtail a company's efforts to operate in China or to even source through Enterprise China. At the same time, conforming to these demands could lead to significant damage to the company's global reputation.

"When in Rome" has been a mantra of global executives for millennia. However, in today's social media–fueled world, the ramifications of an offense—real or perceived—can be significant and create lasting consequences to a company's global reputation. A misstep in China can lead to the company being stigmatized by customers, suppliers, and government officials both inside and outside China. When this happens, the knock-on effects are difficult to calculate. Researchers at Harvard Business School and the US Military Academy describe the dilemma:

> *Stigmatized companies may be mocked in the media, have their charitable donations rejected, see employee morale plunge, and experience an exodus of talent. And organizational stigma is contagious, not only for employees but sometimes even for other companies in the same industry that have done no wrong.*[21]

In November 2021 China upped the stakes for those committing the offense of supporting the independence of Taiwan or Hong Kong. The government announced that it "will hold those who support Taiwan independence criminally liable for life."[22] The first individuals named for this special criminal designation were Taiwan Premier Su Tseng-chang, Parliament Speaker You Si-kun, and Foreign Minister Joseph Wu. The government further stated that individuals so designated would be prohibited from entering Mainland China, as well as Hong Kong and Macau. In addition, any blacklisted individuals would "not be allowed to cooperate with entities or people from the mainland, nor will their companies, or entities which fund them, be allowed to profit from the mainland."[23]

Mitigate Reputational Risks
Mitigating the reputational risks associated with interfacing with the Chinese state and by extension Enterprise China is not an easy task. A good starting

assumption is that a foreign firm's actions in China involving employment, the environment, customer and supplier relations, database management, and government regulations will become known and subject to review by all. Likewise, foreign business leaders should assume that communications—both public and increasingly private—will spread far and wide at the click of a mouse.

Beyond this, navigating relationships with Enterprise China necessitates a clear review of and public commitment to core corporate values, standards, and policies. Deciding what values, standards, and policies are off the table—even in China—and what are open to local interpretation is difficult and often unsettling. Once this is done, leaders need to define the associated behaviors and consequences that are appropriate at all levels of the organization, including front-line employees. To ensure consistency and limit the risks of damaging misconduct or communications, foreign companies need to double and even triple their education and training efforts necessitating the direct involvement of the CEO and all members of the senior leadership team.

3. Strengthen Your China-Centric Leadership Competencies

Given the challenges of competing in China, especially if a firm operates in one of the targeted sectors, having experienced and competent leaders is critical. As we discussed in Chapter 5, Honeywell's Tedjarati shows the influence that a single executive can have. Could Honeywell have been as effective with its "In China, For China" strategy with a less experienced and dedicated leader? We don't think so. Does that mean that every company needs an expatriate leader to learn Chinese and live there for two decades? Maybe not, but clearly much more needs to be done to strengthen China-centric leadership competencies.

The traditional "fly in, have a quick look around, and fly out" trip that potentially served a purpose in the past is in our estimation insufficient going forward. In the past these trips often kept executives in a visitor's bubble defined by stays at a Marriott, Hilton, or Kempinski hotel, getting picked up and driven around town by a company car, and attending meetings in high-rise office spaces that might as well have been in Boston, London, or New York. To make matters worse, executives often spent much of their free time connected to headquarters via their smart devices while at the same time battling severe jet lag. They were physically in China, but their exhausted minds were only half-way present. Some, in moments of candor, recognized the minimal value of these visits. Others saw only the hardships imposed. In an unguarded moment, one CEO who had committed to his board that he would travel to China at least once per year—but who privately told us he stretched it out to 18 months—reported:

> I hate being in China with all the noise, crowds, and bad air. As soon as my two days of meetings are over, I try to get on the first flight out. The best part of

the trip is when the driver picks me up at the hotel to take me to the airport to fly home.

With this kind of mindset, it isn't surprising that China and its culture and people have remained misunderstood and elusive to some foreign business leaders. Given the rise and ambitions of Enterprise China, this can be dangerous.

Develop Longer and Deeper Commitments

For top expatriate executives in China, the traditional role of representing the company's interests and knowing how China fits within the company's global strategy and positioning still matters but may not be sufficiently comprehensive going forward. Likewise, the traditional three-year assignment may not be sufficient. Top expatriates likely will need a deeper understanding of China in general, and Enterprise China in particular, before being assigned there. The effective length of assignment may need to be closer to five years, not three. In addition, while achieving full Mandarin fluency is likely not possible for most executives, a wide and solid command of greetings, well wishes, and other conversation competencies is well advised.

Some companies have recognized these needs and sent ethnic Chinese raised in Taiwan or even places like California who have full language fluency. This may solve some challenges but can raise others. For example, we spoke to one regional CEO of a *Fortune* 500 company who was ethnically Chinese, raised in Taiwan, and who later became a US citizen after pursuing a graduate degree at a prestigious East Coast university. He commented on the limitations of expatriates:

> *They will never be accepted as insiders in China. No matter how fluent they may be, the Chinese will always consider them to be outsiders. Even I, someone who is a native Mandarin speaker, have serious problems being fully accepted. They can tell by my accent where I come from. And they are always suspicious and guarded.*

Utilize Local Chinese Managers

All these adjustments relative to top expatriates aside, foreign firms in China may need to rely more and more on local Chinese managers to succeed. Just as a foreign firm's top expatriate executives need to understand not just the firm's operations in China but how China fits into its global operations, the same is true when those positions are occupied by Chinese executives. To gain that understanding and broad expertise, those Chinese leaders will need some experience outside China. Unfortunately, precious few US and European firms have native Chinese in senior ranks of management outside China. One firm we worked with, a US-based consumer products giant, employed only three native Mandarin speakers *anywhere* in the world at the rank of vice president or above. Other companies employed dozens or even hundreds of lower-level native Chinese managers outside China—most hired out of university—but these managers were not yet ready for senior leadership responsibilities in China.

Poaching Chinese leaders from other firms both in and outside China may be an option, but when most firms have the same need and the supply of globally experienced Chinese business leaders is low, competition becomes intense, and prices rise. These outside hires may not have familiarity with the industry or key technologies; by definition, they lack internal networks in the global firm, and their lack of experience in the firm can leave them with initial credibility challenges. Thus, external hires may come with the advantage of understanding China in general, and Enterprise China in particular, and come with language capabilities, but at the same time their lack of internal networks, credibility, and experience with the firm may make the actual implementation of the strategy, including gaining collaboration from the firms functions and units outside China, difficult.

Build China-Centric Leadership Competencies

Given this, we are often asked, How can we accelerate the development of more effective leaders to deal with Enterprise China? What can we do to ensure that we are not taken advantage of or caught off guard? To build these competencies, we offer several recommendations.

1. **Improve top executive experience in China:** When top global executives travel to China, structure the visit such that they experience China and get outside the executive bubble. A great example of this was John Pepper, twice CEO of Procter and Gamble (P&G), who used to insist on visiting real families to see firsthand how they washed their clothes, cooked their food, and cleaned their homes so that he could better understand how P&G's products could be of value to them. Sometimes gaining insight into China requires getting outside key gateway cities. China is incredibly diverse with the most rapid growth now coming from the hinterland. Often this is facilitated by contracting with someone who can assist with local learning, not just language translation. Developing relationships with key external stakeholders (customers, suppliers, Enterprise China officials, and the appropriate representatives of the state) requires a certain frequency of visits and time beyond official and highly orchestrated "meet and greet" sessions.

2. **Improve expatriation:** Given that the practice by foreign firms of sending expatriate executives to China is likely to continue, it is important to select executives who have not only the technical or business qualifications but also a genuine interest in understanding China and are not just looking to punch their "worked in China" ticket. These leaders do not need to

master the Chinese language, but developing some rudimentary competency can go a long way to conveying commitment. These expatriates should also have as part of their objectives the development of future local Chinese leaders. In many cases, it is wise to reach deep into the global organization in search of appropriate expatriates and not confine opportunities to just top positions. This can help strengthen the human network between the global organization and China. Nestlé provides an interesting example. Nestlé has over 2,000 expatriates around the world at various levels in its operations, but more than 85% of them are not Swiss. This stems from the company's passport-blind perspective in selecting and deploying expatriates. Nestlé seeks to send the best executives to countries where they are needed and where they can further develop themselves regardless of the leader's nationality. Many of these assignments are done early in a leader's career both to develop and to test the person's global mindset and potential.

3. **Develop middle and upper-level Chinese managers in China:** To ensure that a foreign firm has the local Chinese leaders needed for tomorrow, it should have started to identify and develop them yesterday. In some cases this may require "inpatriation," or bringing Chinese leaders to the foreign firm's headquarters on assignment. Again, Nestlé is a good example. Of its nearly 2,600 employees at its headquarters and surrounding offices in Vevey, Switzerland, an estimated 800 of these are foreigners. This level of inpatriation helps develop the individuals, brings diversity and breadth of perspective to the company, builds networks, and fosters trust. In our work over the past 30-plus years, this level of systematic inpatriation is rare, though Lenovo is an example of a Chinese company that systematically brings Western managers into China to build their experience and connections. Effective inpatriation can also increase the career opportunities of Chinese leaders outside China, which in turn can make the foreign firm more attractive to globally minded Chinese leaders because they don't have to view their careers as confined to China.

4. **Develop Chinese and non-Chinese leaders together:** There is wisdom in aligning the development of high-potential Chinese leaders with leaders from across the firm's global operations. Formal development programs that bring high-potential leaders together from various geographies, functions, and businesses can be transformative. The fundamental objectives typically are to (1) extend and strength the human networks across the company, (2) elevate the individual leadership capabilities of the participants, and (3) broaden and deepen the leadership pipeline for the company. These aims are best achieved when the programs are part of a larger development system that includes mentoring/coaching and developmental jobs and assignments. For a firm's Chinese leaders, such programs can

help contrast the common leadership development approach in China, which is lecture-based, theoretical, and "check the box" in nature, with the more interactive, experiential, practical, and transformative approach that Western firms are increasingly taking. These programs can also help contrast the dominant leadership model in China, which is typically more autocratic and hierarchical, with the more collaborative and empowering style increasingly common in many foreign firms. These programs typically include multiple learning modules that bring participants together more than once and have projects and other activities that keep participants connected even while they are back home and physically separated. Many leading companies mandate participation in these global leadership programs as a prerequisite for advancement to the most senior ranks of the company.

These four recommendations can elevate the development of high-potential Chinese leaders in three ways. First, these actions can help build Chinese leaders "In China, For China." In turn, they can draw out the best performance of Chinese workers and managers. Second, they can develop Chinese leaders for China who can more effectively interface with the foreign firm's leaders from various parts of the world. Third, these recommendations can develop Chinese leaders who can be more effective outside China. As Nestlé so aptly illustrates, global firms need the best and brightest at their executive levels regardless of nationality and therefore need to take a passport-blind approach to all high-potential leaders.

For a firm's non-Chinese leaders, the recommendations listed above can also help in three ways. First, these actions can help build non-Chinese leaders who more deeply understand China and the firm's operations there. Second, these actions can spark an interest in China that would serve the individual well later if assigned to work in China. Third, these actions can develop and identify non-Chinese leaders who can more effectively interface with the firm's operation in China and its leaders there.

All of this traveling and training achieves another important purpose. It helps focus the attention not only of the people directly involved but the broader organization as well.[24] From the confines of a comfortable office at headquarters, putting thoughts of China into the back of your mind is easy. Getting serious about Enterprise China requires paying attention to and thinking about China *a lot*. Isaac Newton was once asked how he came to realize the law of gravity and what has become known as Newtonian physics. His response: "I thought about it all the time." By regularly interacting with Chinese leaders, by traveling with the purpose of learning, China is more likely to receive the attention warranted, especially when it is easy to be distracted by the familiar and proximate. And when leaders pay attention to China, a spillover effect spreads to the broader organization.

CONCLUSION

The three pillars of China's competitive strategy have transformed both the country and global commerce. In the coming decade, China is poised to overtake the United States as the world's largest economy. The good news for foreign firms is China's market will only get larger and richer. The more troubling news is China's successes have resulted in a large and growing list of powerful new competitors built on the Enterprise China model that many in the West find difficult to understand and to compete with.

The 2020s and beyond represent turbulent waters for foreign firms competing in and with China. As China moves to center stage, its ability to influence a wide range of business norms will certainly grow. Even foreign firms with no operations in China, which focus singularly on their home country's market, are likely to find themselves in competitive battles with Enterprise China in the coming years.

Like the pebble thrown in the pond, the ripples from an assurgent Enterprise China will continue to roll into the future. The exact impact of these ripples is hard to fully predict. Enterprise China has the ambition of competing and influencing globally by not only leading in the future standards wars but also through its Belt and Road Initiative. In addition to the ties that these "belts" and "roads" create back to China, an open but important question emerges. To what extent will the countries on the other side of the "belts" and "road" emulate the Enterprise China model? Will greater and broader success of the Enterprise China model inspire decision makers in Russia, Brazil, Indonesia, Korea, and other countries to take up or revise the model? Will the success of Enterprise China lead to a long-term decline of the free-market models or simply intensify the competition between the alternatives?

Through all this, China is facing its own challenges with the risk of internal conflicts rising as the state cracks down on free enterprise. In unveiling dozens of new regulations that reined in the country's own tech companies in 2021, Xi has said, "China has entered a new stage of development . . . [with the goal of turning China into a] modern socialist power."[25] The immediate consequence of this new wave of regulations was a loss of $1.1 trillion in market capitalization for Chinese firms during the first half of 2021. The impact on Chinese *and* foreign investors has been significant in the short term and raises concerns about how the state plans to assert its interests in the long term.

To be certain, not everything Enterprise China touches turns to gold. Enterprise China is now facing growing headwinds from less than cooperative governments in North America, Europe, Japan, Korea, and Australasia. Mounting resistance will amplify and not dampen the uncertainties about the ultimate impact of Enterprise China. Nonetheless, deepening an understanding of the nature of Enterprise China and its competitive strategies and tactics will help foreign executives plan and prepare for the future.

In pressing forward, we offer several questions for your consideration:

- To what extent is your company dependent on China for sales, technologies, and supply chain nodes? Are you comfortable with this level of dependency and interdependency?
- Are you paying enough attention to China, given not only your company's current operations but the potential of Enterprise China to disrupt your business model in the future?
- Are you making the necessary anticipatory investments to build and fuel real options that allow you to circumvent this exposure?
- Does the diversity of your company's top leadership team align with the diversity of your company's revenue today and in the future?
- Are you doing enough to prepare the next generation of Enterprise China savvy leaders?
- Are you taking a passport-blind approach to identifying and developing the leaders you need in China, for China, and from China?

As we face the mountain of challenges posed by Enterprise China, it might be tempting to either blame the Chinese or put our heads in the sand and hope the world becomes a safer, more orderly place. Of course, neither of these alternatives offer satisfaction. The only viable option going forward is a deeper and broader understanding of Enterprise China, which can enable you to better anticipate future moves and how they might impact your firm given its current and impending position in or relative to China. These are the foundations of your firm's future strategic options and actions in competing in and with China.

APPENDIX

Japan-Based Fortune Global 500 Executive and Board Composition
(Percentage of Japanese Nationals, 2018)

JPN Rank	500 Rank	Company	Revenue	Exec. %	BoD %
5	55	Nippon Telegraph & Telephone	$106,500	100	100
8	97	Sony	$77,116	80	84
11	114	Panasonic	$72,045	93	100
12	126	Nippon Life Insurance	$68,684	100	100
13	129	Mitsubishi	$68,301	100	100
13	130	Marubeni	$68,057	95	100
16	165	Toyota Tsusho	$58,586	96	94
21	198	Nippon Steel & Sumitomo Metal	$51,164	100	100
23	209	Tokio Marine Holdings	$48,731	82	100
24	221	MS&AD Insurance Group Holdings	$47,095	100	100
27	246	Mitsui	$44,155	100	90
28	250	Sumitomo	$43,570	98	100
30	309	Meiji Yasuda Life Insurance	$37,160	100	100
33	317	Canon	$36,388	98	100
35	329	Aisin Seiki	$35,281	94	100
36	342	Daiwa House Industry	$34,262	100	100
37	347	Sompo Holdings	$34,028	100	100
39	350	Sumitomo Life Insurance	$33,821	100	100
51	462	Chubu Electric Power	$25,753	100	100
52	463	NEC	$25,673	100	100
			AVE %	96.8	98.4

Methodology

We used a random number generator to identify 20 of the Global 500 companies based in each country. Board and executive nationalities for these companies were determined using annual reports, *Bloomberg*, *Wall Street Journal*, and other search tools.

China-Based Fortune Global 500 Executive and Board Composition (Percentage of Chinese Nationals, 2018)

China Rank	500 Rank	Company	Revenue	Exec. %	BoD %
7	31	China Construction Bank	$138,594	100	86
9	40	Agricultural Bank of China	$122,366	100	100
11	46	Bank of China	$115,423	100	100
16	72	Huawei Investment & Holding	$89,311	100	100
22	101	China Energy Investment	$75,522	100	100
23	109	China Minmetals	$72,997	100	100
24	149	CITIC Group	$61,316	100	100
47	227	Shanghai Pudong Development Bank	$46,295	100	100
52	239	HBIS Group	$45,390	100	100
68	295	AIA Group	$38,330	31	73
72	323	Midea Group	$35,794	100	100
85	364	Jiangsu Shagang Group	$32,561	100	100
88	371	China National Aviation Fuel Group	$31,942	100	100
90	375	Xiamen Xiangyu Group	$31,676	100	100
91	381	Xinxing Cathay International Group	$31,078	100	88
95	395	State Power Investment	$29,727	100	100
98	427	Suning.com Group	$27,806	100	100
101	456	Xinjiang Guanghui Industry Investment	$26,106	100	100
102	464	Yango Longking Group	$25,605	100	100
103	496	Henan Energy & Chemical	$23,699	100	100
			AVE %	**96.6**	**97.4**

NOTES

CHAPTER 1

1. According to the World Bank, in 2020 China had 771.3 million people employed of which 50% were employed by the government, including in state-owned enterprises. https://www.businessinsider.com/chart-of-the-day-government-sector-employment-2011-11.

2. According to the World Bank, China had tax revenue of 9.053% of GDP in 2019, and its GDP was $14.28 trillion.

3. Yang, Y. (2019). "China to Invest 800b Yuan in Railways in 2020." *China Daily*, December 27. https://www.chinadaily.com.cn/a/201912/27/WS5e05 94e9a310cf3e3558114c.html.

4. "China's Got a New Plan to Overtake the US in Tech." *Bloomberg*, May 20, 2020.

5. Black, J. S., and Morrison, A. J. (2014). *Failure to Globally Launch*. Global Leadership Press.

6. Black, J. S., and Morrison, A. J. (2020). "Can China Avoid a Growth Crisis?" *Harvard Business Review*, September–October.

7. Rapoza, K. "Intel CEO Quietly Warns of China's 'Great Bay Area' Project." *Forbes*, December 13, 2019. https://www.forbes.com/sites/kenrapoza/ 2020/12/13/intel-ceo-quietly-warns-of-chinas-greater-bay-area-project/?sh=12c2233217d0.

8. Jingrong Lin, K., Lu, X., Zhang, J., and Zheng, Y. (2020). "State-owned Enterprises in China: A Review of 40 Years of Research and Practice," *China Journal of Accounting Research*, 13(1), 31–55. https://www.ualberta.ca/ china-institute/media-library/media-gallery/research/policy-papers/soepa-per1-2018.pdf.

9. Zhang, C. (2019). "How Much Do State-Owned Enterprises Contribute to China's GDP and Employment?" https://documents1.worldbank.org/ curated/en/449701565248091726/pdf/How-Much-Do-State-Owned-Enterprises-Contribute-to-China-s-GDP-and-Employment.pdf.

10. "Profile: Jack Ma, Founder and Executive Chairman, Alibaba Group." *Forbes*. https://www.forbes.com/profile/jack-ma/?sh=73a5b0381ee4.

11. Wei, L. "China Blocked Jack Ma's Ant IPO after Investigation Revealed Likely Beneficiaries," *Wall Street Journal*, February 16, 2021. https://www.wsj.com/articles/china-blocked-jack-mas-ant-ipo-after-an-investigation-revealed-who-stood-to-gain-11613491292.

12. China's Ministry of Finance (2021).

13. Molnar, M., and Lu, J. (2019). "State-Owned Firms behind China's Corporate Debt." https://www.oecd.org/officialdocuments/publicdisplaydocumentpdf/?cote=ECO/WKP(2019)5&docLanguage=En.

14. Belsie, L. (2019). "Favoritism toward China's Former State-Owned Enterprises." National Bureau of Economic Research. https://www.nber.org/digest/mar19/favoritism-toward-chinas-former-state-owned-enterprises.

15. Milhaupt, C., and Zheng, W. (2015). "Beyond Ownership: State Capitalism and the Chinese Firm." *Georgetown Law Journal*, 103, 666–722. https://www-cdn.law.stanford.edu/wp-content/uploads/2017/04/103GeoLJ665.pdf.

16. Mitter, R., and Johnson, E. (2021). "What the West Gets Wrong about China." *Harvard Business Review*, May.

17. As reported in Shikun, M. (2021). "Why Chinese People Support Their Government." *China-US Focus*, May 28.

18. Kipping, M. "The Demise of The 'Middle Kingdom': How a Refresher in Chinese History Might Help US Government." *Forbes*, March 8, 2017.

19. Wang, Z. (2012). *Never Forget National Humiliation: Historical Memory in Chinese Politics and Foreign Policy*. Columbia University Press.

CHAPTER 2

1. Office of the US Trade Representative. (2018). "Findings of the Investigation into China's Acts, Policies, and Practices Related to Technology Transfer, Intellectual Property, and Innovation under Section 301 of the Trade Act of 1974." March 22.

2. *Ancient Civilizations: The Middle Kingdom*. (2019). https://www.ushistory.org/civ/9a.asp.

3. Zhu, X. (2012). "Understanding China's Growth: Past, Present, and Future." *Journal of Economic Perspectives*, 26(4), 103–124.

4. For a full review of the historical decline of China, see Brandt, L., Ma, D., and Rawski, T. (2012). "From Divergence to Convergence: Re-evaluating

the History behind China's Economic Boom." *Economic History Working Papers 41660*, London School of Economics and Political Science, Department of Economic History.

5. Madison, A. (2007). *Contours of the World Economy, 1–2030 AD*. Oxford University Press.

6. As cited by Ljunggren, B. (2017). "Under Xi, China Aims to Be the World's Middle Kingdom." *YaleGlobal Online*, October 31, Yale University.

7. Kotkin, J. (2011). "Rise of the Hans." *Foreign Policy*, January 17.

8. Zheng, W. (2021). "China's Officials Play Pp 'Rise of the East, Decline of the West.'" *South China Morning Post*, March 9.

9. "How Is China Feeding Its Population of 1.4 Billion?" *China Power*. https://chinapower.csis.org/china-food-security.

10. China Strategy Group. (2020)."Asymmetric Competition: A Strategy for China & Technology: Actionable Insights for American Leadership," Fall.

11. Office of the US Trade Representative. (2018). "Findings of the Investigation into China's Acts, Policies, and Practices Related to Technology Transfer, Intellectual Property, and Innovation under Section 301 of the Trade Act of 1974," March 22.

12. Ross, J. (2020). "The Dominance of US Companies in Global Markets." *Visual Capitalist*, February 20. https://www.visualcapitalist.com/us-companies-global-markets/.

13. "2019's Most-Innovative Countries in Nanotechnology." *Statnano*, November 21, p. 201.

14. "Global Photonics Market Size 2021–2025 with Top-Countries Data and Covid-19 Analysis, by Industry Trends, Size, Share, Company Overview, Growth, Development and Forecast." *MarketWatch*, April 26, 2021.

15. "Machinery & Equipment Industry." *Germany Trade and Investment*, 2021; "Germany Machinery and Equipment Industry Is the Top of the World." *Market Prospects*, August 12, 2020.

16. "Taking Stock of China's Semiconductor Industry." Semiconductor Industry Association, July 13, 2021. https://www.semiconductors.org/taking-stock-of-chinas-semiconductor-industry/.

17. "China Opens More Industries to Foreign Investment." *Agence France Press*, June 24, 2020. https://www.barrons.com/news/china-opens-more-industries-to-foreign-investment-01592997006.

18. Friedberg, A. (2022). *Getting China Wrong*. Polity Press.

19. Office of the US Trade Representative. (2018). "Findings of the Investigation into China's Acts, Policies, and Practices Related to Technology Transfer, Intellectual Property, and Innovation under Section 301 of the Trade Act of 1974." March 22, p. 19.

20. Covington & Burling LLP. (Aug. 2014). *Measures and Practices Restraining Foreign Investment in China*. Prepared for the European Commission Directorate-General for Trade 11.

21. American Chamber of Commerce. (2013). "China Business Climate Survey."

22. Crane, K., et al. (2014). "The Effectiveness of China's Industrial Policies in Commercial Aviation Manufacturing." The Rand Corporation, p. 30.

23. National Association of Manufacturers. (2017). *Submission, Section 301, US Trade Representative*, September 28.

24. Lardy, N. (2018). "Does China Force Foreign Firms to Surrender Their Sensitive Technology?" *Peterson Institute for International Economics*, December 10.

25. Deloitte (2020). "Sino-Foreign Joint Ventures after Covid-19: What to Expect." September.

26. Office of the US Trade Representative. (2018), p.19.

27. "2019 Report to Congress." *US-China Economic and Security Review Commission*. November.

28. Ranjard, P., and Misonne, B. (2007). "Study 12: Exploring China's IP Environment." *Study on the Future Opportunities and Challenges of EU-China Trade and Investment Relations 24.*

29. National Foreign Trade Council, submission to the 2018 USTR 301 report, p. 41.

30. Office of the US Trade Representative. (2018). "Findings of the Investigation into China's Acts, Policies, and Practices Related to Technology Transfer, Intellectual Property, and Innovation under Section 301 of the Trade Act of 1974." March 22. P. 48.

31. OECD/EUIPO. (2019). *Trends in Trade in Counterfeit and Pirated Goods*, March 18. https://www.oecd- ilibrary.org/docserver/g2g9f533-en.pdf.

32. US Customs and Border Protection. (2019). *Intellectual Property Rights Annual Seizure Statistics*. https://www.cbp.gov/trade/priority-issues/ipr/statistics.

33. See Jintao, H. (2006). "The International Situation and Our Diplomatic Work.", In *Selected Works of Hu Jintao* (Vol. II, pp. 505–506, 510–515). People's Publishing House.

34. Rosenbaum, E. (2019). "1 in 5 Corporations Say China Has Stolen Their IP within the Last Year: CNBC CFO Survey," March 1.

35. Voo, J., et al. (2020). "National Cyber Power Index." Harvard Kennedy School, Belfer Center for Science and International Affairs, September.

36. "China in Africa: China's Telecommunications Footprint in Africa." *Institute of Developing Economies, Japan External Trade Organization.* https://www.ide.go.jp/English/Data/Africa_file/Manualreport/cia_09.html.

37. "Global Energy Cyber Attacks: Night Dragon," McAfee Foundstone Professional Services & McAfee Labs, February 10, 2011.

38. Volz, D., Viswanatha, A., and O'Keeffe, K. (2020). "U.S. Charges Chinese Nationals in Cyberattacks on More Than 100 Companies." *Wall Street Journal*, September 16.

39. Yehoshua, M. (2020) "State-Sponsored Hackers Target Big Pharmaceuticals." *SC Magazine*, March 5.

40. US District Court, Western District of Pennsylvania, United States of America vs Wang Don, Sun Kailiang, Wen Xinyu, Huang Zhenyu, and Gu Chunhui, May 1, 2014, p. 2. https://www.justice.gov/iso/opa/resources/512201451913235846194

9.pdf.

41. As reported in Miller, M. (2020). "FBI Director Warns That Chinese Hackers Are Still Targeting US COVID-19 Research." *The Hill.* September 24. https://thehill.com/policy/cybersecurity/518051-fbi-director-warns-that-chinese-hackers-are-still-targeting-us-covid-19.

42. Ibid.

43. Office of the US Trade Representative. (2018), pp. 164–165.

44. Office of the US Trade Representative. (2018), p. 172.

45. U.S. Chamber of Commerce. (2012). "China's Approval Process for Inbound Foreign Investment: Impact on Market Access, National Treatment and Transparency," November.

46. U.S. China Business Council, Submission, Section 301 US Trade Representative, October 20, 2017.

47. "The IP Commission Report: The Report of the Commission on the Theft of American Intellectual Property." National Bureau of Asian Research, 2013.

48. Office of the US Trade Representative. (2018), p. 65.

49. De La Bruyère, E., and Picarsic, N. (2019). "CRRC and Beijing's Dash for Global Rolling Stock Dominance." Radarlock. https://www.railwayage.com/wp-content/uploads/2019/11/Raderlock-CRRC-Report-October-2019.pdf.

50. Ibid., p. 19.

51. "Huawei Exquisite and Elegant Light Rail Train Glory Debut." CRRC, May 10, 2018.

52. "National 13th Five-Year Plan for the Development of Strategic Emerging Technologies" (Translation). Center for Security and Emerging Technology. Official Website of the Central People's Government of the People's Republic of China, December 9, 2019. https://cset.georgetown.edu/research/national-13th-five-year-plan-for-the-development-of-strategic-emerging-industries/. Also, see Notice on Issuing the 12th Five-year National Strategic Emerging Industries Development Plan (State Council, Guo Fa [2012] No. 28, issued July 9, 2012).

53. Office of the US Trade Representative (2018), pp. 13–14.

54. "National 13th Five-Year Plan for the Development of Strategic Emerging Technologies."

55. Tang, G. (2020). "China Unveils 'Strategic Emerging Industries' Plan in Fresh Push to Get Away from US Technologies." *South China Morning Post*, September 24.

56. Spuijbroek, M. (2020). "Launch of New SEI Plan (Strategic Emerging Industries)." *Datenna*, September 30. https://www.datenna.com/2020/09/30/launch-of-new-sei-plan-strategic-emerging-industries/.

57. "Is China a Global Leader in Research and Development?" *China Power*. https://chinapower.csis.org/china-research-and-development-rnd/.

58. For more on quantum key distribution technologies, see Gillis, A. (2020). "Quantum Key Distribution (QKD)." TechTarget, January. https://www.techtarget.com/searchsecurity/definition/quantum-key-distribution-QKD.

59. Fitch, A., and Woo, S. (2020). "The US vs. China: Who Is Winning Key Technology Battles?" *Wall Street Journal*, April 12.

60. "Is China a Global Leader in Research and Development?" *China Power*. https://chinapower.csis.org/china-research-and-development-rnd/.

61. World Economic Forum. "Human Capital Report, 2016." https://reports.weforum.org/human-capital-report-2016/.

62. NSF. "Survey of Earned Doctorates," December 1, 2020. https://ncses.nsf. gov/pubs/nsf21308/report/executive-summary.

63. Woolston, C. and O'Meara, S. (2019). "China's PhD Students Give Their Reasons for Misery." *Nature*, 575, 711–713.

64. O'Keefe, K., and Viswanatha, A. (2020). WSJ, "How China Targets Scientists via Global Network of Recruiting Stations." August 20. https://www.wsj.com/ articles/how-china-targets-scientists-via-global-network-of-recruiting-stations-11597915803?mod=searchresults&page=1&pos=9b.

65. Joske, A. (2020). "Hunting the Phoenix: The Chinese Communist Party's Global Search for Technology and Talent." *Australian Strategic Policy Institute*. August 20. https://www.aspi.org.au/ report/hunting-phoenix].

66. Koshikawa, N. (2020). "China Passes US as World's Top Researcher, Showing Its R&D Might." *Nikkei Asia*, August 8.

67. Schoff, J., and Ito, A. (2019). "Competing with China on Technology and Innovation." Alliance Policy Coorination Brief, Carnegie Endowment for International Peace, October 10.

68. https://ccc.technews.tw/2020/12/09/oled-boe-china; http://www.businesskorea .co.kr/news/articleView.html?idxno=56341.

69. Office of the US Trade Representative (2018).

70. As quoted by Osnos, E. (2020). "The Future of America's Context with China." *The New Yorker*, January 6.

CHAPTER 3

1. https://data.gov.sg/dataset/total-visitor-international-arrivals-to-singapore.

2. https://www.hospitalitynet.org/file/152008555.pdf.

3. "China Gas Use to Rise 10pc in 2021: Sinopec, PetroChina," May 3, 2021, *Argus*. https://www.argusmedia.com/en/news/2211256-china-gas-use-to-rise-10pc-in-2021-sinopec-petrochina.

4. For more on national champions, see Morrison, A. J., and Black, J. S. (2014). *Failure to Globally Launch: A Business Parable for Aspiring Market Giants*. Global Leadership Press.

5. García-Herrero, A., and Ng, G. (2021). 'China's State-Owned Enterprises and Competitive Neutrality," Policy Contribution, 05.

6. http://www.gov.cn/guowuyuan/2018-10/19/content_5332515.htm; http://www.xinhuanet.com/politics/2018-11/01/c_1123649488.htm.

7. https://www.piie.com/blogs/china-economic-watch/china-only-nibbling-problem-zombie-state-owned-enterprises.

8. https://www.institutmontaigne.org/en/blog/europe-china-rail-competition-bigger-better.

9. https://world-nuclear.org/information-library/country-profiles/countries-a-f/china-nuclear-power.aspx.

10. https://www.globaltimes.cn/page/202101/1213053.shtml.

11. https://www.theguardian.com/news/2018/jun/29/the-great-firewall-of-china-xi-jinpings-internet-shutdown.

12. Somaney, J. (2015). "Chinese Government Has a Huge Stake in Alibaba," *Forbes*. https://www.forbes.com/sites/jaysomaney/2015/10/18/chinese-government-has-a-huge-stake-in-alibaba/?sh=1d40ed7025b8.

13. https://www.bloomberg.com/features/2016-didi-cheng-wei/.

14. https://hbr.org/2018/09/alibaba-and-the-future-of-business.

15. Ibid.

16. Ibid.

17. Ibid.

CHAPTER 4

1. Osnos, E. (2020). "The Future of America's Contest with China." *The New Yorker*, January 6.

2. Pop, V., Hua, S., and Michaels, D. (2021). "From Lightbulbs to 5G, China Battles West for Control of Vital Technology Standards." *Wall Street Journal*, February 7.

3. Dalton, M. (2021). "Chinese Manufacturers Sidestep Trade Barriers by Buying Factories Overseas." *Wall Street Journal*, May 6.

4. Williamson, P., and Raman, A. (2011). "The Globe: How China Reset Its Global Acquisition Agenda." *Harvard Business Review*, April.

5. https://www.reuters.com/article/china-syngenta-ipo-idAFL2N2OC0BC.

6. Qiao, G., and Conyers, Y. (2014). *The Lenovo Way*. McGraw-Hill Education.

7. Jianhong, Z., and Ebbers, H. (2010). "Why Half of China's Overseas Acquisitions Could Not Be Completed." *Journal of Current Chinese Affairs*, 39(2), 101–131.

8. Rosen, D. H. (2021). "China's Economic Reckoning." *Foreign Affairs*, July–August. https://www.foreignaffairs.com/articles/china/2021-06-22/chinas-economic-reckoning

9. European Commission. (2012). "Commission Staff Working Document of Significant Distortions in the Economy of the People's Republic of China for the Purpose of Trade Defence Investigation 426," December 20, as cited by Office of the US Trade Representative (2018). "Findings of the Investigation into China's Acts, Policies, and Practices Related to Technology Transfer, Intellectual Property, and Innovation under Section 301 of the Trade Act of 1974," March 22.

10. Jost Wübbeke et al. (2016)."Made In China 2025: The Making of a High-Tech Superpower and Consequences for Industrial Countries 7-8." Mercator Institute For China Studies, December.

11. For more on the "Going Out" strategy, Buckley, P., Clegg, L., Cross, A., et al. (2007). "The Determinants of Chinese Outward Foreign Direct Investment." *Journal of International Business Studies*, 38(4), 499–518.

12. European Union Chamber of Commerce in China. (2017). "China Manufacturing 2025: Putting Industrial Policy Ahead of Market Forces."

13. Based on 2018 data. *Forbes*, "The World's Largest Public Companies, 2018" and *Fortune 500* (2018).

14. "Chinese Companies Listed on Major U.S. Stock Exchanges." US-China Economic and Security Review Commission, May 13, 2021. https://www.uscc.gov/research/chinese-companies-listed-major-us-stock-exchanges.

15. Textor, C. (2021). "Capital Stock of Chinese Outward Foreign Direct Investment (FD) from 2010 to 2020." *Statista*, October 28. https://www.statista.com/statistics/865550/china-stock-of-direct-investments-abroad/.

16. "What Was the State of Chinese Outbound Investment in 2019." *EY Greater China*. February 1, 2020. https://www.ey.com/en_cn/china-opportunities/what-was-the-state-of-chinese-outbound-investment-in-2019.

17. Kynge, J., and Liu, N. (2020). "How China Is Setting New Global Rules in Technology That Would Make George 'Orwell Blush.'" *Financial Times*, October 23.

18. Koty, A. C. (2020). "What Is the China Standards 2035 Plan and How Will It Impact Emerging Industries?" *China Briefing*, July 2. https://www.china-

briefing.com/news/what-is-china-standards-2035-plan-how-will-it-impact-emerging-technologies-what-is-link-made-in-china-2025-goals/.

19. Woyke, E. (2019). "China Is Racing Ahead in 5G. Here's What That Means." *MIT Technology Review*. January.

20. "5G: The Chance to Lead for a Decade" Deloitte, 2018.

21. Woyke, E. (2019).

22. Bartholomew, C. (2020). "China and 5G." *Issues in Science and Technology*, 36(2).

23. As quoted by Kyne, J., and Liu, N. (2020). "From AI to facial recognition: how China is setting the rules in new tech." *Financial Times*. October 6.

24. Johnson, K. and Groll, E. (2019). "The Improbable Rise of Huawei." *Foreign Policy*, April 3.

25. Feng, E. (2020). "The Latest U.S. Blow to China's Huawei Could Knock Out Its Global 5G Plans." *NPR*, May 28. https://www.npr.org/2020/05/28/862658646/the-latest-u-s-blow-to-chinas-huawei-could-knock-out-its-global-5g-plans].

26. Johnson, K., and Groll, E. (2019). "The Improbable Rise of Huawei." *Foreign Policy*, April 3.

27. Xue, Y. (2021). "US-China Tech War: Huawei Pushes Licensing of 5G Mobile Technology amid Struggles with Washington's Trade Sanctions." *South China Morning Post*, March 16. https://www.scmp.com/tech/big-tech/article/3125690/us-china-tech-war-huawei-pushes-licensing-5g-mobile-technology-ami.

28. "China Standards 2035 and the Plan for World Domination-Don't Believe China's Hype." *Council on Foreign Relations*, June 3, 2020.

29. "What Was the State of Chinese Outbound Investment in 2019."

30. For more on the BRI see Chatzky, A., and McBride, J. (2020). "China's Massive Belt and Road Initiative." *Council on Foreign Relations*, January 28.

31. "Inside China's Plan to Create a Modern Silk Road." Morgan Stanley, March 14, 2018. https://www.morganstanley.com/ideas/china-belt-and-road.

32. Grosse, R., Gamso, J., and Nelson, R. (2021). "China's Rise, World Order, and the Implications for International Business." *Management International Review*, March 3.

33. Chatzky, A., and McBride, J. (2020). "China's Massive Belt and Road Initiative." *Council on Foreign Relations*, January 28.

34. Curran, E. (2018). "The AIIB: China's World Bank." *Bloomberg*, August 6. https://www.bloomberg.com/quicktake/chinas-world-bank.

35. Jin, F. (2017). "The Belt and Road Initiative: Progress, Problems and Prospects." *Center for Strategic & International Studies*, September.

36. "Dance of the Lions and Dragons: How Are Africa and China Engage, and How Will the Partnership Evolve." McKinsey & Company, 2017.

37. Lai, K., Lin, S., and Sidaway, J. (2020). "Financing the Belt and Road Initiative (BRI): Research Agendas beyond the 'Debt-Trap' Discourse." *Eurasian Geography and Economics*, 61(2), 109–124.

38. Osnos, E. (2020). "The Future of America's Contest with China." *The New Yorker*, January 6.

39. "2020 Report to Congress of the U.S.-China Economic and Security Review Commission One Hundred Sixteenth Congress." Second Session, December 2020, p. 5.

40. Ker, M. "China's High Speed Rail Diplomacy." *U.S.-China Economic and Security Review Commission*, February 21, 2017.

41. Ma, D. "China's Long, Bumpy Road to High-Speed Rail." *The Atlantic*, March 30, 2011. https://www.theatlantic.com/international/archive/2011/03/chinas-long-bumpy-road-to-high-speed- rail/73192.

42. Shirouzu, N. (2010). "Train Makers Rail against China's High-Speed Designs." *Wall Street Journal*, November 17; Anderlini, J., and Dickie, M. (2010). "China: A Future on Track." *Financial Times*, September 23.

43. Cory, N. (2021). "Heading off Track: The Impact of China's Mercantilist Policies on Global High Speed Rail Innovation." Information Technology & Innovation Foundation, April.

44. Lawrence, M., Bullock, and Liu, Z. (2019). "China's High-Speed Rail Development." World Bank Publications. https://documents1.worldbank.org/curated/en/933411559841476316/pdf/Chinas-High-Speed-Rail-Development.pdf.

45. Cory, N. (2021).

46. Kynge, J., Peel, M., and Bland, B. (2017). "China's Railway Diplomacy Hits the Buffers." *Financial Times*, July 17. https://www.ft.com/content/9a4aab54-624d-11e7-8814-0ac7eb84e5f1.

47. "Railway Equipment Manufacturing in China Industry Trends: Market Research Report." *IBIS World*, March 12, 2020. https://www.ibisworld.com/china/market-research-reports/railway-equipment-manufacturing-industry/.

48. Lal, A. (2020). "The CPEC Challenge and the India-China Standoff: An Opportunity for War or Peace?" *The Times of India*, August 9.

49. Kratz, A., and Kingley, M. (2019). "Leveraging the Chinese State against Foreign Firms: Rail and Beyond." Rhodium Group report, March 19.

50. Rogers, J., Foxall, A., Henderson, M., and Armstrong, S. (2020). "Breaking the China Supply Chain: How the 'Five Eyes' Can Decouple From Strategic Dependency." *Henry Jackson Society*, May 2020.

51. Rogers et al. (2020), pp 24, 26.

52. As reported by the "Findings of the Investigation into China's Acts, Policies, and Practices Related to Technology Transfer, Intellectual Property, and Innovation Under Section 301 of the Trade Act of 1974," Office of the U.S. Trade Representative, 03/22/18, pp. 158–159.

53. https://www.scmp.com/news/china/diplomacy/article/3130990/chinas-dominance-rare-earths-supply-growing-concern-west; Simmons, L. (2016). "Rare-Earth Market." *Foreign Policy*, July 12. https://foreignpolicy.com/2016/07/12/decoder-rare-earth-market-tech-defense-clean-energy-china-trade/.

54. https://www.statista.com/statistics/279895/us-rare-earth-import-value/.

55. Cimino, A. (2019). "Shrugging off China Tariffs, Walmart and Target May Be This Season's Jolliest Retailers." *The Motley Fool*, November 25. https://www.fool.com/investing/2019/11/25/   shrugging-off-china-tariffs-walmart-and-target-may.aspx.

56. "10 US Companies with Highest Revenue Exposure to China." Yahoo.com, August 2, 2020. https://www.yahoo.com/lifestyle/10-us-companies-highest-revenue-225350456.html; Swaminathan, A. (2018). "Here Are the Big Stocks with the Most Exposure to China." Yahoo.com. August 1, 2018. https://finance.yahoo.com/news/big-stocks-exposure-china-185734394.html.

CHAPTER 5

1. Bughin, J., and Woetzel, J. (2019). "Navigating a World of Disruption." McKinsey Global Institute, Executive Briefing, January 22, p. iv.

2. https://assets.kpmg/content/dam/kpmg/cn/pdf/en/2018/09/leading-chinese-cross-border-brands-the-top-50.pdf.

3. https://www.npr.org/2019/08/30/756034624/why-many-u-s-companies-have-kept-production-in-china-and-have-no-plans-of-moving.

4. Swithinbank, R. (2021). "China Takes the Lead in Demand for Swiss Watches." *New York Times*, January 14.

5. Johnson, M. (2021). "How Alibaba Makes Money." *Investopedia*, October 13.

6. Engen, John. "Lessons from a Mobile Payments Revolution." https://www.americanbanker.com/news/why-chinas-mobile-payments-revolution-matters-for-us-bankers.

7. https://techcrunch.com/2021/10/14/microsoft-to-pull-linkedin-from-chinese-market/.

8. https://www.gq.com/story/nike-adidas-shifting-production-asia.

9. https://www.cnn.com/2021/10/02/business/vietnam-supply-chain-disruptions/index.html.

10. https://www.cnn.com/2021/03/25/business/hm-nike-xinjiang-cotton-boycott-intl-hnk/index.html.

11. Woo, S. (2022). "Chinese Sportswear Company Anta Gains on Nike, Adidas over Forced-Labor Issue." *Wall Street Journal*, January 5.

12. https://www.nasdaq.com/articles/apple-inc-aapl-q1-2019-earnings-conference-call-transcript-2019-01-29.

13. https://www.inc.com/glenn-leibowitz/apple-ceo-tim-cook-this-is-number-1-reason-we-make-iphones-in-china-its-not-what-you-think.html.

14. Xin, L. (2019). "China and Coca-Cola: A Common Development Trajectory." *China Today*, March 4. http://www.chinatoday.com.cn/ctenglish/2018/et/201903/t20190304_800158961.html.

15. Reuters. (2016). "Swire Pacific to Buy Coca-Cola Bottling Assets in China for $852 Million," November 17. www.swire-pacific-to-buy-coca-cola-bottling-assets-in-china-for-852-million-idUSKBN13D0DU.

16. Knowledge @ Wharton. (2009). "Coca-Cola's Failed Bid for China Huiyuan Juice: The Return of Protectionism? "April 1. https://www.coca-colas-failed-bid-for-china-huiyuan-juice-the-return-of-protectionism.

17. Ibid.

18. Wang, J. (2016). "Coca-Cola's Future More Localized and Diverse in China." *China Daily*. November 22. https://www.chinadaily.com.cn/cndy/2016-11/22/content_27448327.htm.

19. Moss, T. (2021). "Honeywell's Formula for Success in China." *The Wall Street Journal*, October 22. https://www.wsj.com/articles/honeywells-formula-

for-success-in-china-11634911201?st=om3w8u9dfsgcdte&reflink=article_email_share.

20. Ibid.

21. http://www.xinhuanet.com/english/2019-09/25/c_138421326.htm.

22. Moss, Trefor (2021).

23. Ibid.

24. Ibid.

25. Ibid.

26. Shane, D. (2019). "Robot Waiters and Snail Pizza: What US Fast Food Brands Do to Please Chinese Diners." *CNN Business*, June 5.

27. Yum China website, http://www.yumchina.com/brand. Accessed June 23, 2020.

28. "Yum! Brands Announces Intention to Separate into Two Publicly Traded Companies." Yum! Brands press release, October 20, 2015. https://www.businesswire.com/news/home/20151020005767/en/Yum%21-Brands-Announces-Intention-Separate-Publicly-Traded.

29. "Yum China's KFC Partners Sinopec & CNPC to Open Restaurants." Yahooo! Finance. December 19. https://finance.yahoo.com/news/yum-chinas-kfc-partners-sinopec-150803685.html

30. Yum China 2019 Annual Report.

31. "Yum China Named Official Retail Food Services Sponsor of the Beijing 2022 Olympic Winter Games." Yum China Press Release, July 20, 2020.

CHAPTER 6

1. "How Many Companies Exist in the World?" Quora. https://www.quora.com/How-many-companies-exist-in-the-world.

2. "German Business in China: business Confidence Survey 2019/20." German Chamber of Commerce and KPMG. https://mediafra.admiralcloud.com/customer.

3. "British Business in China: Sentiment Survey. 2020–2021." British Chamber of Commerce in China, 2020, p. 10.

4. Kharpal, A. (2019). "Amazon Is Shutting Down Its China Marketplace Business. Here's Why It Has Struggled." *CNBC*. April 18. https://www.cnbc.com/2019/04/18/amazon-china-marketplace-closing-down-heres-why.html.

5. Miaomiao, M. (2019) "Clothes Make the Man." *Beijing Review*, May 13. http://www.bjreview.com/Business/201905/t20190513_800167545.html.

6. Translated from https://www.sohu.com/a/ 396809304_100123330?scm= 1019.e000a.v1.0&spm=smpc.csrpage.news-list.112.1595205589205 xe6or2H).

7. Wernau, J. (2019). "America Is Losing the Chinese Shopper." *Wall Street Journal*, October 12.

8. https://prosperousamerica.org/china-solar-moves-to-se-asia-to-beat-anti-dumping-countervailing-duties/.

9. https://www.reuters.com/business/energy/us-solar-companies-warn-that-proposed-tariffs-would-devastate-new-projects-2021-09-22/

10. Ibid.

11. Ibid.

12. Company documents plus McKay, H. (2020). "How Much of the United States Does China Really Own?" *Fox News*, June 30. https://www.foxnews.com/world/how-much-of-the-united-states-does-china-really-own.

13. "Commission Staff Working Document on Foreign Direct Investment in the EU." European Commission, March 13, 2019.

14. "Foreign Direct Investment (FDI) from China in the United States from 2000–2019." *Statista*, 2021. https://www.statista.com/statistics/188935/foreign-direct-investment-from-china-in-the-united-states/.

15. "China Owns Us." (2021). American Security Institute.

16. Stubley, P. (2021). "China Now Owns £143bn in UK assets, from Nuclear Power to Pubs and Schools." *Independent*, May 3.

17. For more on this story, see Singh, R. K. (2019). "Farm Equipment Maker Deere's Dealers Reel from Trade War, Bad Weather." Reuters, August 9. https://www.reuters.com/article/us-deere-dealers-sales/farm-equipment-maker-deeres-dealers-reel-from-trade-war-bad-weather-idUSKCN1UZ21F.

18. Xiao, E. (2021). "H&M Is Erased from Chinese E-Commerce over Xinjiang Stance." *Wall Street Journal*, March 25.

19. For more on these legal developments, see Hager, N. (2021). "China Retaliates against US Export Restrictions, Adopts new Blocking Rules." Riley Rein LLP https://www.jdsupra.com/legalnews/china-retaliates-against-u-s-export-9612488/.

20. Zhai, K. (2021). "China Plans to Ban U.S. IPOs for Data-Heavy Tech Firms." *Wall Street Journal*, August 27.

21. Pottinger, M. (2021). "Beijing Targets American Business." *Wall Street Journal*, March 26. https://www.wsj.com/articles/beijing-targets-american-business-11616783268?mod=hp_opin_pos_3.

22. Higgs, R. (2008). "The Complex Course of Ideological Change." *The American Journal of Economics and Sociology*, 67(4), 547–566. http://www.jstor.org/stable/27739728.

23. "Who Manufacturers GoPro Cameras?" Quora. https://www.quora.com/Who-manufactures-GoPro-cameras.

24. "GoPro Reiterates Plans to Move U.S. Bound Camera Production to Mexico." GoPro Press Release, May 13, 2019. https://investor.gopro.com/press-releases/press-release-details/2019/GoPro-Reiterates-Plans-to-Move-US-Bound-Camera-Production-to-Mexico/default.aspx

25. Choi, T., Shao, B, and Zhan, M. (2015). "Hidden Suppliers Can Make or Break Your Operations." *Harvard Business Review*, May.

26. Tajitsu, N., Yamazaki, M., and Shimizu, R. (2020). "Source: Japan Wants Manufacturing Back from China, but Breaking Up Supply Chains Is Hard to Do." Reuters, June 8. https://www.reuters.com/article/us-health-coronavirus-japan-production-a/japan-wants-manufacturing-back-from-china-but-breaking-up-supply-chains-is-hard-to-do-idUSKBN23F2ZO.

27. Zhang, J. (2021). "Chinese Smartphone Maker Hopes to Quick-Charge Growth at Home after Conquering Indian market." *South China Morning Post*, December 2.

28. https://asia.nikkei.com/Spotlight/Huawei-crackdown/Chinese-components-double-to-60-in-new-Huawei-smartphone.

CHAPTER 7

1. We are grateful to Robert Theleen, CEO of ChinaVest, for coining these descriptors.

2. Abrami, R., Kirby, W., and McFarlan, W. (2014). "Why China Can't Innovate." *Harvard Business Review*, March.

3. Boeing, Philipp, et al. (2015). "China's R&D Explosion Analyzing Productivity Effects across Ownership Types and over Time." *SSRN Electronic Journal*. doi:10.2139/ssrn.2570736.

4. He, L., and Disis, J. (2021). "Can China Still Lead the World in Tech without a New Jack Ma?" *CNN Business*, June 8. https://www.cnn.com/2021/06/07/tech/china-tech-crackdown-entrepreneurs-intl-hnk/index.html.

5. Abrami et al. (2014).

6. https://www.statista.com/statistics/270325/distribution-of-gross-domestic-product-gdp-across-economic-sectors-in-china/.

7. "Fastest Growing Industries in China by Revenue Growth (%) in 2022." *IBIS World.* https://www.ibisworld.com/china/industry-trends/fastest-growing-industries/.

8. Lardy, N. (2001). "Issues in China's WTO Accession." *Brookings*, May 9. https://www.brookings.edu/testimonies/issues-in-chinas-wto-accession/.

9. USTR, "2020 Report to Congress on China's WTO compliance," January 2021, p. 2. https://ustr.gov/sites/default/files/files/reports/2020/2020USTRReportCongressChinaWTOCompliance.pdf.

10. Bacchus, J., Lester, S., and Zhu, H. "Disciplining China's Trade Practices at the WTO: How WTO Complaints Can Help Make China More Market-Oriented." CATO Institute, policy analysis 856, November 15, 2018.

11. Black, J. S., and Morrison, A. J. (2021). "The Strategic Challenges of Decoupling: Navigation Your Company's Future in China." *Harvard Business Review*, May–June, 49–54.

12. Batarags, L. (2021). "China Has at least 65 Million Empty Homes—Enough to House the Population of France. It Offers a Glimpse into the Country's Massive Housing-Market Problem." Insider, October 14. https://www.businessinsider.com/china-empty-homes-real-estate-evergrande-housing-market-problem-2021-10#:~:text=China%20has%20at%20least%2065,country's%20massive%20housing%2Dmarket%20problem.&text=One%2Dfifth%20of%20the%20homes,house%20the%20population%20of%20France.

13. https://www.nytimes.com/2013/06/16/world/asia/chinas-great-uprooting-moving-250-million-into-cities.html.

14. Black and Morrison (2021). See also "Why are Foreign Tech firms pulling out of China." *Bloomberg*, November 3, 2021. https://www.bloomberg.com/news/articles/2021-11-03/explainer-why-Are Foreign Tech firms Pulling Out-of-china.

15. Xie, S., and Qi, L. (2021). "Chinese Factories Are Having Labor Pains—'We Can Hardly Find Any Workers.'" *Wall Street Journal*, August 25.

16. Stroh, L., Mendenhall, M. J., Stewart Black, J. S., and Gregersen, H. (2005). *International Assignments: An Integration of Research and Practice*. Erlbaum.

17. Black, J. S., and Morrison, A. J. (2020). *The Global Leadership Challenge* (3rd edi. Routledge.

18. Black, J. S., and Morrison, A. J. (2010). *Sunset in the Land of the Rising Sun: Why Japanese MNCs Will Struggle in a Global Future*. Palgrave.

19. Ibid.

20. Black and Morrison (2019).

21. Carpenter, M., Sanders, W., and Gregersen, H. (2001). "Bundling Human Capital with Organizational Context: The Impact of International Assignment Experience on Multinational Firm Performance and CEO pay." *Academy of Management Journal*, 44(3), 493–511.

CHAPTER 8

1. Allison, G., and Schmidt, E. (2021). "China Will Soon Lead the U.S. in Tech." *Wall Street Journal*, December 7.

2. As cited in "CCP 100: Xi Warns China Will Not Be 'Oppressed' in Anniversary Speech." *BBC News*, July 1, 2021. https://www.bbc.com/news/world-asia-china-57648236.

3. Johnson, K., and Gramer, R. (2020). "The Great Decoupling." *Foreign Policy*, May 14.

4. McKinsey Global Institute. (2019). "China and the World," p. viii.

5. GM Reports Strong 2020 Full-Year and Fourth-Quarter Results. (2021). General Motors News Release, February 10.

6. Shukla, V. (2020). "10 Companies with the Highest Revenue Exposure to China." Yahoo.com, August 2. https://www.yahoo.com/now/10-us-companies-highest-revenue-225350456.html.

7. Member Survey: US-China Business Council (2020).

8. Donaldson, J. (2017). "China's Administrative Hierarchy: The Balance of Power and Winners and Losers with China's Levels of Government." In *Assessing the Balance of Power in Central-Local Relations in China* (pp. 105–137). Routledge.

9. As quoted by Brunnstrom, D., and Psaledakis, D. (2020). "Australia Tells U.S. It Has No Intention of Injuring Important China Ties." Reuters, July

28. https://www.reuters.com/article/us-usa-australia-pompeo/australia-tells-u-s-it-has-no-intention-of-injuring-important-china-ties-idUSKCN24T2MP.

10. Pifer, S., (2021). "Rebuilding US-German Relations: Harder Than It Appears." Brookings, March 25.

11. Woo, S., and Hinshaw, D. (2021). "U.S. Fight against Chinese 5G Efforts Sifts from Threats to Incentives." *Wall Street Journal*, June 14.

12. Kelly, M. (2021). "Senate Approves Billions for US Semiconductor Manufacturing." The Verge, June 8. https://www.theverge.com/2021/6/8/22457293/semiconductor-chip-shortage-funding-frontier-china-competition-act.

13. Leary, A., and Davis, B. (2021). "Biden's China Policy Is Emerging—and It Looks a Lot Like Trump's." *Wall Street Journal*, June 10.

14. Leary, A. (2021). "Biden Administration Outlines Measures to Address Supply-Chain Issues." *Wall Street Journal*, June 8.

15. Wong, W. (2020). "McDonald's Apologizes after Restaurant in China Bans Black People." NBC News, April 17. https://www.nbcnews.com/news/nbcblk/mcdonald-s-apologizes-after-restaurant-china-bans-black-people-n1184616.

16. https://thehill.com/policy/finance/464748-nba-sparks-anger-with-china-apology.

17. Gorman, L., and Schrader, M. (2019). "US Firms Are Helping Build China's Orwellian State." *Foreign Policy*, March 19. https://foreignpolicy.com/2019/03/19/962492-orwell-china-socialcredit-surveillance/.

18. Nicas, J., Zhong, R., and Wakabayashi, D. (2021). "Censorship, Surveillance and Profits: A Hard Bargain for Apple in China." *New York Times*, May 17. https://www.nytimes.com/2021/05/17/technology/apple-china-censorship-data.html.

19. Groysberg, B., Lin, E., Serafeim, G., and Abrahams, R. (2016). "The Scandal Effect." *Harvard Business Review*, September.

20. https://www.reuters.com/world/china/china-says-it-will-hold-supporters-taiwans-independence-criminally-responsible-2021-11-05/.

21. Ibid.

22. For more on the topic of global attention, see Morrison, A. J., and Bouquet, C. (2011). "Are You Giving Globalization the Right Amount of Attention." *Sloan Management Review*, Winter, 15–16.

23. As quoted by Wei, L. (2021). "Xi Jinping Aims to Rein in Chinese Capitalism, Hew to Mao's Socialist Vision." *Wall Street Journal*, September 20.

ABOUT THE AUTHORS

Allen J. Morrison, MBA, PhD
Allen.Morrison@thunderbird.asu.edu
Allen J. Morrison is a professor of global management at the Thunderbird School of Global Management at Arizona State University (ASU). Previously, he served as CEO and director general of the school.

Before joining Thunderbird, Dr. Morrison was the holder of the Kristian Gerhard Jebsen Chair for Responsible Leadership and director of the Global CEO Center at IMD in Lausanne, Switzerland. His work at IMD focused on the challenges CEOs face while leading their companies in the global economy. Dr. Morrison has also served as a professor of management practice at INSEAD in Singapore, France, and North America and as a professor and the Associate Dean-Executive Development and Bombardier Professor of Global Management at the Ivey School of Business in Canada. In addition, he was a visiting professor at the Anderson School at University of California, Los Angeles (UCLA), the China European International Business School (CEIBS) in Shanghai, and Tsinghua University in Shanghai.

Dr. Morrison has authored or coauthored more than a dozen books including *The Global Leadership Challenge* (Routledge), the award-winning *Thriving in the Future: A Responsible Leader's Guide to Sustainability* (IMD Press), and *International Management: Case and Text* (Irwin McGraw-Hill). In addition, he has authored or coauthored over 100 articles and case studies. His research has been published in a range of journals including *Harvard Business Review, Strategic Management Journal, Sloan Management Review, Journal of Management,* and *Chief Executive.* He has also been cited in the *Wall Street Journal, Fortune, Newsweek, Business Week,* and *Financial Times.*

Dr. Morrison is a popular keynote speaker on topics of global leadership, leading innovation, responsible leadership, and strategic change. He has conducted capability assessments, organized and delivered executive seminars, and run top management retreats for over 150 multinational companies around the world. Dr. Morrison has been a senior advisor on leadership development to the Royal Court of the Sultanate of Oman and has served on the boards of both NASDAQ-listed and private companies.

J. Stewart Black, PhD
stewart.black@insead.edu
jstewartblack@gmail.com

Dr. Black was previously Professor of Management Practice in Global Leadership and Strategy at INSEAD, specializing in strategy, organizational transformations, and leading change in turbulent times.

Across his career Dr. Black has lived and worked in Asia (Japan and Singapore), Europe, and North America. In Asia, he has traveled to China, including Hong Kong, more than 80 times. Over the years, he has consulted with over 200 organizations and engaged with more than 10,000 executives. Much of this work has been with senior teams as they determined the vision, strategy, culture, and required leadership capabilities of their firms.

He is the author or coauthor of over 100 articles and cases. His research has been published in the most respected academic journals, as well as in those published for practicing managers. Of note he has published five articles in *Harvard Business Review*, of which three focused on China. He has also published articles in and had his work featured in a variety of newspapers and magazines such as *Financial Times, The Wall Street Journal*, and *BusinessWeek*. Dr. Black is also the author or coauthor of 22 books.

Dr. Black started his career on the faculty at the Amos Tuck School of Business Administration, Dartmouth College. Later he was a professor of business administration at the University of Michigan and Executive Director of the school's Asia Pacific Human Resource Partnership based in Hong Kong. He joined INSEAD (Singapore) in 2005, took a three-year leave (2012-2015) as a Professor of Global Leadership and Strategy at IMD in Switzerland before returning to INSEAD. At INSEAD Dr. Black served for four years as Associate Dean of Executive Development Programs for the Americas, as the founder and program director of Leading Change in an Age of Digital Transformation, Learning to Lead. and Leading for Results. He has been the program director for a variety of company-specific programs including Astra Zeneca, BAE Systems, Ciba, Ernst & Young, Lexmark, HSBC, IFF, Jones Lang LaSalle, Manpower, National Commercial Bank of Saudi Arabia, Nissan, NYSE, Rio Tinto, Siam Cement, Shell, SMS Group, Takeda Pharmaceutical, Toshiba, and Western Union among many others.

INDEX

Page numbers followed by *e* indicate exhibits.